Preserving the Old City of Damascus

Contemporary Issues in the Middle East
Mehran Kamrava and Carol Fadda-Conrey, *Series Editors*

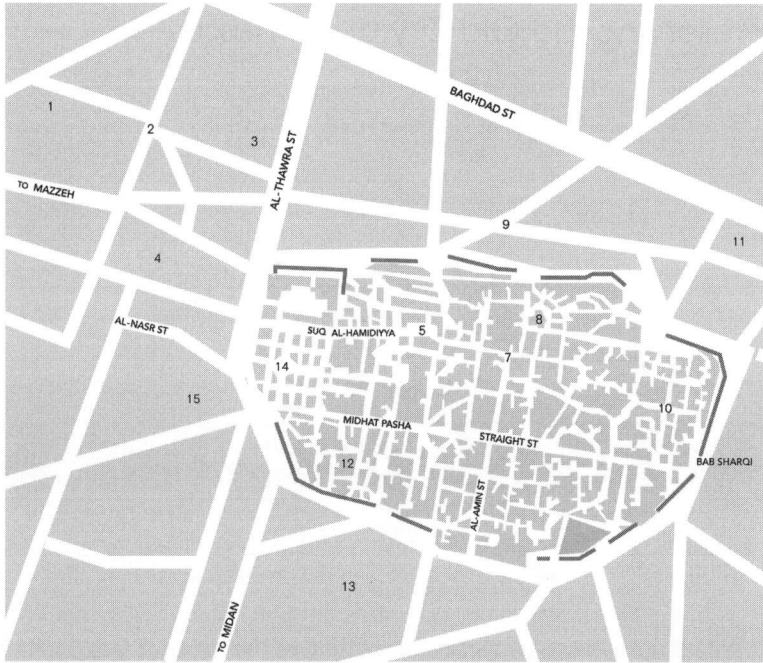

1 SHA'LAN
2 YUSIF AL-'AZMEH
3 SUQ SARUJEH
4 AL-MARJEH
5 UMAYYED MOSQUE
6 'UQAYBAH
7 QIMARRIYYAH
8 'AMARAH JUWANIYYAH
9 'AMARAH BARRANIYYAH
10 BAB TUMA
11 QASA'
12 SHAGHUR
13 SHAGHUR BARRANI
14 AL-HARIQAH
15 QANAWAT

Map of Damascus depicting modern neighborhoods and the Old City. The Old City is the oval-shaped neighborhood.

Preserving the Old City of
Damascus

FAEDAH M. TOTAH

SYRACUSE UNIVERSITY PRESS

All photographs taken by the author.

∞ The paper used in this publication meets the minimum requirements
of the American National Standard for Information Sciences—Permanence
of Paper for Printed Library Materials, ANSI Z39.48-1992.

For a listing of books published and distributed by Syracuse University Press,
visit www.SyracuseUniversityPress.syr.edu.

ISBN: 978-0-8156-3349-5 (cloth)   978-0-8156-5262-5 (e-book)

Library of Congress Cataloging-in-Publication Data
Totah, Faedah M.
Preserving the old city of Damascus / Faedah M. Totah. — First Edition.
pages cm. — (Contemporary issues in the Middle East)
Includes bibliographical references and index.
ISBN 978-0-8156-3349-5 (cloth : alk. paper) — ISBN 978-0-8156-5262-5 (ebook)
1. Gentrification—Syria—Damascus.   2. Urban renewal—Social aspects—
Syria—Damascus.   3. Neighborhoods—Syria—Damascus—Sociological aspects.
4. Sociology, Urban—Syria—Damascus.   I. Title.
HT178.S982D367 2014
307.3'41609569144—dc 3   2014006519

Manufactured in the United States of America

In memory of my father Musa I. Totah and mother Suʿad S. Totah.
And in remembrance of my niece Sandra Ghassan Totah.

Faedah M. Totah is an assistant professor
at Virginia Commonwealth University.

Contents

Illustrations

Preface

"With You Begins and Ends Creation"

This book is an ethnographic account of the recent gentrification of the intramural Old City of al-Sham (Damascus).[1] In 1992, a restaurant opened in a renovated *bayt 'arabi* (vernacular courtyard dwelling), and by 2008, there were more than one hundred, followed by dozens of boutique hotels, several art galleries, and artist workshops in refurbished courtyard houses catering to middle- and upper-class Syrians living outside the wall. Private investors were largely in charge of converting the bayt 'arabi into restaurants and other venues to provide visitors to the Old City with an "authentic" Shami (Damascene) experience although most of the Shuwam (plural of Shami) did not live in the Old City. In fact, the majority of long-term residents in the intramural neighborhoods were of rural descent. In this book I use Shami and Shuwam to refer to the social group that claims its provenance in the Old City even if they no longer live there. Long-term residents refers to the inhabitants of the Old City before the onset of the current gentrification and regardless of origin. By Damascenes, I mean residents of the city outside the wall.

The gentrification of the Old City represents another global instance of how new economic conditions led to urban renewal through the

---

1. Although Dimashq is the Arabic name for Damascus, al-Sham is used colloquially. Al-Sham has many meanings and usages and refers to Syria, in a common Arabic linguistic device where the country is known by its main city (Qasatili 1879; Kurd 'Ali 1983, 8). For example, Misr (Egypt) is also used for Cairo.

rehabilitation of housing for new cultural and social use (Smith 2002). The Syrian regime adapted its own variation of economic neoliberalism creating a "social market economy" to maintain its control of the economy while introducing efforts to encourage direct foreign investment, to promote the private sector, and to facilitate integration into the world economy (Abboud 2009; Hinnebusch 2009; Selvik 2009). The liberalization of the Syrian economy in the late 1980s led to new opportunities for private investment in the historic city center.

Gentrification in Syria was not confined to the Old City or to Damascus but was apparent in many neighborhoods outside the wall and in other cities throughout the country, including Aleppo, the largest city in Syria (Busquets 2005; Ouroussoff 2010). In the Old City of Damascus, the interests of private investors converged with the needs of urban planners for an urban policy that promoted cultural consumption in an urban setting. Although I address the economic and cultural aspects of gentrification in the Old City, I am more intrigued by the ways in which social users navigate transformations in the cityscape to negotiate social change under new economic conditions. How do the various social actors, including investors, long-term residents, Shuwam, and government officials navigate the gentrification of the Old City? Why is urban revitalization taking the form of preserving an idealized Shami identity when many of the Shuwam no longer live in the Old City? Moreover, why do many of the new social users who are not of Shami origin partake in the consumption of a Shami culture? Why is rural culture in the Old City rejected? Finally, the urban–rural binary has long informed the social and political hierarchy in Damascus and Syria. Does this social division have a role in the gentrification process?

Preserving the Old City of Damascus examines these questions by exploring the local processes of "place making," or the ways in which social actors deploy local social hierarchies, cultural discourses, and power relations in the production of space (Tuan 1977; Soja 1989; Lefebvre 1991; Massey 1994; Zukin 1995, 2010; Feld and Basso 1996; Gupta and Ferguson 1997a). The urban transformations in the Old City manifest the economic and cultural aspects of gentrification, especially when market reforms facilitated the flow of global capital into the country. As in other parts of the world, urban space becomes a prime target of global investment, shaping cities to meet the needs of global investors rather than local residents. The space of the Old City is historically and traditionally associated with the Shuwam, but the Shami identity cannot be understood without untangling the urban–rural binary that informs the social hierarchy in Damascus. In addition, the Shami identity informs ways of being and belonging in the city. This includes, but is not limited to, appropriate forms for social interaction and spatial practices as well as moral conduct. As I will demonstrate in the pages that follow, embedded in the urban–rural division are discourses on *hadarah* (civilization) and *takhalluf* (backwardness), where the former is associated with urban dwellers and the latter with rural migrants. Hence, I am also interested in how discursive practices on "civilization" and "backwardness" are repurposed in the recent gentrification of the Old City.

I do not confine my usage of civilization to behavior, lifestyle, or manners that are considered superior to other forms of being but include the historical eras of the Old City. As such, civilization also refers to the numerous ancient, medieval, and modern empires that have left their impact on the cityscape and urban dwellers' psyche. I became acutely aware of the importance of the history of the Old City in the process of place making early in my fieldwork when Syrians frequently asked me about my research. I would answer briefly, outlining my work on the gentrification of the intramural Old City. Since there was no equivalent term in Arabic that encompassed gentrification as it came to be understood in the West, I used examples they were already familiar with, the ways in which the bayt 'arabi in the historic district was converted into a restaurant or boutique hotel. In response, some would refer me to their favorite and, in their opinion, most "authentic" restaurant in the Old City, and others offered suggestions for my research, whom to talk to, or whose home to visit. Yet, invariably, someone would mention how Damascus was considered one of the oldest and continuously inhabited cities in the world. Since it was vying for the same distinction as Aleppo, its rival city to the north, some Syrian historians claimed that Damascus was *the* only oldest and continuously inhabited capital in the world. Other Syrians were more figurative in their interpretation of the city's longevity and waxed poetically that if I excavated anywhere in the city I would see *sabi' tabaqat* (seven layers) of empires that once ruled Damascus.[2] It was a powerful image, and though I was never clear on what constituted the individual layers, since I could come up with more than seven civilizations in the eternal city, my interlocutors were not much help either. It seemed that seven and layers were more significant than their actual components. Yet it is these perceptions and images of the city that are important to how social actors orient and navigate the urban setting (Lynch 1960, 4). I contend that any study of the gentrification of the Old City needs to consider the ways in which social actors imagine and objectify the historic urban core in the restoration and renovation of the courtyard houses.

The Old City is a repository of numerous empires, ancient and modern, that embody the collective national and Arab/Islamic memory. It was first mentioned in prehistoric texts circa 2500 BC but was an established city well before that time (Burns 1999, 75).[3] It has survived countless manmade catastrophes, natural disasters, several pogroms, wars, and famines, and is now a precarious witness to the ongoing civil war. The resilience of Damascus throughout the centuries inflamed the imagination of writers and poets alike. Mark Twain described the city as "a type of immortality" (2003, 336). Nizar Qabbani, the Shami poet and the city's most filial son, perhaps expressed it best when he wrote, "God ordained that you be Damascus / With you begins and ends creation" (1995, 106).

Damascus was the seat of political and economic power for the Semitic Aramaeans in the ancient period, then for the Arab-Islamic Umayyad

2. Seven is a number of layered significance in Arabic and Islamic tradition. It is a holy number in Islam and can be seen throughout Damascus. Other than the imagined seven layers of civilization, there are seven tributaries to the river Barada that fed the fountains found in the courtyards of the houses in the Old City before the advent of modern plumbing. In the Islamic tradition, God created seven heavens, and they are depicted in the Barada panels, the mosaics on the façade of the Umayyad Mosque. According to this same tradition, there are seven gates to heaven and today seven functioning gates to the Old City that was once believed to be paradise on earth.

3. There are numerous histories on Damascus in Arabic and English that cover both modern and ancient periods (Qasatili 1879; Rafeq 1966; Kurd 'Ali 1983; Burns 2005; Degeorge 2005).

Dynasty (661–750 AD), and the short-lived Arab government (1918–1920) under the leadership of Amir Faisal. It was an important provincial capital during the Ottoman period and today is the political, cultural, and economic hub for the Syrian Arab Republic.

Throughout most of its history, Damascus was mainly confined within the wall. It began to expand extramurally and in all directions during the later part of the Ottoman period.[4] As Ross Burns (2005, xx) described, "every layer of history has built precisely on top of its predecessor for at least three millennia. Whereas, for example, the forerunners of present-day Cairo shifted between various sites since Pharaonic times, Damascus has remained planted in one spot, a patch of land less than one by two kilometers." This book focuses on this densely layered neighborhood of modern-day Damascus, which is witnessing cultural gentrification largely because of this intense history.

Damascenes believe the longevity of the city reflects the resilience of their ancestors who did the surviving and the rebuilding. However, the endurance of the Old City was not by chance alone but the result of divine intervention. Al-Sham is considered a blessed city because of its fortuitous connection, no matter how tenuous that connection is to numerous prophets who lived and were buried there. It is a city of *fada'l* (virtues) as the majority of the populace insisted on reminding me. The blessed city is

---

4. Although most of the external neighborhoods came into being during the Ottoman period, Midan, a neighborhood outside the wall, was important to the development of the Old City. This neighborhood connected the Old City to its southern hinterland and agricultural villages. Because Midan was not constricted by a wall, it was able to expand over the centuries, unlike the Old City whose area remained fixed and eventually became overcrowded. The relation between the neighborhoods inside and outside the wall was complementary and symbiotic. Although at times of political crises and economic hardship, it became contentious. For several centuries, rural immigrants moved to Midan before settling inside the wall; therefore, it was considered the first step for adapting to urban life. Today, many Shuwam consider Midan the neighborhood of rural migrants, though some families have been living there for several generations. The relationship between Midan and the Old City has been the focus of several studies that examined the impact of the developments outside the wall on the intramural neighborhoods (Schilcher 1985; Rafeq 1989; Marino 2000).

inscribed in the Syrian imagination and written on the alley walls of the Old City, with epithets such as *Dimashq al-mahrusah* (Damascus under the Protection of God), *al-Sham Allah hamiha* (Al-Sham God is protecting you), and *Allah Hamiki Ya Sham* (God is protecting you O Sham). In the summer of 2006, when the Bush administration and its allies accused Syria of abetting terrorism while Israel bombed Lebanon, the number of these inscriptions increased on alley walls in residential neighborhoods. They were probably written as a talisman against a possible attack on the city. Today, the civil war in Syria threatens Damascus and the Old City. Already, fighting between government forces and armed rebels has devastated the Old City of Aleppo. The Old City of Damascus at this writing has remained for the most part unscathed from the destruction that has devastated entire suburbs and neighborhoods outside the city. However, bombings have been reported in the Christian quarter.

The most momentous endorsement of Damascus came from the Prophet Muhammad, who blessed Damascus when he declared its people the most sincere and upright of any other nation (al-Makdisi 2003, 29).[5] Furthermore, and according to local lore, the Prophet refused to enter the city, preferring to gaze on it from the summit of Mount Qasyun, because he believed there was only one chance for heaven, and he was not forsaking the celestial version for its earthly counterpart. Therefore, it is no coincidence many Damascenes firmly insist their city is heaven on earth. The heavenly aura of the city has been described in literature and in poetry. The medieval Arab traveler Ibn Jubayr (1144–1217) wrote, Damascus is "the paradise of the east. . . . If heaven is on earth then it is Damascus without a doubt. If it is in the skies than surely she is its equal" (1980, 235). Bordering on the sacrilegious, the poet Nizar Qabbani went further: "Damascus is not a copy of paradise / It is paradise" (1995, n.p.). Even Mark Twain (2003), who visited Damascus during his travels in southern Europe and the Near East in 1867, was not immune to its charm, at least from afar. As he gazed on it from "Mahomet's lookout perch," he thought it seemed like paradise;

5. Several cities in the Arab Islamic world were noted for their virtues as well (Watenpaugh 2004, 37).

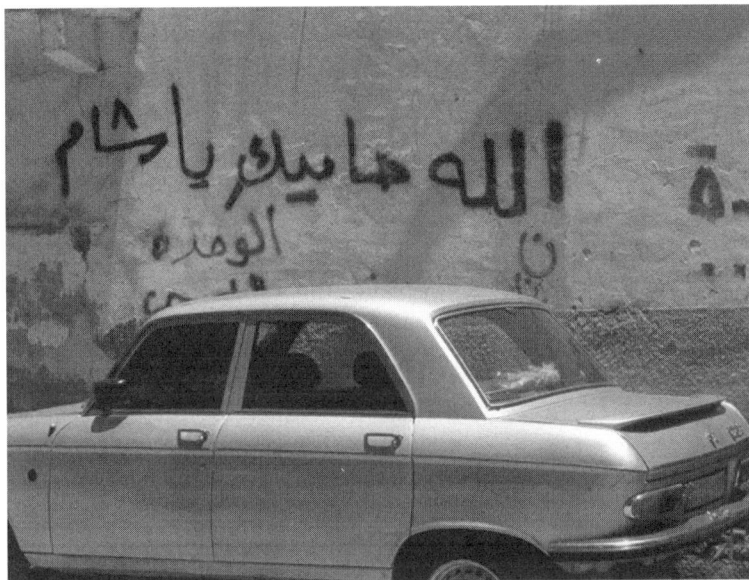

1. "God is protecting you O Sham," written on a wall in the Old City, ca. 2006.

however, he was disappointed when he did step foot there and found the city of the "Arabian Nights" crowded, dirty, and unfriendly and concluded the Prophet "was wise" not to venture into the city (335).

Although the Old City was designated paradise on earth, during the late 1800s and early 1900s, the new neighborhoods built outside the wall began to attract residents from within. After independence from the French in 1946, a division materialized between the neighborhoods inside and outside the wall. During the middle of the twentieth century, the term *old* was used to distinguish between the historic and modern neighborhoods. The Shami middle and upper classes left the Old City and the bayt 'arabi for newly built neighborhoods outside the wall and apartment complexes vacated by the French. The other Shami classes followed once their economic situation improved. However, the intramural neighborhoods were never depopulated because newcomers to the city, especially refugees and rural migrants, found accommodations in the bayt 'arabi. Although the Old City as the site of historical monuments retained its cultural importance, it lost its political and social clout.

Nadia Khost (1989), a novelist and longtime advocate for the preservation of the Old City, wrote *Hijra min al-Jinna* (*Exodus from Paradise*) to decry the abandonment of the historic neighborhoods. As the Old City began to decay and the once celebrated paradise was tarnished with overpopulation and congestion, the middle and upper classes avoided the intramural neighborhoods. Government officials ignored the needs of the residents, and rural migrants moved out once their situation improved. The Old City suffered from neglect, but its historical sites were maintained for cultural and economic reasons. The monuments of past Arab and Islamic rulers not only conferred legitimacy on political regimes but also were important for promoting heritage tourism. In the early 1990s, the restaurants and cafes in newly refurbished courtyard houses in the Old City lured the "new" middle class back to the Old City by restoring the bayt 'arabi to emulate a Shami upper-class environment before the influx of the rural migrants (Salamandra 2004). Although many of the new visitors to the Old City were not Shuwam, they supported the rehabilitation of the Shami city. Damascus is the sum of the numerous civilizations that left their traces on the landscape and in urban dwellers' consciousness. In social actors, the longevity of the city also developed a form of civility, manners, practices, and social interactions suited to this urban space laden with historical significance. According to the Arab medieval historian Ibn Khaldun, the survival of the city is contingent on the sophistication of its founders and inhabitants to forge civilized social relations that allow them to continue their urban lifestyle under different rulers (Mahdi 1964, 210–11). This could explain the survival of Damascus and how being "civilized," or becoming "civilized," is inherent in the process of place making.

In *Preserving the Old City of Damascus*, I examine how the "rediscovered" Old City becomes a metonym for "civilization" and "civilized behavior" that in turn informs social relations and spatial practices in the city (cf. Shannon 2005). In this context, the moral value of "civilization" conflates the historical significance of the city with a civility associated with an idealized and ahistorical Shami presence in the historic district. Social actors are labeled "civilized" (*hadari*) or its antithesis "backward" (*mutakhalif*) based on how they inhabit, experience, and imagine the Old City. Although constructed pasts are nothing new in the historic preservation of heritage sites (Herzfeld 1991; Handler and Gable 1997), in this instance the idealized past is created and consumed largely by non-Shuwam. Although some Shuwam may be involved in the commodification of their culture, most investors rehabilitating the bayt 'arabi cannot claim the Shami 'asl (origin). Rather, what is fascinating in this instance is that the appropriation and appreciation of Shami culture for both the producers and consumers of urban heritage allow them to identify as civilized. Therefore, gentrification of the Old City of Damascus through historic preservation is not merely the rehabilitation of dilapidated courtyard houses and the creation of a sanitized environment for visitors but also the restoration of "civilization" (hadarah) and promotion of "civilized behavior" by removing "backwardness" (takhalluf) and "backward" practices. I argue "civilization" and "backwardness" become the new social binary in Damascus under new economic conditions and a modification of the urban–rural division that has long defined being and belonging in the city.

I use these terms with caution because they are not only problematic but also easily challenged: One person's "civilization" could easily become another person's "backwardness." The flexibility of these terms reflects local contestation over space and its meaning under new socioeconomic conditions and becomes most apparent in the rehabilitation of the bayt 'arabi where disagreements over the "true" form of the Shami home results in accusations of "backwardness." Although the aim of gentrification is to promote the Shami city, how this should be achieved varies from one social actor to another, leading to confrontations over who has the moral authority and power to determine the future of the Old City. Furthermore, the parameters for the binary "civilized"–"backward" are continuously redefined from one historical moment to another not only to explain, to interpret, and to justify social change but also to enforce social hierarchies and power relations. Hence, my usage of the quotation marks when these terms refer to the new social binary. Yet what remains pertinent to this study is that local discourses on "civilization" are commensurate with being *in* and *of* the Old City. They are constructed through the ways in which social actors imagine, experience, and embody the Old

City; therefore, as I will illustrate throughout the book, the history of the urban core becomes an important forum for identity construction under new economic conditions.

Locating Damascus

The present-day capital of Syria is a series of intertwined modern and traditional neighborhoods. The historic neighborhoods inside and outside the wall are distinguished by the *harah* (neighborhood) of winding narrow streets, from which branch lanes, alleys, and cul-de-sacs. In the residential neighborhoods, the arterial streets are lined with tightly compressed courtyard houses usually two stories high. The identical blank exterior of houses makes it difficult to tell where one house ends and the other begins, though the wall is punctuated with doors and windows of the individual homes. New neighborhoods are notable for their wide, straight, and perpendicular streets, with sidewalks and rows of apartment buildings several stories high. But the distinction is not just physical; the historic neighborhoods tend to index "tradition" and "authenticity," whereas new neighborhoods tend to indicate "modernity" (Shannon 2005).

These days ring roads create a rupture between the intramural neighborhoods and their natural expansion in Qanawat, Suq Sarujeh to the west, Midan and Shaghur Barranni to the south, and 'Amarah Barranniyyah and 'Uqaybah to the north. The predominantly Christian neighborhood Qasa' in the Northeast sits outside Bab Tuma, the traditional Christian quarter inside the wall. Suq Sarujeh connects with Salihiyyeh, once a separate village but now, like Mazzeh farther west, incorporated within the boundaries of Damascus. Between Salihiyyeh and Mazzeh, in the former gardens of the Ghutah that surrounded the city and gave its paradisiacal appeal, are Abu Rummaneh and Malki. Wealthy Damascenes live here, and even the Syrian president's apartment is in Malki.[6]

---

6. For a different topography of Damascus, see Salamandra (2004) who emphasized the social class composition of the different neighborhoods.

The Old City is distinct from other neighborhoods in Damascus, not only by the wall and the ring of traffic that separates it from the rest of the city but also by its built environment. This area has the highest concentration of ancient and medieval monuments and religious buildings that underscores the historical significance of Damascus. In chapter 1, I will demonstrate that the modernization of the city was an attempt to create a rupture with this past. For many social actors, the Old City stands for continuity not only in time and in space but for a process that introduces new rural migrants to the city and initiates them into its ways (Mahdi 1964, 212). Hence, one cannot understand the social hierarchies in modern-day Damascus without understanding the Old City's role in the socialization process of rural migrants into proper urban dwellers.

Although there are numerous historic neighborhoods outside the wall, none are designated old or historic, except for the intramural quarter known by several appellations: *al-balad al-qadimah* (Old City), *Dimashq al-qadimah* (Old Damascus), or *al-Sham al-qadimah* (Old Sham). I have opted to use Old City in this book because it is usually associated with the intramural neighborhoods, whereas the other terms could be used for the historic districts inside as well as outside the wall. However, in everyday conversations with Syrians, the different neighborhoods and districts within the wall are mentioned: shopping in Suq al-Hamidiyya or Buzuriyyeh, visiting relatives in Bab Tuma or Shaghur, going to the shrines in Qimarriyyah or 'Amarah. As a result, the different neighborhoods retain their peculiarity and distinction in relation to one another and with Damascus at large. This difference does not emerge when saying, "Old City."

Damascus is a city of civilizational palimpsests—ancient, medieval, and modern all visible in the cityscape, especially in the Old City. Ancient Roman columns stand next to Byzantine arches leading to the Umayyad Mosque with its Mameluke and Ottoman minarets. The Ayyubid mausoleums and schools (*madrassah*) throughout the city were refurbished by Ottomans and restored by the postcolonial Syrian state. Ottoman bathhouses still operate in the historic districts. The cityscape promotes the myth of fluidity from one civilization to the next until the French

Mandate (1920–1946) when the colonial administration created the first rupture in the cityscape. The French colonists designed a "modern" square in the Old City with perpendicular roads leading toward the residential areas, lined with office buildings of several stories high that loomed as an anomaly from the rest of the Old City's built environment. Although the French were introducing modern urban practices in Damascus as part of their "civilizing mission," they were also trying to eradicate the traces of destruction they incurred when they bombarded this neighborhood to quell the local rebellion (Fries 1993; Degeorge 1995). Unlike earlier attempts at modernization, the French square never blended with its surroundings and remained "a foreign element, a section hard to integrate with the city structure" (Sack 1998, 194). The Haussmannization of the Old City by the Ottomans through the construction of Suq al-Hamidiyya to connect the intramural neighborhoods with the new administrative center outside the wall did not leave a lasting rupture. The suq is now one of the main features of the Old City and an important tourist destination. However, the area constructed by the French is still known as al-Hariqah (fire) the name adopted by the inhabitants of the city after the French destroyed Sidi ʿAmud, the neighborhood that once stood there.

It is therefore no coincidence that this city with significant cultural value became a UNESCO World Heritage Site in 1979. The designation not only protected the intramural neighborhood from modernization as Damascus expanded in all directions outside the wall, but also called for the preservation of its unique built environment. Government agencies assumed the responsibility of maintaining and restoring monuments and buildings of historic significance though the vernacular buildings were excluded from these efforts. Although the Old City is a protected heritage site, it remains a vibrant urban center with workshops, schools, places of worship, and medical clinics like any other neighborhood in the city. As with any urban setting, the Old City faces congestion, overpopulation, and pollution as well as balancing the needs of long-term residents with the need to preserve national heritage. However, current gentrification has elevated heritage preservation over the needs of long-term residents who remain marginalized from most of the efforts to revitalize the historic district.

Peeling Layers

To understand the Old City as a lived and imagined experience and how these perceptions contribute to the discourses surrounding "civilization," "backwardness," and gentrification, I resort to peeling layers (*tabaqat*). Tabaqat (layers or rank) is anything related to something else to form a collection.[7] Tabaqat hadariyyah (layers of civilization) are mentioned to encompass the civilizational longevity of the Old City. In the historical preservation of houses, tabaqat of paint and plaster are removed to reveal "authentic" Shami ornaments and decorations hidden by the modification to the house by uninformed dwellers. Tabaqat refers to social classes and the social hierarchy in the city. In Damascus, the urban–rural binary defined the social layers of the city and though the Shuwam in the Old City were of different socioeconomic and religious backgrounds, the current gentrification privileges the elite and mainly Sunni Shuwam. Rural migrants are not all poor, and several have been in Damascus for decades yet are still referred to as outsiders.

Many who live in the Old City in a bayt 'arabi dream of a *tabiq* (flat) because it is considered to be more suitable for a modern lifestyle. A flat in a modern building is layered vertically, unlike a bayt 'arabi, which is horizontally linked with other courtyard houses. Moving into a tabiq is a vertical move, both figuratively and literally. The movement from a traditional to a more modern lifestyle symbolizes social mobility as a result of improvements in the family's economic conditions. It is also a spatial movement from the two-story courtyard house at the street level inside the wall of the Old City, to a flat in a multistory apartment building outside the historic center, where stairs lead to the home or, in upper-class apartment buildings, an elevator. Therefore, the following pages will examine the ways in which gentrification becomes another layer in the local social discourse on social mobility and construction of identity. This book will unravel the social, economic, and cultural layers that make the current gentrification possible.

7. *Encyclopedia of Islam*, 2nd ed., s.v. "Tabakat."

Situating Fieldwork

This book is the result of several years of intermittent fieldwork beginning in 2001 through 2008 that allowed me to chronicle the urban transformations in the Old City. During my first trip to Syria during 2001–2002, I lived in an apartment in Sha'lan, a neighborhood outside the wall built during the French Mandate and near the current center of the city, but I spent much time visiting the Old City. My second trip to Syria lasted from October 2003 to December of 2004, and I lived in the Old City. I traveled to Syria again in the summer of 2006 for two months and in May 2008 for three weeks. During both of these trips, I also lived in the Old City.

In 2003–2004, I lived in Harat Hananya in the quarter of Bab Tuma in the Old City.[8] Harat Hananya is a predominantly Christian neighborhood that lies between Bab Tuma and Bab Sharqi, two of the seven functioning gates in the northeastern section of the Old City. The city wall forms the eastern boundary of Harat Hananya, and some houses in the neighborhood actually sit on the wall. One main street leads from Straight Street to the neighborhoods, and several alleys branch from the street, ending in cul-de-sacs.[9] Therefore, the street is the only way in and out of the neighborhood. The street is wide enough for one small car moving in one direction, and it was interesting to see what happens when two drivers from opposite directions tried to negotiate who reverses first. The street is also an extension of many homes where children played, and old men amused themselves playing backgammon or visiting one another. On warm evenings, young men congregated at street corners to joke with one another and to wait for a group of young women to take their daily strolls through the neighborhood. The presence of people in the street throughout the day and well into the night gave Harat Hananya a homey feeling.

8. Harah is used when talking about neighborhood or the neighborhood, but *harat* in the construct state as in Harat Hananya.

9. To simplify matters and to avoid confusion, I will use "street" to describe a route that can be traversed by a car. Alley is the route that is too narrow for cars and used mainly by pedestrians.

Since the nineteenth century, the neighborhood Church of St. Ana-nias, which according to local lore was built over the house of Ananias where Paul became a follower of Christ, has been a tourist attraction. Tourists walked to the church amid children playing in the street and old men sitting outside their stores but did not upset the residents' daily rhythm in the neighborhood. This scene was an example of how "tourism [was] added without making it disappear, to traditional and customary uses of space and time, of monumentality and the rhythms of the other" (Lefebvre 1996, 238). But with the introduction of neoliberal economic policies, the ability of local communities to adapt to tourism has been compromised. In 2004, a new law removed rent control, making it easier for property owners to evict long-term residents, even when they were willing to pay higher rent. The decline in the residential population in Harat Hananya was evident in 2008 when many long-term residents, especially those living along the street, moved, as their homes were slated for conversion to restaurants and hotels.

Harat Hananya served as my home base. It offered opportunities for "thick description" (Geertz 1973) of quotidian life in the Old City where I have gotten to know several residents, shopkeepers, and restaurant owners. During my stay in Harat Hananya, I also became very familiar with the challenges of living in a bayt ʿarabi. These challenges were part of the local discourses on the "backwardness" of the Old City that led many long-term residents to exchange the traditional courtyard dwelling for a modern apartment. Having lived in Shaʿlan outside the wall in an apartment during my stay in 2001–2002, I was able to compare the lifestyles in both neighborhoods and in two types of housing. The different embodied experiences of living in a tabiq versus a bayt ʿarabi were especially noticeable by the amount of contact with other inhabitants. In the courtyard house, sharing the entrance, courtyard, and, in some instances, the amenities meant more forms of interaction with neighbors than in an apartment where, other than sharing the entrance to the building, there was not much contact with other residents.

I appreciated how many Damascenes thought the lifestyle in the Old City and in a courtyard house was inconvenient and full of hardships when compared to modern neighborhoods and apartments. The seasons exaggerated the pronounced differences between an apartment and a bayt 'arabi. It was hard to keep a room in a courtyard house warm during the winter, and the trudge home in rain and sleet along narrow alleys inaccessible by cars was wretched. In a courtyard house, I lost the battle to keep my room clean, especially from dust on windy dry days. As we will see in chapter 4, cleanliness became a serious inducement for many families contemplating abandoning the Old City.

Although I lived in a predominantly Christian area, I visited with long-term residents of other persuasions throughout the Old City. The topic of my research undermined sectarian differences because most of those who lived in the Old City had similar experiences and observations, and they all shared a strong pride in their city. It was interesting to see how sectarian differences were interpreted in the gentrification of the Old City. Some investors believed that Christian neighborhoods were more tolerant of strangers in their midst and, therefore, sought investment opportunities in these areas. I address in chapter 5 the perceived difference between Christian and Muslim long-term residents when it came to the social impact of restaurants in the Old City.

I Spy

Although I had no prior connection to Syria before my first trip in 2001, fieldwork was a fascinating tutorial in the ways I was forced to navigate ethnicity, nationality, and citizenship. I too like Michael Herzfeld in Greece could proclaim, "I was hard to place" (1991, 47), which both hindered and facilitated my research. Syrians perceived me as some kind of "native" since I looked "Arab" and spoke colloquial Arabic fluently but with a Palestinian dialect.[10] As an American woman of Arab and especially of Palestinian descent, I found myself juggling several identities

10. My experiences in the field are part of a growing trend by Arab and Arab-American women ethnographers working in the Middle East (L. Abu Lughod 1986; Altorki and el-Solh 1988; Ghannam 2002; Deeb 2006; Sawalha 2010).

during fieldwork; some of which invariably influenced the ways I conducted research not unlike other women ethnographers with a similar background (Abu Lughod 1986; Ghannam 2002; Sawalha 2010). I encountered some Syrians who suspected I was a spy because I was an American and others who simply resented more Palestinians in their country whom they considered potential agents of political agitation.[11] I learned to accept Syrian suspicion of foreigners as part of life under an oppressive regime and resisted my own growing paranoia that all Syrians I encountered were part-time government informants. Such sentiments were common among the expatriate community in Damascus, and self-censorship was heavily enforced, especially in public. Nonetheless, ethnographic fieldwork was mostly a thoroughly enjoyable experience, and most Syrians I met were welcoming and empathetic to visitors.

I was fortunate with the contacts I made at the two agencies that supervised the Old City: the Department of Antiquities for the Old City, under the aegis of the Ministry of Culture, and the Committee for the Protection of the Old City of Damascus (CPOC), under the direction of the governorate of Damascus, through the executive office of the Damascus Governorate Council. These two bodies worked in tandem since their mandates overlapped in the management and preservation of the Old City. The Department of Antiquities focused on documenting and monitoring the material heritage in the Old City. The CPOC, or Maktab Anbar as it was commonly known after the courtyard house in which it was headquartered, administered the daily management of the Old City, and its mandate was restricted to the areas within the wall. They enforced the preservation guidelines for buildings and issued the required permits and licenses for long-term residents and investors to rebuild, fix, or refurbish courtyard houses. The CPOC's technical staff inspected construction sites

---

11. Salamandra (2004, 4–7) had a different experience conducting fieldwork in Syria though she too was suspected of being a spy. However, being accused of espionage is not only levied against ethnographers in Syria. Michael Herzfeld (1991, 47–54) encountered similar accusations while in Greece; however, in his case, he was thought to be spying on behalf of the Greek government against the Rethemniots among whom he worked. In Italy, he was also accused of being a spy (2009, 194).

while work on rebuilding and restoration was in progress. Moreover, the CPOC conducted surveys and studies, either individually or with other government agencies that documented the built environment for planning purposes. In addition, the CPOC had a team of architects and engineers responsible for the conservation and preservation of several historic monuments and "treasure" houses that it expropriated over the past three decades (Keenan 2000). Several of these houses have been restored to their "original" condition as national heritage sites, such as Bayt Nizam and Bayt Siba'i. During my last visit in 2008, these houses were being considered for conversion into hotels, with the assistance of the Agha Khan Fund for Economic Development (al-Malouf 2004; Wise 2012).

In both agencies, I was able to meet and interview directors and staff members, but at CPOC, I had gotten to know some of the architects and archivists who took me on field visits to construction sites and walks in the Old City. I am grateful for the assistance of staff members who patiently explained in detail unique architectural features of the bayt 'arabi that not only made the Old City come alive but illustrated how the historic city center was imagined and experienced by the people who were in charge of its protection.

In this project, I examined archives, perused newspapers, mapped the new establishments in the Old City, and watched TV series that dealt with the Old City. In addition, I used the ethnographic tools of participant-observation and interviews to understand the process of place making and place attachment. I spent time socializing with neighbors and their friends in their homes or restaurants and paid attention to how people spoke of the Old City, life in the bayt 'arabi, the longing for a tabiq (apartment), and they ways they explained the transformations in their built environment. Part of my ethnographic research methodology was to visit as many courtyard houses in the Old City as possible, some private and some under government control. The employees of the CPOC were generous with their time and took me to see many of the "treasure" houses, some of which were not open to the public. Several people I had gotten to know during my stay in the Old City invited me to their homes, and I would accompany my landlady or neighbors when they visited friends and relatives who also lived in the Old City. These trips allowed me to observe the ways in which social relations were spatially arranged.

I also spent much time being in the Old City, walking its many streets and alleys in an attempt to absorb the sounds and smells of the intramural neighborhoods. I trekked numerous times from Harat Hananya to Suq al-Hamidiyya and onto Sha'lan and other parts of the new city rather than riding a bus, service (the minivan that connected different neighborhoods of the city), or taxi. At times, walking was faster than being trapped in traffic, which worsened with each visit.[12] Walking allowed me to experience fully the many neighborhoods of Damascus at the street level and to revel in the "intriguing conflation of social, political, technical, and artistic forces that generates a city's form" (Celik, Favro, and Ingersoll 1994, 1). During these walks, I met shopkeepers, bathhouse attendants, shoppers in the many suqs and makeshift markets inside the wall, workmen, custodians of mosques, Palestinian refugees and Shami Jews living in the same neighborhood, Shiite pilgrims from Iraq and Iran visiting the holy shrines, and children playing in the streets who followed me until they heard my Arabic and then lost interest. I also discovered new restaurants and hotels that were in the process of starting. I loved walking in the suqs especially near Bab al-Jabya in the southwestern part of the Old City where the secondhand clothing stores were located and not many tourists ventured. I was able to get a glimpse of the quotidian life in the historic district before gentrification. As I will elaborate in chapter 1, walking was an indispensible research methodology for understanding the different meanings and uses of urban space, especially between new and old neighborhoods.

I conducted semistructured interviews with individuals associated with the gentrification and preservation of the Old City of Damascus, some of whom were working with the CPOC, Ministry of Culture, or Department of Antiquities. During these sessions, I asked about the importance and significance of the Old City, the urban transformations

---

12. A new law in the early 2000s removed the heavy duties and taxes on imported cars, which encouraged many Syrians to buy new cars.

and their impact on residents, and the role of the government in gentrification. I also interviewed architects and contractors at construction sites
and spoke to long-term activists, historians, and friends of al-Sham.

Interviews for the most part were conducted in Arabic. Although I
speak a Palestinian dialect, I could understand the various colloquial Syrian dialects. The proximity between the Syrian and Palestinian versions
of Arabic made me easily understood; however, my fluency in Arabic led
me at times to assume my interlocutors' intended meaning. When I realized this, I became more careful and asked social actors to explain what
they meant by a term or a concept. Because of my demonstrated language
fluency and cultural knowledge, some interlocutors thought I was being
deliberately obtuse and were offended by my questions![13]

The situation in Syria has changed dramatically since my last visit in
2008, and it is my deepest fear that this book will become "salvage anthropology," which was never my intention. The troubling image of violence
sweeping Syria has not abated since March 2011 when the regime began
battling an insurgency throughout the country, targeting both armed and
unarmed civilians. Following the Arab uprisings in North Africa and
Yemen, Syrians also demanded political reforms and an end to autocratic
rule. An armed conflict has morphed into civil war, with strong sectarian
undertones. Most worrisome is that there is no indication that the violence
will subside as both the regime and the insurgents outdo one another in
committing atrocities against civilians and exchanging accusations while
they destroy cities, kill thousands, and displace many thousands more.
The current situation also highlights the sharp social divides in Syria,
as manifested by the support some social groups extend to the regime,
even as it attacks civilians. A further complication is that the conflict has
morphed into a proxy war for regional powers, pitting Sunni against Shia,
with serious ramifications beyond the Syrian border.

This book's intent is to focus on social dynamics in Syria beyond sectarian and rural–urban binaries and to look at how neoliberal urbanism
has allowed older prejudices about "civilization" and "backwardness" to

13. Sawalha (2010, 18) in Beirut recounts a similar experience.

gain new expression and meaning in the current conflict. Many Syrians I have gotten to know attribute change in their communities to either "civilized" or "backward" forces, not to obscure the class and sectarian differences but to undermine them in an attempt to build a society that encompasses and thrives on difference. Many Syrians want to see their country, of which they are proud, take its rightful place among the nations of the world. Therefore, they attribute efforts to arouse sectarian and class differences to "backward" and "ignorant" forces bent on destroying the civilization that is Syria. I remain hopeful these forces do not gain the upper hand in the ongoing conflict.

Acknowledgments

First, I express my deepest and sincerest gratitude to the many Syrians who made this work possible. Although I would have loved to name them individually, I have decided because of the civil war in Syria to thank them anonymously. I thank the Syrians who received and welcomed me in their homes, offices, and stores, who took me on walks in the Old City and who agreed to be interviewed. They were most gracious with their time and patient with my persistent questions. To my neighbors and friends in Harat Hananya and Sha'lan, thank you for allowing me to be part of your community for the duration of the time I lived there. I am indebted to the staff and directors of the Committee for the Protection of the Old City (CPOC) and the Department of Antiquities as well as to the Institut Français du Proche-Orient/Damas (IFPO) for their help and assistance in all matters related to research. Posthumous thanks to those who have left their trace on my work. I hope the following pages have done justice to all of those who shared with me in different ways their Sham, for they deserve the credit for all that is good and useful in the pages that follow, but the faults and shortcoming are entirely mine.

Research was funded by the IIE Fulbright (2001–2002) and Fulbright-Hays Dissertation Award (2003–2004). I made additional trips to Syria in the summers of 2006 and 2008 with support from the Palestinian American Research Committee (PARC) and Virginia Commonwealth University (VCU).

This work began as part of my PhD work at the University of Texas at Austin and still owes tremendous debt to my advisers, mentors, professors, colleagues, and friends in the Anthropology Department. At VCU, I was fortunate to find more supportive colleagues and friends.

I thank my sister, brothers, and their families for their support. My brothers Abraham (Bebe) and Faris who by constantly saying, "You're still not done?" as only brothers lovingly can, motivated me to finish. I also would like to thank my sister-in-law Carol who always made sure I had a home away from home and my wonderful supportive cousins-in-law Alya Sahouria and Gugu Totah as well as their families.

Dawn Chatty, Jonathan Shannon, and Elyse Semerdjian read parts of the manuscript and offered valuable suggestions for the rewriting. Lauren Wagner provided me with references for gentrification in Morocco.

My Richmond friends, especially my downtown YMCA buddies, Sue Story, Penny Sedgley, and Stacey Moulds, deserve much thanks for encouraging me to go to yoga even when I insisted I should be writing. Their delightful company in and out of exercise classes helped keep me sane and centered. Namaste.

Since my time at Georgetown University where I worked on my master's degree, Yvonne Haddad has been an amazing mentor and role model. I am beholden to her for the continued interest in my work and my development as a scholar.

My friends from around the world were supportive in their different ways and at different times. I would like to especially mention Lee Wasiluk, Shareah Taleghani, Ronda Brulotte, Lamia Midanat, and Jennifer Najera. Ferdous Ahmad is the best guy friend a woman can ever have. He reached out by phone, e-mail, or text, and always forgave me for being terrible at keeping in touch. Hanan Saadeh and Elyse Semerdjian gave new meaning to "time-space compression" by constantly being there even when they were thousands of miles away and in different time zones. It was through their virtual handholding that this book made it to publication. There are no words that can express my appreciation for their amazing sisterhood.

Elizabeth Knowles (aka Irina Birch) was able to follow my incoherent instructions to make a wonderful map of Damascus. J Whaley provided much needed editing and proofreading to the manuscript in its earlier stages. Deanna McKay at Syracuse University Press was a pleasure to work with. Two reviewers for the press offered valuable suggestions for revising and improving the manuscript.

My late parents had the biggest influence on me and my work, and I still miss them. My father would have been especially proud with the publication of this book, and I regret he is unable to regale me with his own tales about his trips to Damascus in the 1950s. The premature passing of my beautiful and wonderful niece, Sandra, left me with a void that I doubt I will ever fill. The book is dedicated to the memory of both my parents and my niece.

And, finally, how does one thank a city? Can one thank a city? Damascus old and new, inside and outside the wall inspired me from the beginning. To paraphrase the poet Nizar Qabbani Damascus affected me in ways I cannot comprehend and being in the city, though at times trying and frustrating, was a wonderful thing. I always looked forward to going back. I still do. As much as this ethnography can be, it is my own modest attempt at a "thank you" to the city and its people that encouraged me to seek new ways for understanding the urban process. May al-Sham always be protected.

A Note on Transliteration

I followed a simplified system for transliteration based on the *International Journal of Middle East Studies* (*IJMES*) for formal Arabic words and popular names where I eliminated the diacritical marks except (') for the '*ayn* and (') for the *hamza*. As for colloquial words in Shami Arabic, I adhered to the *IJMES* system, but for words ending with a (h), I have added (eh) to approximate the local pronunciation. As is common in colloquial transliteration, I used the *qaf*.

Individuals who are identified in the text by first name only are pseudonyms to protect their anonymity. However, full names that appear in the book refer to actual individuals who have given their verbal consent to be included and/or who express views that they have publicized elsewhere. Where full names do not follow the transliteration system above, it is because I used the English version individuals themselves have adopted on their business cards.

All translations from Arabic and French into English, including interviews and texts, are by me.

Preserving the Old City of Damascus

Introduction

Gentrification, a "Civilizing" Process

In early 2004, while I was walking in the alleys of the Old City, I stumbled upon a construction site where yet another bayt 'arabi was being converted into a restaurant. There was no sign, but through the open door, I saw several men working on the finishing touches for a courtyard designed for an opulent restaurant. The restaurant, called Opalin, became the newest trendy destination for Syria's middle and upper classes who lived in the posh neighborhoods outside the Old City. I asked one of the workers if I could look inside, and he referred me to the manager who was somewhat forthcoming about the project. I was able to discern that the bayt originally belonged to a Shami who sold the house to a group of investors that included the sons of the vice president of Syria at the time. Perhaps the restaurant's connection to the upper echelon of political power in Syria contributed to its success.

According to the manager, a daughter-in-law of the vice president designed the restaurant's interior by blending a variation of the "traditional" elite Shami home with a *One Thousand and One Nights* theme. The main architectural elements of the bayt 'arabi, the courtyard, fountain, and *'iwan*, or *liwan* (three walled room), were visible but altered to evoke a fantasy setting directly from the Arabian Nights. The courtyard had a glass ceiling that allowed sunrays to filter in but prevented the rain and cold air from disturbing the serenity of the interior. Eventually, fresh flowers would float in the fountain. Translucent white curtains covered the *'iwan* whose walls were intricately and extensively decorated with *'blaq* and *'ajami* found mainly in courtyard homes to indicate the wealth and status of the owner.[1] A solitary table set for two was placed on the second story overlooking the courtyard, whereas other dining tables were on the first and second floors in rooms that surrounded the courtyard. The faux wood ceiling paneling of the larger rooms resembled the traditional décor in some of the wealthy Shami homes of the late nineteeth century.[2]

The owners of Opalin and other similar restaurants were rehabilitating courtyard houses that were supposedly damaged by long-term residents, 67 percent of whom were renters (Pini, Repellin, and Miglioli 2008, 14). It was common for investors to blame tenants for the dilapidated conditions of much of the housing in the Old City. However, such accusations ignored the reality of the living conditions for many of the long-term residents who leased rooms in courtyard houses from landlords not particularly interested in the preservation of their property. Nora, one of the long-term residents I have gotten to know, lived with her family in a rented room in a communal bayt that housed up to six other households. Four families lived in rooms surrounding the courtyard, and three other families used the courtyard to access their rooms on the second floor. The only decorations in the courtyard were the patterns of dust and soot on the graying white wall. Walking in from the street one was greeted with a whiff of urine from two Turkish toilets that lined the corridor leading to the courtyard. Nora and her family shared one of these toilets. Across the courtyard, opposite her front door, was the kitchen with only one water tap that ran cold, a stove top, and a refrigerator. Nora's family washed and bathed in the kitchen, heating water on the stove and using a large plastic tub. The landlord refused to improve the house and did not interfere to settle differences among the tenants. Nora dreamed of moving outside the

1. 'Blaq is a geometric pattern carved and filled with a paste of powdered colored stone, usually red and black. 'Ajami is a floral and geometrical pattern painted on wood around the walls and ceiling. For a detailed and excellent account of the decorations found in these Damascene guest rooms, see Mathews (1997) and Daskalakis (2004).

2. The restaurant also had a room near the entrance set aside for a fortune teller. The fortune teller was an excellent example of "auto-orientalism" (Mazzarrella 2003, 138) that illustrated how the upper classes were experiencing popular Syrian culture in a sanitized environment.

2. The balcony in Opalin restaurant, ca. 2004.

Old City to an apartment with modern conveniences once her economic situation improved.

I invited Nora to Opalin after it opened as a token of my appreciation for her hospitality and generosity during my numerous visits to her home. She reluctantly agreed and refused to discuss her hesitation. We had numerous conversations about the restaurants in the Old City—there were several in her neighborhood—and how she rarely could afford these places.[3] When we entered the restaurant Nora was visibly mesmerized by the interior design and barely recognized the bayt in Opalin. Although we

3. Going to restaurants such as Opalin became a new cultural practice in the early 1990s. Most Syrians distrust the quality of food in restaurants and prefer home-cooked meals (Salamandra 2000, 198). Furthermore, eating is a social activity, and many families privilege the privacy of the home where the quality of food is controlled and where socializing is not under the gaze of outsiders. However, dining in an expensive restaurant such as Opalin is a marker of social status.

3. Courtyard in a bayt 'arabi inhabited by long-term residents, ca. 2008.

found a table in one of the rooms, she insisted on sitting in the courtyard, which only served drinks, to absorb the ambience of the restaurant. She wanted to "people watch," intrigued by the upper classes dining in Opalin who she rarely saw in her neighborhood or in the Old City prior to the new restaurants. She refused to eat anything but slowly and deliberately sipped her lemonade. I realized that she might feel out of place in the ostentatiously redesigned bayt 'arabi that made her even more conscious of her social status. I began to regret bringing her to Opalin but then she turned to me and said, "*Khay!* Now we pay to enter a bayt 'arabi."[4]

4. Khay is a colloquial expression of thanks.

Gentrification and Social Status

I proceed from Nora's incisive comment on gentrification and the dissonance in the ways social actors experience the bayt 'arabi to explore how the refurbishment of the traditional vernacular dwelling for cultural consumption reflects social and economic change in Syria. Not only did the gentrification of the Old City bring into sharp contrast the aesthetic differences between courtyard houses used for entertainment and habitation but it also created new forms of social distinction between the upper and lower classes under new economic conditions. Gentrification of the historic city center began in earnest when the government initiated economic reforms to integrate the Syrian economy into the global market. Among these initiatives were Law No. 10 of 1991 that encouraged foreign investment and the repatriation of expatriate wealth, as well as a rent law that took effect in 2004 and allowed rent to be determined by the market. These laws found tangible expressions in the heritage industry of the Old City, especially in the real estate market for courtyard houses. Investors purchased courtyard houses to transform them into tourist destinations that preserved, through selective reinterpretation, an idealized elite Shami presence in the Old City but which excluded the lived experience of all other groups, including the current long-term residents. What is fascinating is that investors saw gentrification as "saving" the Old City from the people who lived there. The aim of urban renewal was to encourage heritage tourism to the Old City, but tourism accounted for only 2 percent of the gross domestic product and did not employ more than 5 percent of the workforce in 2004 (Daher 2007, 23).[5] Tourism to Syria has always been

5. I do not deal explicitly with tourism because its impact on the social transformation of the Old City was minimal during the period of my fieldwork. In an interview with the *Wall Street Journal* in 2005, the Syrian minister of tourism stated that tourism to Syria had increased by 50 percent in 2004, a figure he hoped to see rise further in the coming years (Sovich 2005). However, the Israeli invasion of Lebanon in 2006 and the uprising in Syria have reversed the trend. Since tourism as an engine of economic growth has never been reliable or consistent, new restaurants in the Old City relied heavily on Syrians who lived outside the Old City. Nonetheless, tourism is important for understanding the

unpredictable and susceptible to internal and external factors; therefore, many restaurants in the Old City catered to local consumers, members of the "new" class that emerged with the liberalization of the Syrian economy (Perthes 1991).

The Old City of Damascus was not the only historic center in Syria undergoing urban change and transformation. Aleppo, its sister and rival city to the north, had undergone a fifteen-year comprehensive urban rehabilitation project much earlier, beginning in 1992. The project was a joint venture between the German Organization for Technical Coopera-tion (GTZ) and the Aleppo municipality, with funding from the Kuwaiti Arab fund (Khechen 2005, 55). The aim of the project was to revitalize the historic urban center, improve living conditions for long-term resi-dents, and integrate the historic center with the wider Aleppo metropolis (Busquets 2005). Eventually, the interest in the historic center of Aleppo led to its gentrification, and restaurants as well as boutique hotels opened several years before they became popular in Damascus.[6] Moreover, the rehabilitation of Aleppo was a municipal effort with international sup-port, whereas development in Damascus was largely spearheaded by private investment. Therefore, the Aleppo project was designed with the participation of different stakeholders, including long-term residents, to ensure the sustainability of the project (Khechen 2005; Ouroussoff 2010). The rehabilitation of the historic center in Aleppo, though a "civic task,"

---

renewed economic interest in the Old City as well as other heritage sites in the country. In the Middle East, tourism has become one of the many ways in which Arab countries engage in economic liberalization without transforming the authoritarian nature of their regimes (Hazbun 2008). In Syria, as in other parts of the region, the focus was on heritage tourism (Shackley 1998). Daher (2007) also places the development of heritage tourism in Syria within the context of regional interest in pursuing tourism as a strategy for national economic growth and modernization. In 2005, the government allowed private invest-ment in more than one hundred tourist sites in the country (Daher 2007, 22). Syria has partnered with the European Union in the Euromed Heritage Project that encourages cultural tourism to the southern Mediterranean. For more information, see http://www.euromedheritage.net/index.cfm?menuID=13.

6. During the civil war, parts of the historic center in Aleppo was damaged by the fighting between rebel forces and the Syrian army.

encouraged local public–private collaboration (Khechen 2005, 60). In Damascus, some banks offered loans to renovate homes; but those loans could not be used for courtyard houses (Shatta 1999). GTZ eventually opened an office in Damascus to replicate parts of its Aleppo project in Damascus, including loans to long-term residents to renovate their homes (Pini, Repellin, and Miglioli 2008, 22). On the basis of some conversations I had with Damascenes, the Aleppo project allowed urban planners to determine the location of hotels and restaurants to maintain privacy of residential neighborhoods. In Damascus, gentrification was proceeding at a much faster pace than local planning efforts, with investors introducing hotels and restaurants in predominantly residential neighbors. Some Shuwam complained that they were marginalized from the decision-making process, whereas Aleppines were more involved. Damascus was the seat of power for the Ba'th regime, and the contentious relation between the Shuwam and the regime limited their involvement in urban planning. This is not to say that Aleppines had a closer relation with the regime, rather that the distance between Aleppo and Damascus accorded them some measure of freedom in revitalizing their city in ways that expressed local needs while not threatening the regime's authority.

The local tension between "native" elite urbanites and the regime is a defining feature of urbanism in Syria, where urban planning is not strictly controlled by state and local officials but is influenced by regional interests, whether Shami or Aleppine, who seek to control the development of their cities to promote their social and political interests. Although other groups live in these cities, they are not considered as vested in the development of the city as groups that claim their origin in the city.

Moreover, Nora's comment accentuated her surprise at how the Old City became a fashionable destination for the upper classes who previously avoided the historic center. The Old City, as will be demonstrated in chapter 2 and prior to its recent "rediscovery," was considered a dirty, poor, and "backward" neighborhood of modern Damascus. Many studies on repackaging the urban experience for cultural consumption have shown how cities strive to provide visitors with a unique urban experience in a safe and sanitized environment where they can partake in the local history and culture that has been carefully manufactured and displayed for their enjoyment (Zukin 1995, 2010; Alsayyad 2001; Davila 2004; Hill 2004, 2007; Herzfeld 2009). As suggested by these works, the commodification of urban sites, history, and culture raises concerns about long-term residents' moral right to the city, as they are denied access to these new sites, thereby eroding their claim to urban space and attachment to the city.

The complication in the Old City of Damascus is that many of the long-term residents aspire to leave the historic site to search for "modern" accommodations, a desire fueled by these new venues of cultural consumption that reinforce the inferiority of their homes compared with the idealized elite Shami abode reproduced by restaurants and other cultural destinations. Moreover, the current interest in the traditional courtyard house presents new economic opportunities for homeowners as well as renters to improve their social status, which will be discussed in chapter 4. Not all long-term residents were forced to leave. The new rent law stipulated that renters could remain in the property if they agreed to pay market-price rents; however, property owners were more interested in the amount investors were willing to pay for vacated properties. The new rent law could significantly reduce the number of inhabitants in the Old City with serious ramifications for the vitality and viability of the historic core. Unfortunately, the current civil war will probably have a bigger impact on the future of the Old City than the rent law and gentrification.

The Old City is considered the provenance of the Shuwam regardless of where they live, whereas most long-term residents in the historic city are either rural migrants or refugees. Hence, the displacement of long-term residents is elided in local discourses on the current gentrification because it is widely perceived these residents do not belong in the Old City anyway; displacement could only take place when the "original" inhabitants are forced to relocate. Therefore, in my work, I examine whether a claim to a place can be made by a social group without their actual being there. Intertwined with the perception that the Old City is the patrimony of the Shuwam, a claim not without merit, is the urban–rural binary that has informed much of Syria's modern social and political history. Hence, a key aim of this study is to understand the local perceptions that surround the division between the Shuwam and rural migrants and how these discourses are manifested spatially and articulated in the scope and scale of the gentrification of the Old City of Damascus. In other words, I am interested in how social actors involved in the gentrification process—investors, long-term residents, government officials, and visitors to the newly refurbished bayt 'arabi—deploy the transformations of the Old City to negotiate identity and social interactions with other users of the city under new economic realities. Some key questions that will be addressed in this book include: How are social hierarchies and categories informed by the urban setting? Why did the bayt 'arabi emerge at this moment in time as the embodiment of an idealized Shami identity? And most important, whose Shami identity is it? Thus, another aim of this study is to explore how transformations in the built environment are a commentary on social change.

Dwelling in Place

These questions cannot be fully tackled without a full comprehension of how social actors embody space. The distinct architecture and layout of intramural neighborhoods when compared with modern neighborhoods engender different experiences of the city in daily users of urban space, which translate into a set of meaning and symbols deployed to negotiate social change and to navigate identity. Yet how social actors come to understand and interpret the physical landscape is determined by cultural discourses on place making and "ways of seeing" (Berger 1972). Therefore, "imageability," as used by Kevin Lynch (1960) to describe the impact of cities on their dwellers, is particularly useful to my project. Lynch defined imageability as the "quality in a physical object which gives it a high probability of evoking a strong image in any given observer" (9). He described cities as "highly imageable," thereby allowing social actors to experience urban space through a layering of familiar images that result in forms of attachment to place and space (10). However, the imageability of the city privileges the sense of sight over other senses, and the act of seeing is "affected by what we know or what we believe" (Berger 1972, 8). Moreover, as John Gluck (1963, 197) illustrates, Lynch's imageability is influenced by the social class and cultural background of people that determines not only the ways the image of the city is processed but also the ways it is made relevant to their lived experience.

For both Lynch and Gluck, how the city is experienced through sight is determined by the ways it is embodied and the dialectics between seeing and embodying bring forth the cultural process of "becoming" (Richardson 2003, 88). In my work, embodied space is the "existential and phenomenological reality of place: its smell, feel, color, and other sensory dimensions" (Low and Lawrence-Zúñiga 2003, 5) or the "being-in-the-world" as put forth by Miles Richardson (2003) and Keith Basso (1988). Both authors elaborated on how social actors construct and experience the physical and natural environment they live in so that it comes to "dwell" in them (Richardson 2003, 74; Basso 1988, 122).

Richardson's understanding of being-in-the-world comes from Heidegger, where the dialectical relationship between being engaged with and being detached from the setting formulates one's identity (75). Basso is more interested in being-in-the-world, put forth by Ricoeur, as an act of speech rather than as an actual embodied experience. By examining the ways the Western Apache "talked" about their landscape, Basso determined it was "employed strategically to convey indexical messages about the organization of face-to-face relationships and the normative footings on which these relations are currently being negotiated" (102). He explained how speech acts about the landscape; the expressions and representations used invariably reflected the relationship social actors have with place, but this relationship informs their place in the world and their interaction with others (101). Talk was done by place-names readily recognized by other Apache members as certain localities but with wider social and cultural connotations, of "mental and emotional associations" (103). This shorthand for speaking becomes an important social discourse on being-in-the world, a dialectical relationship between the Apache and their landscape, "in which individuals invest themselves in the landscape while incorporating its meanings into their own most fundamental experience" (122).

Richardson is interested in the semiotics of the built environment where the symbols then reference specific cultural experience. He examines the difference of experience in the plaza versus the market in Cartago,

Costa Rica, where the material culture of each environment indexes a different cultural experience. The "dialectic tension" between these two forms of being allows for the construction of Spanish–American culture (88). He describes the experience of "being-in-the-market" as *listo*, or savvy, while "being-in-the-plaza" as *cultura*, or cultured (86), and it is these two different experiences associated with two different environments reflected in the cultural dynamics in Costa Rica that explain what it means to be South American. Whereas the market calls for "engaged participation, intense action, and offstage performance," the plaza is the setting for "disengaged observations, serene action and onstage performance" (85). Hence, the contradiction between being cultured and street smart, each triggered by the material culture of a specific place that itself is constructed by social actors, allows social actors to "be." Setha Low (2000) conducted similar research on the different meanings of public space also in San Juan, Costa Rica, where she similarly observed different forms of social behavior linked to two different plazas, constructed at different historical moments and for different purposes. She found that the semiotic difference encoded in the built environment of each plaza led to different spatial practices and meanings (157). Therefore, the material culture of each plaza encouraged a different embodied experience that in turn social actors used to navigate cultural meaning.

The new neighborhoods and the Old City such as the plazas and market in Costa Rica are also semiotically encoded with the cultural concepts of "civilization" and "backwardness" that "speak" to social actors. However, tensions between being "civilized" and being "backward" are both found in the Old City. Hence, the contradiction is not only between the new and old neighborhoods and their distinctive built environment but also within the singular space of the Old City, especially between the monuments and vernacular architecture—Shami past and rural present. Therefore, the dialectics of embodiment in Damascus is layered, where the spatial tension between the Old City and the modern neighborhoods creates the distinction between "civilized" and "backward." Within the Old City, there is the temporal tension between the illustrious civilizations of the past embedded in the monuments and the decaying present of the vernacular residential neighborhoods that represent "backwardness." Added to this spatial and temporal layering of "civilization" and "backwardness" is the social dimension that the "civilized" live in modern neighborhoods but the "backward" inhabit the Old City. In addition, the illustrious past is associated with the Shuwam, whereas the decaying present is the result of long-term residents of rural origin.

In conclusion, though both Richardson and Basso explore the dialectics between place making and cultural meaning in different settings, they are concerned with the ways social actors create their world, not only so they may live in it but also so it "speaks" on their behalf. The world is constructed to reflect its social builders and users. Through different means of embodiment, social actors understand their cultural selves. Yet what both authors imply but do not dwell on is the cultural act of seeing and how the semiotics in the built and natural environment are relevant according to what social actors are conditioned and expected to see.

Furthermore, both Basso and Richardson neglect the "multilocality" and "multivocality" of place (Rodman 1992), where there are often numerous and contradictory meanings and "talks" associated with one place. This is where "being-in" the Old City becomes fraught with tension because it speaks in different voices. Monuments and historic buildings are seen not only as civilization but also as the legacy of the Shuwam, whereas backwardness is seen in the dilapidated residential neighborhoods of long-term residents. Hence, the gentrification of the Old City underscores the dialectic tension between these two embodied and contradictory experiences associated with the Old City, one that celebrates the history and heritage of the site associated with a Shami through a contested civilizational past, while the other denigrates the popular lifestyle and lived experience of its long-term residents. Gentrification proceeds because social actors see "backwardness" where there should be "civilization." Moreover, the fascination of "dwelling" in the Old City does not necessarily mean having a physical presence in the intramural neighborhoods. The Shuwam claim the Old City while they dwell elsewhere. The long-term residents actually live in the Old City, but their essence remains located elsewhere. It can be said that the Shuwam dwell in the image of the Old City that becomes more important than the real city overrun by rural migrants.

In *Preserving the Old City of Damascus*, I build on the work of Richardson and Basso and examine gentrification through the multiple ways the Old City is seen, imagined, and lived to bring about being-in-the-Old City. The Old City's built environment has created strong images and visual cues in its daily users that influence their perceptions of the heritage site even without having lived there or visited. The images of the Old City are propagated by popular television series, memoirs, novels, and newspaper articles that influence and determine the ways many social actors come to embody the historic urban core.

Moreover, under new economic conditions, the causes of decline and decay in the Old City were no longer restricted to rural immigrants but to those who were unable to demonstrate "cultural affinity" for the heritage site, which can only come about when non-Shami social actors become "Shamified." Hence, the stewards of this heritage were not necessarily the Shuwam in the genealogical sense but were the investors and consumers, regardless of their origin, who privileged and promoted Shami culture. The Old City becomes the provenance of social actors who see its "civilizational" aspects embodying the courtyard house and traditional neighborhoods as Shuwam instead of as long-term residents. As a result, I complicate the binary Shami-rural by introducing the duality "civilized" and "backward," and I do so with the full awareness that binaries are problematic. As analytical categories, they provide insight into how local actors organize their social world and see themselves in it (Herzfeld 2005a, 15; Harms 2011, 223). Binaries should be approached with caution because they tend to reduce cultural differences to stereotypes; yet, they provide insight into features of the world we are trying to understand (Herzfeld 2005a, 219).

Gentrification Generalized

Gentrification of the Old City is significant for how social actors deploy the "civilized"–"backward" binary in the transformations of the bayt 'arabi to create new spaces that bespeak social change. Gentrification illuminates the process of social change when social actors embody space in new ways that illustrate how they negotiate class and status. Therefore, the gentrification of the Old City is part of a wider urban phenomenon that is occurring in different parts of the world. Broadly conceived, gentrification referred to how private capital rehabilitated dilapidated or abandoned housing in economically depressed neighborhoods, a process that resulted in demographic and cultural change (Zukin 1987, 1995; Smith 1996; Lees 2000; Redfern 2003). The process of gentrification was relevant for how the transformations in the cityscape accentuated the shifting relationships between capital, class, and space under new economic conditions (Smith and Williams 1986, 3). The late Neil Smith (2002, 2006) explored the spread of gentrification as "global urban policy." He explained how globalization allowed an urban phenomenon specific to postindustrial cities in the West to extend to cities around the world with a different history. The political-economic restructuring under neoliberalism adopted in many parts of the world has resulted in "an entrepreneurial style of urban governance" that encouraged the adaptation of gentrification to solve urban problems, spur revitalization efforts, and posit the middle class as "saviors" of the city (Atkinson and Bridge 2005, 4; see also Harvey 1989; Smith 2002). In numerous examples from around the world, neighborhoods with a distinct physical environment and history were targeted by gentrification, especially through heritage preservation where the elite ownership of the past was essential for how the privileged class reasserted their moral authority over urban space (Zukin 1987, 134–35; Jones and Varley 1999; Herzfeld 2009; Sawalha 2010).

Smith (2002, 439) is quick to note that the "experiences of gentrification are highly varied and unevenly distributed" and "spring from quite assorted local economies and cultural ensembles and connect in many complicated ways to wider national and global economies." However, the "generalization of gentrification" creates "urban landscapes that can be consumed by the middle and upper middle classes" while dismissing the lower classes claim to space (Smith 2006, 199–200). Hence, gentrification under neoliberalism reasserts middle- and upper-class interests in the city and, in the process, marginalizes, criminalizes, and displaces the lower classes from the urban core. This process of dispossession has been described as a "hegemonic discourse" (Redfern 2003), "new forms of urban colonialism" (Atkinson and Bridge 2005), and "revanchist city"

(Smith 1996) to accentuate the violence associated with gentrification and the decrease in the diversity of social users in the urban core.

Class as a social category needs to be "problematised rather than taken for granted" in any study of gentrification (Redfern 2003, 2355). Gentrification is more than the new or middle class displacing the working or lower class because "class" is never static and self-contained but rather constantly undergoing reformulation and negotiation (Jager 1986, 78). As Michael Jager (1986, 79) explains in his study of gentrification in Melbourne, Australia, "social distinction" is created by how social actors transform dilapidated houses. Redfern (2003, 2362) posits that the difference between the gentrifier and the displaced is the control over the urban "experience of class," though differences become serious during times of crisis and change. Therefore, gentrification is the class with the most means and power to assert its moral authority onto the cityscape to determine how the city should be embodied.

The urban middle class in the Middle East has suffered from the collapse of nation-building projects accompanied by the decline of economic opportunities and social mobility. As a result, the middle class in the region seeks to differentiate itself from other groups through lifestyle and behaviors (Taraki 2008, 62). However, the middle class as a social category has developed from the work of Karl Marx based on his study of capitalism; in the Middle East, social association and power relations were not explicitly linked to economic status (Bill 1972, 420). Therefore, and as Handler (1988, 25) has written, "the persistence of disputes concerning attempts to identify classes and fragments of class suggest that 'class' itself is not an objective and verifiable reality, but depends on analyst's models." In the following pages, I demonstrate how social distinction in the gentrification of the Old City is not only linked to lifestyle and practices but also determined by place of origin where an urban descent confers more status than rural lineage.

Although with globalization, gentrification reveals the middle and upper classes' anxieties over their moral authority and social status, especially during uncertain times, how this anxiety is articulated and negotiated is clearly a local issue. Anna Tsing (2000) has cautioned that "the cultural process of all 'place' and all 'force' making are *both* local and global" and that, if anything, globalization enforces the differences that exist among cultures (352; emphasis in the original).

Several recent works on the "global force" of gentrification resisted the homogenization of globalization by emphasizing how local conditions determined the process of place making to express local anxieties and class interests. In Puebla, Mexico, gentrification reduced the anxiety of the Spanish middle class who feared their Spanish patrimony was being diluted and polluted by the poor and the working class of indigenous origin (Jones and Varley 1999). The social category with the most power mounted a "reconquest" of the historic urban center to impose their moral authority over the historic core by reversing the supposed "decline" caused by the poor and indigenous classes. Through nonresidential conversion of buildings, the Spanish middle class was able to assert its presence in the historic core without having to live there. Alternatively, in Istanbul, the "new" middle class, many of whom were migrants to the city, led to the gentrification of the historic districts in the city. The new middle class was engaged in cultural and heritage consumption to cement its new status and claim to the historic urban sites in Istanbul as well as to the cultural practices associated with a cosmopolitan urban lifestyle (Keydar 1999; Islam 2005; Potuoglu-Cook 2006). These new claims to urban space raised serious questions over the ownership of the past and its representation in Istanbul. With the rise of Islamists in Turkey, gentrification privileged the Ottoman period, which resulted in contestation among social actors over which of the many pasts of the city should be preserved (Bartu 1999). In Damascus, social actors elide the Ottoman past but promote an idealized Shami identity and material culture, especially in the form of the bayt 'arabi from that period. The denigration of the Ottoman past in Syria is congruent with postcolonial nation-building attempts at seeking a mythologized past that serves specifically Syrian national interests.

Yet man-made disasters can create new anxieties in the rebuilding of the urban core, as in Beirut. The destruction of the historic city center during the civil war allowed the appropriation of the urban center by the private–public company Solidere, which created an entertainment complex in the historic site (Sawalha 2010). Although this was gentrification at its extreme, the rejuvenation of Beirut after the end of the civil war resulted in new tensions over the meaning and memory associated with place and pitted the architects of the Solidere plan and their allies against long-term residents and displaced families. Whereas Solidere was interested in creating a new urban center to showcase global Beirut and to attract international visitors to the city, opponents to the plan were concerned about maintaining their claim to urban space. They were the long-term residents who had lived through the civil war and saw their neighborhoods and communities decimated by the fighting. They were not willing to see their memories eliminated as well. They also wanted to ensure that any reconstruction considered the ethnic plurality and social relations among diverse groups that once lived there (Sawalha 2010, 23).

In addition to gentrification as generalized urban policy, we see that planning for heritage sites also converges under globalization. As more countries around the world adopt tourism as an engine for economic growth, cities endowed with a unique and historic built environment are targeted in gentrification. The historic urban core achieves added significance in the global market of heritage consumption when it is designated as a UNESCO World Heritage Site.

UNESCO World Heritage Sites and Globalized Gentrification

The designation of an urban core as a UNESCO World Heritage site shifts the focus of the government and social actors to global cultural tourism (Di Giovine 2009). This in turn redefines the relationship between long-term residents and the state on the one hand and investors and the state on the other. A point of contention in the gentrification of heritage sites is the struggle between residents and the state over the definition of *heritage* and its stewardship, especially when heritage sites are designated for tourism (Herzfeld 1991; Robinson 2001). In his work on Rethemnos, Michael Herzfeld demonstrated how the state narrowly defined heritage to further its own political aims and in the process imposed restrictions on residents who wanted to restore, renovate, and live in their homes. Moreover, the process pitted residents against the representatives of the government—the architects and bureaucrats overseeing the preservation process. Residents not only contested the arbitrary historic preservation laws the government imposed on them but also challenged the government's authority to do so.

Matthew Hill (2004, 2007) describes how the globalization of historic Havana was associated with its designation as a UNESCO World Heritage Site. The promotion of an idealized colonial past over other possibilities came about because Cuban officials thought it would appeal most to foreign tourists. Therefore, the historic center of Havana became a space for the exclusive use of foreign tourists, and long-term residents lost access to public spaces in the historic core. In addition, their property was expropriated to build hotels and restaurants for global elites. The gentrification of the historic urban core in Havana showed how national patrimony is redefined for universal ownership when it acquires the UNESCO designation, invariably marking it for global consumption.

The influx of tourists to the historic center of Marrakesh, Morocco, was instrumental in its eventual gentrification; however, in this case, foreigners purchased second homes to restore (Kurzac-Souali 2007). As in Havana, the historic core of Marrakesh is a UNESCO World Heritage Site, and gentrification was complicated by nonnational ownership of universal patrimony. Although elite Moroccan families abandoned the richly decorated and ornate ancestral homes, locally known as *riad*, they became the object of desire for foreigners, who, in the process of historic preservation, could lay claim to the Moroccan patrimony. Meanwhile, Moroccan families that remained experienced a decline in community as Marrakesh became the part-time home for foreigners. In Damascus, heritage tourism is supported by the highest political levels, and several expatriates have purchased courtyard houses and painstakingly restored them to their former glory (Keenan 2007). However, the gentrification of the Old City has focused largely on creating new venues of consumption that overwhelmingly attracts other Damascenes and Syrians.

The gentrification of the working-class district and historic center Monti near the ancient ruins in Rome, also a designated UNESCO World Heritage Site, demonstrates the effect of neoliberalism on established communities. Newcomers who proclaimed themselves "guardians of a national heritage" and the possessors of its "majestic civilizational status" (Herzfeld 2009, 3–5) displaced Monti's long-term, working-class residents, thereby saving it from the contamination and destruction of the working class. Such discourses were common among many private investors in the Old City who claimed their investments were "saving" the bayt from residents while "preserving" it for future generations (see chapters 4 and 5).

Fear of contamination or transgression was apparent in the gentrification of Lima, where Daniella Gandolfo (2009) has shown the revitalization of the Peruvian capital expressed through discourses of transgression and decency based on local attitudes to city life. Middle-class Limenos associated urban living with cleanliness, order, and beauty, since the massive urban growth in the 1940s (33–34). Hence, the gentrification of Lima's historic center, another UNESCO World Heritage site, expressed these anxieties over urban space, as the city became populated with Indians from the Andes. The gentrification of Lima was an attempt to "recapture" its idealized colonial *Criollo* past. Yet non-Shuwam are implementing the gentrification of the Old City of Damascus to recreate the idealized Shami past, which leaves many Shuwam ambivalent about the process. Although there is satisfaction that their past is being preserved, which reinforces its superiority to all others, the Shuwam have no control over its representation because much of the historic preservation conducted by non-Shuwam has reduced the Old City's diverse and rich cultural history to stereotypes and generalizations.

The generalization of gentrification has led to transformations in historic neighborhoods around the world, where heritage, stewardship, and ownership are contested in the global marketplace of cultural experience. Yet local conditions determine how the global flow of ideas and capital induce change, especially in how these new spaces of cultural consumption are to be experienced. The role of the middle and upper classes, who tend to benefit the most from globalization, also has the most impact on how urban space is reconfigured and reimagined under new economic realities because how they see and embody urban space dominates over other ways of being in the city.

Gentrification of Damascus

Recent works on the gentrification of Damascus have followed the main contours of the cultural and economic aspects of urban revitalization in other parts of the world (Salamandra 2004; Sudermann 2012). Christa Salamandra (2004) took a cultural approach, focusing on middle- and upper-class Damascenes' consumption of heritage; however, Yannick Sudermann (2012) approached gentrification as another instance of authoritarian resilience with economic reform targeting loyal private investors.

Sudermann examined gentrification as "authoritarian upgrading" in which the Ba'th regime co-opted the new middle classes to its economic and political agenda through granting patronage in the form of access for investors to the Old City. Investors recreated the "experience of origins" in the idealized Shami environment of restaurants and hotels, which appealed to visitors of the historic center.

The seminal work by Salamandra on the commodification of the Old City was among the first ethnographies to address the cultural gentrification of the historic urban core in an Arab city. She described the desire of elite Damascenes, by which she refers exclusively to the Shuwam, "to return to the old (*'awda lil-qadim*)" in search of "authentic" Damascene "customs and traditions" (3). The gentrification of the Old City, as described by Salamandra, results in an "authentic" city, one that is able to "create the *experience* of origins" by "branding neighborhoods in terms of distinctive cultural identities" (Zukin 2010, 3; emphasis in the original). In Damascus, the concept of "origin" ('asl) provides insight on how social actors experience the Old City. Although the concept of origins, according to Sharon Zukin, implies "a moral right to the city that enables people to put down roots" and "not just consume it as experience" (2010, 6), in Damascus, 'asl transcends Zukin's definition and implies an origin associated exclusively with the Shuwam who can trace their genealogy to a neighborhood inside the Old City or to its natural extension beyond the wall.

In Salamandra's account, the gentrification of the Old City demonstrates the "marketable ethnicity" (Davila 2004) of a refined, depoliticized,

and ahistorical Shami identity that appeals to Damascenes and other Syrians. The association of an urban place with a specific ethnic identity is
the topic of the work of Arlene Davila (2004) on the gentrification of East
Harlem. Davila explores how even though urban revitalization of the
neighborhood was due to its Latino culture, the process of urban change
led to the displacement of its Latino residents. Therefore, and according
to Davila, Latinos no longer needed to live in East Harlem for it to be
marked as a Latino space, and any claim by the Latino community for the
right to remain in the neighborhood was "discredited as discourses of the
past that needed to be superseded if real development was to be obtained"
(2004, 209). The "authentic" cultural ethnic experience promoted in the
gentrifying space allows origins to become associated with social actors
who want to inhabit the space commensurate with neoliberal urbanism.
As a result, long-term residents of Latino descent, who maintain spatial
practices referencing a pre-neoliberal urban environment, are encouraged
to move. A similar process is taking place in the Old City of Damascus.
The historic urban core becomes significant for its Shami culture even
though the Shuwam have already relinquished their physical presence by
relocating to modern neighborhoods. It is ironic that the Shuwam's voluntary relocation is recast as forced removal by the "backwardness" of the
Old City attributed to rural migrants. The World Heritage Site designation
preserved the built environment and physical space associated with the
Shuwam and allowed them to retain their moral authority over the space
even when they no longer lived there. The strength of their claim to the
Old City was due to the influence of 'asl in local discourses on identity and
behavior. Rural migrants lacked the 'asl to live in the Old City, and the
intramural neighborhoods remained an exclusive Shami space and can
only be inhabited by "Shamified" social actors.

Davila's account of the gentrification of Spanish Harlem focused on
the ethnic and cultural marginalization of long-term residents, who, under
neoliberal urbanism, saw investors profiting from their cultural identity.
As Salamandra and Sudermann have observed, the Shuwam are marginalized from political power even though they retain cultural and social
capital, and though rural migrants may attain political power especially
when they are members of the regime, they are culturally subordinate

to the Shuwam (Salamandra 2004, 8; Sudermann 2012, 50). Though my work offers a similar observation, I am also aware how the culture of the elite being marketed for mass consumption complicates the relationship between elite and nonelite Shuwam and elides the latter in the remaking of the Old City.

Salamandra's account explicitly focused on the return of the elite Shuwam, who lived outside the wall, to the Old City. Their consumption of tradition distinguished between them and other classes, especially those of rural descent and, by implication, the leadership of the Ba'th regime. In Sudermann's account, the Old City appealed to the new classes and not exclusively to the elite Shuwam living outside the wall (29). I too noticed that the new classes were interested in the Old City. My and Sudermann's observations may have diverged from Salamandra's when our work was conducted. Salamandra's research occurred in the early 1990s, whereas our work was almost a decade later. What started as an exclusively Shami return may have expanded to other social groups seeking class distinction through cultural consumption.

Sudermann examines how gentrification has enabled authoritarian upgrading under new global conditions. He explored the production of gentrification both at the state and at the private investor level and how the lack of trust between the two groups can result in a complicated relationship, even though the interests of both sides converge (41). The bureaucratic process both hinders and facilitates the work of private investors in an attempt to demonstrate the authority of the regime. Yet government workers are not sure of the policy concerning hotels and restaurants in the Old City that allows investors to use this uncertainty to their advantage (44). Moreover, investors thwart any attempts at a master plan that restricts restaurants to nonresidential areas. They preempt planning by purchasing houses outside the plan and create new realities on the ground (43). Sudermann concludes with how the recent uprising in Syria did not attract many supporters in Damascus among middle- and upper-class Damascenes, largely because the ability of the regime to conflate its interests with the business community (52).

Preserving the Old City of Damascus builds on the work of Salamandra and Sudermann and addresses several of the issues raised in their research on the gentrification of the Old City, especially the cultural consumption of a Shami city and the complex relation between local bureaucracy and investors. Where I differ from both accounts is in my privileging the physical Old City as the subject and object of gentrification. Although Salamandra's account is of the Old City, it remains the background for elite Shuwam to maintain their distinction, and she does not address how speaking about al-Sham is about "shared understandings of how, in the fullest sense, they know themselves to occupy it" (Basso 1988, 101). Her interpretation of a Shami identity is contingent on its opposite, the rural identity, especially the Alawites. Although social actors in Damascus engage in stereotypes based on origin and sectarian affiliation, Salamandra maintains the political and class divisions social actors use to define themselves or others as "Sunni," "Shami," "Alawites," and so forth and undermines the internal discord within each category. Social actors who use stereotypes are aware of the "political value of being able to deploy stereotypes of themselves by way of explaining away perceived weakness or claiming particular strengths"; therefore, stereotypes "are interesting for what they tell us about the relationship between daily social life and the intellectual imagination" (Herzfeld 2009, 80).

For Sudermann, the Old City remains incidental to the resilience of the Baʻth regime, serving again as the backdrop for the middle- and upper-class business community to promote their interests under authoritarianism. However, because of the history and cultural significance of the historic urban center, it is important for the regime to cement its legitimacy. As a result, gentrification of the Old City is about the ways power relations are manifested in urban space.

I agree with Salamandra that a return to the Old City is taking place. However, I contend that the return is for "civilization" (hadarah) to displace "backwardness" (takhalluf). The physical experiences of being in the Old City and the ways of seeing the material culture in the built environment inform identity and relationship with others. For many social actors, the Old City is hadarah (civilization) not only in the temporal layering of the various dynasties that at one point claimed Damascus and whose remnants remain visible in the urban palimpsest but also in the ways the city informs a specific form of sociability and civility. The city as such is a "civilizing process," transforming rural migrants into urbanites by instilling in them refined social ways (Mahdi 1964, 209–16). This civility as I will argue conflates with the Shuwam but can serve as the basis for a new Syrian identity, that addresses social change under new socio-economic conditions. In this instance, the Shami identity is shorn of its political significance and historical contextualization when it is reduced to how urban place should be experienced and embodied. Although some Shuwam may see this as another instance of how the regime undermines their culture, identity, and attachment to the Old City, it is in keeping with the ways space and culture are reconfigured under neoliberal urbanism (Davila 2004; Zukin 2010).

On "Civilization" and the City

Being of and belonging to the Old City is about spatial and social practices that promote not only refined manners and civility but also an appreciation for certain aesthetics that revolves around the traditional architectural elements in the bayt 'arabi. Embodying the courtyard house and the Old City as a Shami engenders in social users an appreciation for luxury, refinement, and "civilized" social practices; hence, restaurants such as Opalin maintain the tradition of a "civilized" Old City. Therefore, and as Ibn Khaldun asserts, "civilization" and "civilized" are urban qualities and can only be attained by living in cities (Mahdi 1964, 201–2). However, in the West, to be "civilized" applied to individuals based on their manners, regardless of their origin and place of residence (Sennett 1990, 80). The civilizing process, according to Norbert Elias (1978), began in the courts of the middle ages and continued through the centuries, where, in the project of modernity, it spread beyond the upper classes. It is constantly moving forward. Unlike Ibn Khaldun's "civilization," which finds its highest expression in the city but the "primitive" lived outside the city, Elias points to a process that continues to progress and move forward, labeling what occurs before it as "barbaric" (Mennell and Goudsblom 1998, 14).

Western understanding of "civilization" and "civilized" behavior was linked to the new emergence of the modern individual as a pacified and cultured subject (Paul 1998). The emphasis was on controlling sex-ual desire and bodily functions in the presence of others, the imposition of order, demonstrating constraint in social relations, and renunciation of basic instinct gratifications that subjugated the will of the individual to the will of society, a process that resulted in alienation (Freud 1946). Therefore, civilization was about personal constraints in modern society, it involved a measure of artifice in dealing with difference both social and personal in public encounters (Sennett 1990, 81).

"Civilization" and culture, once used interchangeably, have come to refer to two different experiences (Williams 1977; Elias 1978; Sennett 1990). According to Raymond Williams (1977, 14), "civilization" and "culture" diverged in meaning in the late eighteenth century when the former came to stand for the "superficial" and "external" as opposed to the "natural" and "internal" of "culture." Williams's historicized account of "culture" and "civilization" demonstrated the process of modernity in creating difference, especially with what came to be labeled as barbaric or savage though he neglects the impact of colonialism in the new under-standing and usage for these two concepts (Massad 2007, 3).

Richard Sennett (1990) brings this binary to urban space where he explained that the difference between the internal self and the "out-side" was projected on the urban street where social actors of different backgrounds met and interacted. This interaction required some com-mon manners to guide the social relations that created "a certain kind of disguise," which reconciled personal belief and morality with outside influences (78–79). "Civilization" became the way "to encompass social and personal differences, especially when these might make for invidi-ous comparisons" (81). In the western city, social actors are susceptible to alienation and moral dissolution because the urban brought together individuals from disparate backgrounds that shared no common values or morals, resulting in perfunctory social relationships (Wirth 1938, 12; Sennett 1990, 198). This alienation from living in the city is in keeping with the alienation of the modern subject, especially since urbanization in the West was the result of the modernity project. However, I will dem-onstrate how "civility" in the Old City is about overcoming alienation and smoothing social relations to create harmony in the urban community through finding commonalities. The argument lies in the embodiment of space. If social actors are raised in the same space, then they develop the same norms and values that guide their interaction with one another. Difference occurs when an encounter takes place with someone raised in a different urban or nonurban space, and hence the urban–rural binary inherent in the social hierarchies and categories in Damascus. Next, I will illustrate the historical evolution of this binary as contingent on the relationship between the city and the country. Moreover, I will explain how difference was overcome when rural migrants underwent the "civilizing" process in Damascus, or "Shamification." Through Shamification, migrants to the city can also acquire urban civility and contribute to the enhancement of the urban setting.

In what might be a Mediterranean aspect of urbanism, Michael Herzfeld (2009, 3–5) illustrated how in Rome civility and civilization were about "good manners" that facilitated social interactions and were an essential component of being Roman and of Rome. Hence, being of and living in Rome are associated with specific forms of social interaction that determine the basis for social exclusion and inclusion. Good social manners, Herzfeld demonstrates, were also important in interactions with city authorities. Therefore, the ability of long-term residents to resist the gentrification of their neighborhood was restricted at times by the code of civility when dealing with the civic. Tensions between city bureaucrats and long-term residents during meetings that discussed eviction and displacement were contained when each side strove to maintain the decorum of being Roman. As Herzfeld noted, "the civic does not entirely displace the civil; on the contrary it must draw on it in order to be effective and this means that norms of civility channel and contain the uses of civic procedure as well" (212). The ruthless use civility, to evict, to intimidate, and to threaten (217). In my work, civility is associated with how the Shuwam embodied the unique built environment of the Old City, resulting in forms of sociability and social relations that overcame difference. Therefore, civility is not just about social relations in the city but also about moral conduct and values defined by the urban setting; the Shuwam built a city that made them.

Organization of the Book

As an urban ethnography, *Preserving the Old City of Damascus* contributes to our understanding of the gentrification of historic urban cores in developing countries. The layered meanings and history of urban space are continuously reinterpreted by social actors to meet new social and economic realities. This study will unravel the different layers of "civilization" and "backwardness" as they are seen, lived, and experienced by social actors and at different historical junctures. The pages that follow offer insight into one of the many *Damascuses* that exist for "cities are always *in process,* always on the move, always changing, always growing, never static" (King 2007, 2–3; emphasis in original). I have attempted to capture a glimpse of the urban process during a particular moment in time. To live for a long time in any urban setting is to know it in fragments composed of fleeting moments. I am narrowing my knowledge of the city to a certain theme at a moment in time. Hence, my knowledge of the city can only be partial because, as any practitioner of the city knows, the city is reduced to familiar neighborhoods, routes, and processes that are not the whole city. Therefore, this account is my effort to do justice to the gentrification of the Old City that I experienced during my stay there.

Preserving the Old City of Damascus is divided into two parts to address the local cultural discourses on hadarah ("civilization") and takhalluf ("backwardness") and how they inform the current gentrification of the Old City. The first part is an overview of the three layers necessary to unravel the social process of gentrification: the Old City, the Shami–rural binary, and the bayt ʿarabi. In this section, I interpret the different ways social actors embody and see the historic urban core as both a site of "civilization" and "backwardness." The second part analyzes how current gentrification reinterpreted and renegotiated social discourses on "civilization" and "backwardness" in the rehabilitation of the bayt ʿarabi for residential and nonresidential use. It also describes how the new social users of space developed new forms of attachment to the heritage of the Old City that maintained the relevance of urban heritage in negotiating identity under new socioeconomic realities. The book concludes with remarks on the future of the Old City, especially in light of the civil war.

Chapter 1 introduces the Old City temporally and spatially through a walking tour, during which new and modern images from the city are gathered and interpreted against the cultural discourses of "civilization" and "backwardness." This chapter brings to the forefront how the cultural dynamics of this binary are found in the cityscape, and it is through the embodied practice of walking and seeing that they can be analyzed to make legible the social formation of the city. My approach to the urban setting was inspired by Walter Benjamin's practice of image analysis for urban sights in an attempt to comprehend how "the city's formation becomes legible within the perceived experience" (Buck-Morss 1999, 27). Furthermore, I use walking as a social analytical category in addition to a research methodology to better appreciate how the cultural tensions between "civilized" and "backward," as expressed in the built environment, result in social hierarchies and categories.

Yet the cultural dynamics of "civilized" and "backward" have been historically constructed during the past century in an attempt to address social change and political transformations. Therefore, chapter 1 expounds on the creation of the "Old City" by illustrating how the urban setting is "the product of both hegemonic and subordinate cultures and, at the same time, as the site for their production (Agnew, Mercer, and Sopher 1984, 7–8). Beginning with the late Ottoman period, I trace how the intramural neighborhood emerged as the forum for debating, negotiating, "civilized" and "backward" in the process of nation-building. Much of these debates were taking place in the context of resistance to Western domination, and local discourses were cast as modernity-tradition to reference contact with the modern West. Although the process of creating modern subjects has always been rooted in the transformations of the Old City as a result of contact with the West, reducing cultural dynamics to modernity-tradition neglects the importance of the city prior to the modern period. There is continuity in the ways social actors constructed notions of self and the other through their urban experience prior to the modern period. Therefore, I opted for the dyad "civilization"–"backwardness" by altering the point of reference for understanding social processes away from the West toward local forms of knowledge (Chakrabarty 2000).

In chapter 2, I explore the urban–rural binary in Damascus and how it contributes to understanding the development of the social categories "backward" and "civilized." Damascus developed as a city because of its interactions with the countryside. Although the rural–urban division is common in many cities around the world, in Damascus, social and political transformations, especially in 1963 when the Baʻth party came to power, created a more insidious differentiation between the Shuwam and rural migrants. With many of its leaders from rural areas and affiliated with the minority Alawite sect, the Baʻth regime disrupted the urban Sunni monopoly on power in Damascus and allowed for new divisions to arise within the Shuwam and between them and other regional groups. Yet this binary is also located in place; therefore, much of the understanding of how the Shami identity is differentiated from the rural/Baʼth/Alawite is in the ways the Shuwam dwell in the Old City. This leads to the discussion of ʼasl (origin) and how it is associated with distinct behaviors and social interactions. I conclude this chapter with the Shami merchant (tajr) as the metonym that brings together the historical evolution of the Shami identity, with specific social behaviors and urban practices. The commercial transactions among Shami merchants became the standard for social relations in the city. The merchant embodied not only the quintessential Shami markers of an urbanity and a civility but also the courtyard houses targeted in the gentrification are renovated to approximate the ideal home that once belonged to the wealthy merchants.

The bayt ʻarabi, the main focus of chapter 3, is discussed as an example of how the traditional dwelling informs our understanding of local social and cultural processes. Analyzing the courtyard house within its cultural and historical context sheds light on social, sexual, and cultural hierarchies in Damascus, and I further address the cultural differences between the Shuwam and rural migrants through dwelling in the bayt ʻarabi. This analysis adds another layer to the cultural differentiation between the Shuwam and rural migrants, and it contributes to our understanding of the wide appeal of the current gentrification. I analyze the architectural elements of the traditional house, especially the courtyard and the exterior wall, in how they engender a unique Shami sensibility. Essentialist

Shami qualities as a result of dwelling in the courtyard house are prob-lematic; therefore, I insist they must be viewed in the context of political conditions in Syria.

This chapter also provides an interpretation of how "backwardness" became associated with the courtyard house regardless of its inhabitants. I continue the discussion I began in chapter 2 on the reasons for leaving the Old City by explaining how the bayt 'arabi played a role in pushing the Shuwam outside the Old City. I highlight the role of gender in the abandonment of the Old City since it continues to inform the decision of many long-term residents to move outside of the wall. With this chap-ter, I conclude the discussion on the social construction of "civilization" and "backwardness" that provides the background for the second part of the book in which I examine how gentrification maintained the cultural differentiation between the Shuwam and long-term residents who were reduced to rural migrants.

The second part of the book explores how investors continued to uphold local discourses on the Old City and the bayt 'arabi in their gen-trification projects. The concept of return ('awda) is discussed, as the Old City is rediscovered by the new classes for its potential in the heritage industry. However, this return is not merely driven by economic consid-erations but underlies local social processes that make sense of new socio-economic realities. The Old City remains an important forum for debating change, and the gentrification of the Old City brings forth local anxieties over social hierarchies and power relations. Hence, in chapters 4, 5, and 6, we see the different manifestation of civilizational anxiety as the return to the Old City is contested on several levels and by various groups.

I divide the investors into two categories: the "returnees" and the *mustathmirin* (investors) since they articulate their return in different but complementary ways. In chapter 4, I focus on the returnees, who, in their gentrification of the Old City, maintain the function of the bayt as a residence unlike the mustathmirin in chapter 5 who prefer nonresiden-tial use as either restaurants or hotels. Returnees uphold the significance of the bayt 'arabi, as the accumulation of a Shami identity and preserve this 'asl in the "ruined" houses they purchase. In this chapter, we see how 'asl is applied to the bayt rather than to the social actors in an attempt

to shift belonging to the Old City from individuals with a Shami genealogy to those with an appreciation for the Shami culture. The appreciation
emerges in how returnees restore, renovate, and reconstruct the traditional
Shami dwelling. Returnees seek not only to preserve the bayt 'arabi but
also to differentiate themselves from long-term residents. Therefore, they
deploy the same tactics of the Shuwam in creating distance with other
social groups—not necessarily because of a different origin but because of
a cultural affinity for the Old City. Nonetheless, returnees are a contested
group, and their presence in the Old City has raised serious concerns over
what is being preserved and whether lacking a Shami 'asl can be overcome
with cultural affinity. In chapter 4, I begin the discussion on civilizational
anxiety based in the fear that some returnees are destroying the integrity of the Shami city; therefore, like rural migrants, their presence in the
Old City is damaging. I attribute this civilizational anxiety to blurring the
social hierarchy as defined in the Shami–rural binary.

In chapter 5, I illustrate how the mustathmirin, like the returnees,
present themselves as "saviors" of the bayt but by converting it for nonresidential use. Although there are different new uses for the bayt in this
chapter, I focus on restaurants because they were the first form of nonresidential use and the most prevalent. However, they were also designed
for local consumers, especially those from outside the wall. Moreover,
they have been in existence since the early 1990s, which allows for a better
assessment of their social impact than hotels and art galleries that came
much later. I address how mustathmirin navigate local controversy by
articulating their investments within the local discourses on the Old City.
This includes an analysis of how the architectural elements of a courtyard
house are refurbished in a restaurant to evoke a Shami identity. Therefore,
restaurants combined economic and cultural power in the gentrification
of the Old City. Restaurants proliferate throughout the Old City, and their
profitability is based on marketing an "authentic culture" in an attempt to
restore "civilization," in its many forms, to the Old City.

Chapter 6 concludes with the wider social and political ramifications
of civilizational anxiety as more officials, long-term residents, Shuwam,
and even investors question the current gentrification and heritage preservation in actually safeguarding the Old City's unique history and built

environment. These concerns are framed within fears over cultural invasion (*ghazu thaqafi*), which unlike a military invasion, is perpetrated from within and by local social actors who are ignorant of the heritage of the Old City and its meaning. Their ignorance leads to innovations on the Shami culture, which is more dangerous than an enemy attack because ignorance undermines society from within. Moreover, there is criticism leveled at different government agencies that oversee different aspects of the Old City especially the contradictions and confusion in government policy over how to preserve the Old City.

Although such criticism has its merit, what needs to be addressed are wider regional and international forces, especially an understanding of how global capital has restructured cities. The neoliberal economic policies initiated in the late 1980s have encouraged the linkage between the local and global economy, but 9/11 intensified this link. The new banking regulations implemented to prevent the flow of funds to terrorist organizations and the anti-Arab and Muslim sentiment in the West have led Gulf companies, especially those working in construction, to seek other venues to invest their capital and much of it flew to the region (Daher 2007; Elsheshtawy 2008). Global "flow is only effective to the extent it enters into relationships with others" (Lefebvre 1991, 347), we therefore, see how the Old City became the location of civilizational anxiety over globalization. The lack of control over these global forces by the government and the regime again questions the commitment of the Ba'th to the protection of the Old City. Notwithstanding the current civil war, the intramural neighborhoods will remain central to any discussion on new global, local, and regional challenges facing Syria.

1

Unlocking the Secret of the Old City

Shortly after I arrived in Damascus in October 2003, Ramadan started and I was able to indulge my passion for Syrian TV serials, which dominate the airways the entire month. One series that especially caught my attention was *Dhikryat Al-Zamn Al-Qadm* (*Memories for the Time to Come*) (hereafter *Dhikryat*) directed by Haitham Hakki and filmed in part in the Old City. The TV series dealt with the social and political impact of economic liberalization in Syria and included some aspects of the recent gentrification of the Old City.[1] I recognized some of the sites in the Old City, including the homes and restaurants where the series was filmed, and the story arc included a dramatization of some of the social and political issues I hoped to address in my own work. There was the trend of 'awda (return) to the Old City by members of the upper classes that lived outside the wall. One protagonist, a successful artist, who lived in a modern

---

1. In several postcolonial societies, television has been important for producing national culture, and in the process of nation-building, directors and writers see their role as modernizing agents with a pedagogical mission to create "good" citizens (L. Abu Lughod 2005). Although Syrian television is not a free medium but rather controlled by the state through censorship, funding, and other means, it remains pertinent for understanding the ways in which local social issues are publicly debated. Moreover, many serials, especially those aired during Ramadan, have an overt political and social message. The recent work by Christa Salamandra (2008, 2011) introduces the ways Syrian TV series address contemporary sociopolitical issues. She has also studied the role of television in creating an idealized Shami Old City (1998, 2000, 2004).

apartment, returned to his parent's bayt 'arabi in the Old City to open an art studio and gallery. New immigrants to the city became part of the transient population in the historic quarters that included students, single young professionals, and soldiers, who eventually moved once their status changed. The powerful images of life in the Old City compared to the modern neighborhoods created a difference I already knew was reductionist. The rich lived in comfortable apartments equipped with modern conveniences in the neighborhoods outside the wall where they owned and drove cars. The poor, disabled, and frustrated were confined to dilapidated houses in the Old City where they walked.

Watching *Dhikryat* I wondered: Why did the director use the transformations in the Old City to address social change? How is the gentrification of the Old City important for understanding the socioeconomic dynamics in Syria? How does the Old City configure in the ways social actors identify themselves and relate to others? Answers to these questions depend on understanding the ways social actors experience the built environment and navigate their identity inside and outside the wall. The powerful mental images of the Old City revolve around "civilization" overrun by "backwardness." Though *Dhikryat* is critical on the causes and sources of decay and decline in the Old City, the serial nonetheless uncritically portrayed the marginalization of the intramural neighborhoods from the rest of Damascus.

Many social actors in Syria had their experience of the Old City mediated through TV series filmed there, such as *Dhikryat* (Salamandra 1998, 2000, 2004). *Dhikryat* was instrumental in promoting the intangible heritage of the Old City—the civility and solidarity among long-term residents, which supposedly disappeared in the modern neighborhoods. Many Syrians "rediscovered" the Old City after watching popular series that caught the national imagination when they capitalized on the public's nostalgia for the idealized past in traditional urban quarters. Upscale restaurants further encouraged Syrians outside the wall to "venture" to the Old City. For Damascenes whose parents and grandparents had lived in the Old City, it was a form of return, even though it did not include their actual relocation to the Old City.

How social actors negotiate identity through imagining and experiencing the city is the subject of the brilliant and beautifully written monograph *Picturing Casablanca* by Susan Ossman (1994). Ossman extrapolates on how Moroccan cultural and social change can be understood through an analysis of the historic images of the city that remain in mass circulation. It is an interesting approach to the study of tradition and modernity in the Middle East through exploring the "aesthetic power" (191) and how images and representations reorder social hierarchies and transform social actors' relationship to one another and the nation-state (12). The role of the senses in navigating modernity has also been documented in Syria in listening to traditional music (Shannon 2006).

However, in Ossman's account social actors engage with the symbols of tradition and modernity of Casablanca. There is no indication of their actual presence in the city. The city is the backdrop on which social actors project their anxieties and concerns as they negotiate identity construction in modern times. As a result, Casablanca is never an actual location but remains as loosely linked images in the minds of social actors. The city is incidental to the aesthetic power of images and could easily be replaced by other material cultural forms to understand the social debates on modernity and tradition.

Darrow Zenlund (1991) used a semiotic analysis of Aleppo to understand the interplay between tradition and modernity, especially the city's reduction to a set of symbols that social actors deploy to "evaluate urban life" (6) and declare social distinction (9–11). Zenlund notes that there are many different meanings ascribed to Aleppo that reflect the local contradictions over urban space and social identity (28). In Aleppo, as well as in Damascus, the dialectic tension between the new and old city creates in social actors a dichotomy between modernity and tradition. Zenlund, like Ossman, is interested in how moral value is articulated through spatial practices, especially as residents of Aleppo seek to establish social hierarchies mediated through their understanding of the different neighborhoods of the city and who lives in them (10). In both accounts, seeing becomes a "choice" (Berger 1972, 8) social actors employ to assign meaning and purpose to their lives. However, in Zenlund's account, both the old and new neighborhoods of Aleppo remain abstract concepts, and there is no indication of how social actors interacted with the built environment to develop images of tradition and modernity that they then associated with the different neighborhoods of the city to construct cultural difference.

The Old City needs to be understood through an embodied experience that underscores the "phenomenological reality of place" (Low and Lawrence-Zúñiga 2003, 5). I have found that walking from the modern neighborhoods to the Old City and through the intramural neighborhoods creates contrasting images that define "civilization" and "backwardness" as cultural and social categories. As Susan Buck-Morss (1999, 27) wrote on the work of Walter Benjamin in Naples: "images, gathered by a person walking the streets of a city, can be interpreted against the grain of idealist literary style. The images are not subjective impressions, but objective expressions. The phenomena-buildings, human gestures, spatial arrangements-are 'read' as a language in which a historically transient truth (and the truth of historical transiency) is expressed concretely, and the city's social formation becomes legible within perceived experience."

Walking allowed for a specific way of seeing and image gathering that reflected the difference between the new and old neighborhood at the street level. Moreover, walking was the only form of mobility in Old City, with its narrow winding alleys that constricted the use of other modes of transportation. Yet this difference between roads for cars and routes for pedestrians was significant in the creation of cultural difference. Mobility in general is fundamental to any study of the Old City, especially because the return to the historic site for the consumption of heritage includes movement. New classes that want to project themselves as "civilized" visit the new venues in the Old City, whereas long-term residents overcome the "backwardness" of the intramural neighborhood by moving out. Therefore, movement in and out of the Old City indexes social actors as "civilized" or "backward" based on the direction of the move.

I begin this chapter by describing the different meanings and images of the Old City created through walking and how these images become important in defining social actors and social acts as "civilized" or "backward." It is here that being-in-the-Old City and being-in-the-new-city create the dynamics of cultural becoming. However, the dialectics is not only between the two different neighborhoods outside and inside the walls but also within the Old City where the temporal tension between the past and present of the intramural neighborhoods also informs cultural becoming. Yet the very difference between the intramural and extramural neighborhoods was socially constructed over the course of the past century as Damascus expanded and modernized. Hence, the second part of this chapter will deal with the making of the Old City into the distinct urban space it is today. This historical overview will include a discussion of the debates on tradition and modernity that were instrumental in the production of a historic urban space during social and political transformations. The making of the Old City is also about "placenaming" (Basso 1988) for what it means to be simultaneously "civilized" and "backward" in today's world. The struggle in Syrian society is between these two modes of being, and they are negotiated in the gentrification of the Old City.

Walking the Old City

I was fortunate to eventually meet Haitham Hakki, the director of *Dhikryat*. Hakki is a famous Syrian TV director and producer whose work is shown all over the Arab world. He is well known for using television and film for social activism to address contemporary societal concerns. He was gracious enough to discuss his work and to explain how the Old City figured as a major protagonist in his series. During our interview, Hakki insisted the Old City could not be understood without "dwelling" there. He himself lived in the extramural neighborhood of Suq Sarujeh when he first moved to Damascus from Aleppo to study at the university:

When I first came [to Damascus] I lived in Mazzeh. How is Mazzeh different from Hay al-Sabil (Sabil neighborhood) in Aleppo? It is not different. . . . But there are Damascene social relations that you can only understand in the Old City. I lived [in the Old City] and understood this. . . . My relations with the Old City had a secret, and I found the key. What does the Old City do especially when you live in an area like Suq Sarujeh? Most of the movement is by foot. There is always movement. You leave Suq Sarujeh and you are in Salihiyyeh in two minutes walking. You cannot take a car. There is no car so all your movement in the city within the neighborhoods is on foot. If you lived in Qimar-riyyah you walk two steps and you are in [Suq] al-Hamidiyya and two steps in Bab Tuma. You are in the heart of the city but you cannot take any [transportation].

There are at least two important observations in Hakki's account on being-in-the-Old City. Though he lived outside the wall in the historic district of Suq Sarujeh, the physical environment was similar to the intra-mural neighborhoods, and his observation applies to the Old City. He demonstrated the ease of moving from outside to inside the wall when the extramural neighborhoods were an organic growth from the intramural city. He said that the modern neighborhoods of Aleppo and Damascus were indistinguishable, and he could not "see" what it meant to be in and of Damascus by living in modern neighborhoods. Therefore, the images to be read against the grain do not emerge from the new neighborhoods, and the difference between Aleppo and Damascus cannot be discerned from living there. To understand how the city is socially formed is contingent on historical moments that can only be glimpsed in the unique space built before the advent of modern urban planning and construction material that not only transformed the cityscape but social relations as well.

Hakki succinctly described how social and topographical differences between the modern and traditional parts of the city could only be scru-tinized through walking. Walking as a "spatial ability" leads to "spatial knowledge when movements and changes in social locations can be envi-sioned" (Tuan 1977, 67). Incidentally, several Syrians took me on walking tours of the Old City when they wanted me to understand the difference between the new and old neighborhoods or to appreciate their passion for the historic quarters. Hence, the Old City has to be walked before it could be understood.

When Ahmad who worked with the Committee for the Protection of the Old City (CPOC) wanted me to understand the "urban palimpsest" of the Old City and the ways in which one civilization bleeds into the next he took me on walks. Although Andreas Huyssen (2003, 7) cautioned the "trope of palimpsest is inherently literary and tied to writing," he conceded that it could be "used to discuss the configurations of urban spaces and the unfolding in time without making the architecture and the city simply into texts." Ahmad, however, insisted that no understanding of the city could take place without understanding the "basic vocabulary" of the city and walks were my tutorial in the reading of the palimpsest of architectural elements that referenced certain civilizations and were repeated over the centuries. Chapter 6 will demonstrates how civilizational continuity was threatened with the current gentrification and the political and social ramifications of this threat. Ahmad explained how the monuments and historic buildings stood comfortably next to the vernacular structures that he believed led to the cohesive urban fabric and social solidarity. Civility that existed inside the wall was largely the result of the built environment that instilled in its daily users a sense of harmony, whereas the new neighborhoods did not. Although Ahmad was not a Syrian, he was nonetheless "invested" in the Old City and what it said about "matters of importunate social concern" (Basso 1988, 122).

Several memoirs and books on the Old City of Damascus demonstrated how walking led to an appreciation of the intramural neighborhoods. In his *Dimashq al-Asrar* (*Secrets of Damascus*), Nasr el-Din Al-Bahra (2001) took his "friend" for a walk in the Old City, pausing at monuments and other sites of historic interest. The trip is not only a history lesson for the friend and, in turn the reader, but also the dialogue between the two becomes a commentary on the importance of the city's cultural heritage to the present and therefore a plea for its preservation. Nadia Khost walked to the important houses and sites in her books *Al-Hijra min al-Jinna* (1989) (*Exodus from Paradise*) and *Dimashq: Dhakirat al-Insan wa al-Hajr* (1993) (*Damascus: Memories of Humans and Stone*), expounding on their historical and national significance in her appeal for the preservation of historic neighborhoods in Damascus. Incidentally, she took me on two walks to demonstrate her precise meaning. Khost insisted the Arab city was distinct from other cities in the world because it was a city built for pedestrians (1993, 29). Therefore, the images that informed social actors' spatial and temporal understanding of the Old City came from the walking. They employ these images to construct cultural discourse on "civilization" and "backwardness."

Therefore, walking became the only way to effectively research the Old City. I walked Damascus, connecting the city spatially and temporally. As a result of all my walking, I became Lefebvre's (1996, 228) "rhythm-analyst," wandering the streets of Damascus with all my senses and thoughts fully engaged, not always by choice but as a tactic to maneuver the crowded streets. At times, I walked "aimlessly" as suggested by Walter Benjamin who, as one of the most consummate practitioners of the city, believed that "the first and most important thing you have to do is feel your way through a city so that you can return to it with complete assurance" (Benjamin as quoted in Gilloch 2002, 165). As a result of all my walking, I felt, with some measure of confidence, that I was able to always return to Damascus.

Come Walk with Me

On September 19, 2001, two days after arriving in Damascus for the first time, I walked to the Old City from the hotel where I was staying in Sha'lan, one of the neighborhoods built during the French Mandate that became popular with Syrians after independence.[2] This neighborhood mixed commercial and residential buildings, many of which adhered to the French building code of four stories, resulting in a pleasant modern neighborhood. The wide streets in the modern neighborhoods had sidewalks, but they were usually occupied by parked cars that pushed pedestrians onto the street and into oncoming traffic. Following a route I plotted on a city map I had purchased from a bookstore near the hotel, I made my way past Yusif al-'Azmeh Square, the bustling financial district, carefully negotiating the vehicular traffic that reluctantly stopped for walkers, even at pedestrian crossing lanes. The map was not drawn to scale, but by walking in the general direction of the Old City, I eventually arrived there. I walked through al-Bahsa with the 'abraj (towers), the

2. For more information on the French Mandate in Syria, see Philip Khoury (1987) and Elizabeth Thompson (2001). For more information on World War I and the creation of the modern Middle East, see David Fromkin (1989).

local name for multistory buildings. This area was once part of the historic extramural neighborhood Suq Sarujeh of courtyard houses and narrow lanes. Before preservation activists were able to halt destruction of the historic neighborhood, parts were demolished during the 1970s and 1980s to erect modern commercial buildings.[3] Today, it is a mix of traditional built environment and looming office towers, combining in one location the struggle between urban development and conservation. I walked to Al-Marjeh Square using the pedestrian bridge over May Twenty-Ninth Street (when the Ba'th came to power).

Al-Marjeh Square was built by the Ottomans toward the end of the nineteenth century in their efforts to modernize the city and shift the center away from the intramural neighborhoods. Here, the Ottomans built modern institutions such as the municipality and post office using cement and iron beams that allowed for larger and taller structures than the buildings of the Old City. The new building material and architecture marked one of the first ruptures with earlier civilizations and the beginning of the distinction between neighborhoods inside and outside the wall. Surrounding the square today are tourist offices, souvenir shops, sweet shops, nut shops, and budget hotels, some of which double as brothels. I continued past the square toward the wall of the citadel and walked along al-Thawra Street until I reached Suq al-Hamidiyya, which today is inaccessible at street level. Perpendicular to al-Thawra was al-Nasr Boulevard, built by Jamal Pasha, the last Ottoman governor of Damascus, as a ceremonial avenue for military parades to connect the Hijaz Railway station to the entrance of the Old City, where Suq al-Hamidiyya now stands. In 2002, as part of the restoration of the suq, a pedestrian tunnel was built underneath al-Thawra Street, and iron railings were installed along the sidewalk facing the entrance to push pedestrians into the tunnel so that cars on al-Nasr and al-Thawra Streets did not stop for pedestrians. The foot patrols

3. Siham Tergeman and Nadia Khost, two advocates for the preservation of historic Damascus, were raised in this neighborhood, which they lovingly depicted in their memoirs of life in the traditional neighborhood and courtyard house. Their books decried the demolition of historic neighborhoods in Damascus in the name of modernization.

4. Yusif al-'Azmeh Square on a quiet Friday morning, ca. 2008.

in this area control the crossings and prohibit young men from jumping over the railings.

The walk from the entrance of Suq al-Hamidiyya to the Umayyad Mosque in the center of the Old City covered a shorter distance than the walk from Sha'lan to the Old City but offered a denser temporal overview of the city and a deeper appreciation of the urban palimpsest. The suq built in the late Ottoman period in the style of the European arcades, ended beneath the remains of the Roman propylaeum, still impressive after two millennia. The Corinthian columns that once marked the entrance to Jupiter's temple now signaled the end of the suq. They were uncovered in 1983 when the houses and stores that surrounded the Umayyad Mosque were demolished to create a ceremonial square for visiting dignitaries (Sack 1998, 187). Past the Roman columns are the Byzantine arches for the arcade to the Cathedral of St. John that replaced Jupiter's Temple when the Roman Empire embraced Christianity. The cathedral itself replaced the Roman temple for Jupiter, and the temple was built on an Aramaean shrine, the first ancient civilization to declare Damascus a capital city.

5. The entrance to Suq al-Hamidiyya and the Old City from al-Nasr and al-Thawra Streets during a lull in traffic, ca. 2004.

The Roman columns are almost as high as the metal Ottoman roof of Suq al-Hamidiyya, and both dwarf the Byzantine columns that lead to the mosque past shops of Suq al-Miskiyyah built during the Mameluke period. The government in 2003 attempted to remove the shops from the entrance to the Umayyad Mosque and replace them with tourist police and visitor information booths. The owners protested this decision and resisted moving from the shops that have been in their family for generations. The government relented, but the official position remained that the selling of religious books, paraphernalia, and holiday streamers at this suq was an unacceptable representation of the nation to visitors to the Old City.

Beyond al-Miskiyyah stood the main entrance to the Umayyad Mosque used by Muslim worshipers. Visiting tourists entered the mosque through a gate to the left of the main entrance. They are charged a fee, and unveiled women are given a long nondescript, drab green or gray robe

6. The square in front of the Umayyad Mosque. In the center are the Roman columns, Byzantine arches leading to the mosque, and the metal dome covering Suq
al-Hamidiyya, ca. 2004.

with a hood that makes them look like characters from a science fiction
movie. The mosque replaced the Byzantine cathedral honoring St. John
the Baptist and was built during the Umayyad period by Al-Walid who
was seeking to imprint Damascus with an Arab-Islamic identity.[4]

This short walk covered nearly 5,000 years of history and offered one
of the densest palimpsests of the numerous ancient and modern civilizations. Here, the Ottoman, Roman, Byzantine, Mameluke, and Umayyad
civilizations are etched in the cityscape, and a main reason the walled
neighborhoods became a World Heritage Site. Moreover, this walk inside
the Old City cuts through what Schilcher (1985, 12) called the "central

4. For an excellent and fascinating interpretation of the sociopolitical reasons
behind the construction of the Umayyad Mosque, see Finbarr Flood (2001).

rectangle," or the area that includes the historic, religious, and economic hub of the city. Beyond the central rectangle are the residential quarters, with cul-de-sacs and narrow alleyways lined with courtyard houses facing inward and away from the street. These neighborhoods until recently were mainly restricted to their residents. To the north of the mosque was 'Amarah Juwaniyyah (Inner 'Amarah), a Sunni neighborhood that connected both Qimarriyyah and Bab Tuma. To the east of the mosque lay Qimarriyyah, a predominantly Muslim neighborhood that linked Bab Tuma, the Christian quarter in the northeast, with the central rectangle. To the south of Bab Tuma and Straight Street is Harat al-Yahud (Jewish Neighborhood) separated from Shaghur by Amin Street. Harat al-Yahud is also known as Hay al-Amin, perhaps because most of the Jews who lived there left in the early 1990s. Nonetheless, this neighborhood was one of the most mixed areas in the city whose inhabitants included Palestinian refugees, Syrian Shiites, Armenians, and Christians.

Through walking, I connected the old and new neighborhoods, as well as the past and present, bringing forth the dueling images of modernity and tradition in the cityscape. The walk also highlighted the differences between "civilization" in the monuments of the Old City and the "backwardness" of the residential neighborhoods. Moreover, while I was moving through the city, I realized walking was an analytical category as well, illustrating social and gendered differences in Damascus. Walking was the only form of mobility in the historic neighborhoods, but it was discouraged in modern neighborhoods where cars occupied sidewalks and the street. There was also the gendered notion of walking and although women did not usually walk alone, I felt relatively safe in the streets of Damascus. I did not stand out as a foreigner by my appearance, and my fluency in Arabic led some to think that I was some kind of local.[5] For the

5. With my generic ethnic looks, I could pass for Syrian, but, according to a friend, I walked "Syrian," which meant I did not walk like a tourist strolling about or looking lost but with a purpose. Moreover, since I looked local and was "brave" enough to be in the streets by myself, some Syrians may have interpreted this as being "connected." According to my friend, I would not be there if I was not confident that I was somehow protected and if anyone harassed me, they risked repercussion from "my connections." Walking

most part, I was left alone during my walks, though, at times, I felt the piercing stares of men, and I did receive a fair amount of verbal harassment but nothing that proved threatening. I was especially cautious of my surroundings in neighborhoods known to be more conservative, and where women were not usually seen unveiled and unaccompanied walking in the street. But I was also an anomaly in the more open but upper-class neighborhoods with wide sidewalks people rarely used, since residents in those neighborhoods drove or were driven everywhere. In this instance, walking highlighted a class difference. Imposed by the narrow alleys that were built pre-vehicles, walking remained the main form of mobility in the Old City. The site was protected; many of these narrow alleys could not be widened to accommodate cars. Therefore, the Old City became a site of "backwardness" because people walked even if they could afford cars.[6]

Walking and Civility

Michel de Certeau and Walter Benjamin both expounded on the role of walking in understanding the modern city. According to de Certeau, walking was as a "tactic" employed by ordinary practitioners of the city to overcome the "Concept city" and impose their own meaning and order on space (1984, 93–96). Benjamin, however, espoused a more detached approach to walking the city in the "flaneur" and "whose way of life still conceal[ed] behind a mitigating nimbus the coming desolation of the big-city dweller" (Benjamin 1999, 10). The city becomes the stage or background for the flaneur to comment on the state of modernity. The

---

also provided me with fascinating insight on the social construction of confidence where in Syria it emanated from faith in family connections rather than from personal abilities.

6. Even in streets where cars could be driven in the Old City, it was impractical and the streets could only accommodate traffic in one direction. Nonetheless, some people in the Old City would drive their cars in these narrow alleys and would take a long time maneuvering in and out when it was easier just to walk. Traffic in the Old City was one of the major problems for conservationists as well because the vibrations and the exhaust fumes were damaging to the fragile built environment. Yet any ban on cars in the Old City was met with mass protests from residents and businesses inside the wall.

modernity project in the city introduced new social relations and spatial practices that disrupted earlier forms of forging connections with the urban environment and other users of space. Walking was an attempt to negotiate spatial transformations and social alienation of modernity. For the ordinary practitioners of the city "walking which alternately follows a path and has followers, creates a mobile organicity in the environment" that reinforces their presence in the city (de Certeau 1984, 99). Furthermore, walking in the Western modern city was dangerous. It could lead to encounters with difference that could be dangerous; therefore, being in the street was fraught with real and imagined fear for city dwellers (Sennett 1990, 197–98).

If we return to Khost, al-Bahra, and Hakki in their recounts of walking and the city, there is a sense that the premodern Arab city grew out of the need of its dwellers to build a livable city that they could find themselves in. In their description of Damascus, urban alienation is overcome by walking because it brings people of different neighborhoods in contact and makes the urban setting familiar to its users. Walking in the old neighborhoods is not an act of resistance, social alienation, or detachment but forges and enforces connections with others. It affirms the shared values of urban dwellers.

In my own walking tour, the images I gathered of the city where I highlighted different ways of being-in-the modern and being-in-the old neighborhoods and how the dialectic interplay between these two modes of existence allow for an understanding of how "civilized" and "backward" come to stand for the cultural dynamics in Damascus. Walking also demonstrates one layer of the interaction between place and behavior through the "symbolic communication" of the built environment in how culture "becomes" (Richardson 2003).

However, another layer in the interaction between place and behavior is not a spatial but a temporal dialectical relationship. In my walk within the Old City, I focused on how the history of Damascus is visible in the cityscape. It is these images that index a civilizational component to the intramural neighborhoods. However, the residential neighborhoods undermine this aspect of city and index a decaying present. Nonetheless, it is within the wall that certain sociability was forged among social users of this urban space. The traditional materials of straw mud and wood that are used in the construction of the Old City did not allow for more than two stories; therefore, walkers in the Old City were not overwhelmed nor overshadowed by looming multistory buildings.

Walking the Old City established social connections and encouraged social interactions breeding familiarity and enhancing solidarity. When I walked with my landlady, she took me through alleys in the Old City that were too narrow for cars so we were not squeezed into doorways to make room for them. We passed neighbors and shopkeepers, and she greeted all of them because, according to local adage, a greeting is for God. However, greetings were not only for familiar faces but also for people we passed in other neighborhoods. Walking made the unfamiliar less threatening with the greeting. These were some of the "Damascene social relations" Hakki mentioned that can only be appreciated when living in the Old City that integrated newcomers to the city. In modern neighborhoods where street life is less intense and where social relations have been transformed in the new environment, greetings are less necessary. The difference between the new and old neighborhoods is due to not just the built environment but also the ways in which visibility is more concentrated in the narrow alleys and cul-de-sacs that results in the unfamiliar becoming familiar.

When I lived in the Old City, there was only one way to get to my front door, whereas in Sha'lan, there were several options to arrive at the entrance of my building. If I wanted to avoid someone near my building, I could take a different route home but that was not an option in the narrow cul-de-sac in which I lived. Visibility is also a form of social control and surveillance. I used to half-joke with friends that, if I was struck with amnesia, I would have no problem keeping to my daily routine because people in my neighborhood, even those I only recognized by sight, would be able to reconstruct it for me. Walking in the Old City rendered me seen by the community and whether or not I chose to I was, on a certain level, integrated into the daily experience of the neighborhood. By being visible when walking, the socialization process of the Old City integrates and monitors newcomers to the urban setting.

Walking in the Old City was at times an unpleasant experience as I became aware of open sewers, getting wet from laundry dripping on my head, or inhaling the smoke in the winter from the *suba,* the heater that burns diesel fuel and covers everything with soot. I avoided dirt from the crumbling houses and the garbage in alleys because the government sanitation services were intermittent in the marginalized parts of Damascus. I saw bags of trash ripped apart by cats. In the alleys, I was careful of open doors because I learned how things may come flying out as I walked by—a used paper handkerchief, a cigarette butt, water used for mopping, or spit. In modern neighborhoods, these incidents were rare because sidewalks are wide and doors are not always at street level.

As cars became important for the modernization of the city, roads superseded pedestrian routes, drivers supplanted walkers, and modern neighborhoods were privileged over historic districts. Several long-term residents complained that they wanted to own cars, but it was difficult to park them. Although some alleys in the Old City had been widened during the past century to allow vehicular traffic, especially for security reasons, the narrow lanes of the Old City recall a prevehicular lifestyle. Those who had horses and carriages tended to live outside the wall where there was more space. The Ottomans widened roads to accommodate new forms of transportation, such as tramcars from and to the intramural city. Bab Tuma and al-Amin Streets were widened to improve traffic circulation and movement (Sack 1998, 191). In 1898, many lanes in the Old City were widened to allow Kaiser Wilhelm II and his entourage to visit the intramural quarters.

The French were also involved in a plan to beautify and expand the city through the construction of boulevards that connected the Old City to the new neighborhoods built farther away from the town center (Khoury 1987, 190). The French built the first roads that surround the Old City, beginning the process of isolating it from the rest of the neighborhoods (Khoury 1987, 190–191; Thompson 2000, 65–66). Roads were associated with open spaces that were more hygienic than the densely built intramural neighborhoods. The emphasis on hygiene and transportation in urban planning required the demolition of courtyard houses to reduce the congestion of the Old City. However, the French, like the Ottomans, were interested in opening roads in the Old City to enable their troop's access to neighborhoods in times of civil unrest.

Many of the policies begun by the French concerning the Old City continued under the independent state. Notions of modern urban planning and French urbanism were internalized in the minds of Syrian urban planners who were trained by the French or in France (Zeifa 2004; Thompson 2000, 65). Syrian planners further sought to "open" the Old City to traffic and reduce the tortuous streets in the intramural area. Celik (1997) reported that in Algeria, French colonial urban policy was considered modern and part of the modernization project that the nation-state continued after independence. However, the roads brought about a rupture in the flow of people from the Old City to the surrounding neighborhoods and enforced the differences between the lifestyle inside and outside the wall.

In this section, we saw the distinction between the intramural and modern neighborhoods through the embodied experience of walking and the images gathered during the walk. These images are what social actors deploy in their cultural discourses on social hierarchies and change. Yet since these images are embedded in the built environment, it is necessary to understand how this physicality came to stand for old, new, modern, tradition, "civilized," and "backward." In the next section, I explore the ways in which space functions as "a kind of neutral grid on which cultural difference, historical memory, and societal organization is inscribed" (Gupta and Ferguson 1997b, 34). The Old City is such a "neutral grid" on which social actors project local discourses on tradition, modernity, "civilization," and "backwardness" where these social discourses are also about place making. The making of the Old City begins with the modernization of Syria during the late Ottoman period when questions on the role of the past in the present were first asked, questions that remain pertinent today.

Familiar and Alien Pasts

According to Lowenthal (1985), the past has become an unfamiliar territory that induced mixed and often contradictory reactions among social actors. It could be both empowering and a source of pride but also impoverishing and alienating. Whereas some individuals developed attachments to the past, others were burdened by the physical remains of previous eras that cluttered their landscape and controlled the shape of their present living space—no cars in the Old City for instance. Furthermore, Lowenthal observed that the past could be threatening when individuals deprived themselves of experiencing the present (65). In cities, the past took on a new dimension, with historic preservation and conservation movements that sought to protect districts or buildings from demolitions for their perceived historic value. As cities became possessed by the past, this obsession led to "underlying tensions between current and previous inhabitants; between local history and world history; between user and visitor; between internal and external space; between depth and superficiality" (Orbasli 2000, 8, 15). In many instances, historic preservation and conservation of the built environment eclipsed the current needs of residents, and as result, residents in heritage sites were often vying either with the past and history for recognition or with government officials for control over their built environment (Herzfeld 1991, 2009). In Damascus, ownership of the past became a struggle between the Shuwam and the regime over the meaning of the Old City, and both parties excluded long-term residents. Whereas the Shuwam claim the Old City as their patrimony, the Ba'th regime seeks to legitimize its power by controlling how urban heritage serves its national project.

Since Hakki dealt with issues of the past and the Old City in his work, I asked him about its role and place in Syrian society. Hakki spoke of "people who wanted a rupture with the past. All of it because it is takhalluf (backwardness)." He explained that this was not a unique Syrian condition but that "all over the Arab world there was a struggle over the past" and how the past "is strongly present in the life of the Arab people." He continued, "There are people who want *tahdith* (modernization). If you see the films during Abdul Nasser [Egyptian President, 1956–1970] you see in one of them old neighborhoods. The film ends with bulldozers destroying all these neighborhoods and in their place building boxes [apartment buildings]. These boxes are modernization. This point of view remains present in many of the conversations today: take away all of this old world and build modern cities like the cities in Europe."

It is familiar to hear of attempts by the state to overcome societal problems through modernization (J. Scott 1998). Hakki mentioned Arab modernizing agents had the same objectives in their respective countries. The desire to destroy the past stemmed from its image as an obstacle to progress, and this sentiment became stronger after the Six Day War of 1967, which resulted in a resounding Arab defeat and the loss of more Arab territory to Israel. In Syria, several leading intellectuals and writers disavowed the past—all of it—as "backwardness" and claimed it was the direct cause of the defeat in 1967 (Shannon 2006, xvi). What became significant about this historical period was that "backwardness" was no longer confined to the economic or political aspect of society but now included the cultural patrimony (Massad 2007, 20).

In Syria, the state did only lose the war but lost national territory, the Golan Heights, to the enemy. This defeat led to much soul-searching among political factions seeking an explanation for the defeat, not only in economic, political, or military terms but also in cultural terms. Whereas right-wing and religious groups blamed the defeat on the supposedly godless and avowed secular Ba'th regime that came to power in 1963, the regime saw tradition as the true culprit. It called for a new society: "the need to sweep away the crippling traditions of the past" and to relegate religion, capitalism, feudalism and values of old society to the "museum of history" (Petran 1972, 197). The progressive agenda of the Ba'th party supported overcoming ethnic and sectarian divisions in local society for a pan-Arab socialist identity that also undermined its political opponents. However, the Ba'th leadership never completely overcame regional and sectarian affiliation that could readily be mobilized in times of crisis. In the current civil war, the regime can mobilize members of the Alawite community as well as other minorities by stoking their fear of Sunni oppression, which is embedded in the collective memory of these groups. Hence, a break was sought with the past to create a new, strong society that would withstand outside aggression, but such a break was never completed. Some Syrians argue it was never fully embraced by the regime.

Nonetheless, the debate over the role of the past in the present was fundamental to the conservation of the Old City and other historic neighborhoods in Damascus. There was a backlash against the Old City and the courtyard houses, believed to support a traditional and "backward" lifestyle that stifled creativity and innovation, because supposedly it encouraged extended patriarchal families, gender segregation, submission of individual will, and religiosity that could border on the extreme and radical. Courtyard houses were typically described as closed to the outside and open to the inside. This enclosed structure, according to some observers, reflected the insular and antiprogress mentality of those who inhabited them. Thus, as the inheritors of the Old City, the Shuwam, were seen as part of the reactionary forces keeping Syria "backward" and defeated as they clung to their traditional city. The winding alleys and narrow lanes, incompatible with modern transportation needs, had to be destroyed to bring about national progress. Modernizing agents regardless of their political affiliation believed that any attempt to create a modern society necessitated the destruction of the Old City to create a new urban space and with it a modern urban and national subject. Urban planners in Syria were searching for their own Baron Haussmann or Robert Moses to modernize the city as these men respectively transformed Paris and New York. (Berman 1983; Harvey 1988). And he came in the form of the French urban planner Michel Ecochard, but before I explain his role in transforming the Old City, we need to understand modernity in the process of place making.

Modern Cities

What remains pertinent in the call to destroy the Old City was the appeal of modernity as a panacea for contemporary social and urban problems, particularly during times of crises. Modernity, as Paul Rabinow (1989, 9) aptly noted, is difficult to define or to conceptualize, and "it would seem more heuristic and modern ethnographic, to explore how term has been understood and used by its self-proclaimed practitioners." Hence, modernity needs to be addressed within the context of specific historical moments. According to Timothy Mitchell (2000, 1), modernity is *of* place, the West, where presumably it had its origins, and being modern became synonymous with being Western (see also Knauft 2002, 18). But modernity is also located *in* place, specifically the urban environment where it is expressed and articulated in the landscape. As several scholars have demonstrated, the modernity project was largely an urban project (Berman 1983; Holston 1989; Harvey 1990), and it is the congested and impoverished European cities of the 1800s that led to new "modernist practices and thinking" (Harvey 1990, 25). As the cityscape became the canvas on which ideas and behaviors were implemented in an effort to create new modern subjects several European cities such as Vienna and Paris were rebuilt along modern lines for that purpose (Schorske 1979; Harvey 1985). For example, the Haussmannization of Paris ushered in new forms of public spaces and spatial practices that reorganized social and economic life in the city (Harvey 1985, 73), and eventually, such practices led to the creation of the "Concept city" that "is simultaneously the machinery and hero of modernity" (de Certeau 1984, 95).

With the rise of colonialism, urban planning became a "strategy" (de Certeau 1984, xix) or the basis of control and domination of local subjects by the occupying forces, through the juxtaposition of old and modern cities built by the colonial power (J. Abu Lughod 1980; Rabinow 1989; King 1990; Wright 1991; Fuller 1992, 2007; Celik 1997). But the practice of using urban space to monitor, to control, and to dominate urban subjects was not confined to the colonial period, and after independence, many of the newly minted nation-states continued in this practice. As Holston (1989), in his seminal work on Brasilia, explained, the building of a new capital was premised on the belief that it could engender a new social order and a Brazilian national subject. Therefore, the values that underlined city design could be used as a "blueprint for change" in national development (Holston 1989, 4). Films made during Nasser's rule in Egypt that Hakki mentioned reflected a similar notion, where the destruction of traditional neighborhoods and their replacement with modern ones will result in new citizens. Farha Ghannam (2002) describes this process in the relocation of working-class residents of a historic neighborhood in central Cairo to the outer edge of the city. The residents were accused of being a blight to the modernizing city, and their presence marred the representation of Egypt to the global community. However, the relocated residents used their new surroundings to redefine themselves as modern subjects based on their interpretation of modernity rather than succumb to the official discourse.

For a brief period, between 1958 and 1961, Egypt and Syria joined to form the United Arab Republic under the leadership of Nasser, and urban planning policies popular in Egypt during that time influenced Syrian city planners (Verdeil 2012, 256). However, when the Ba'th regime came to power it favored socialist urban planning and even appointed Eastern Europeans from socialist countries as urban planners (Verdeil 2012, 256).

The example of Brasilia was echoed in different parts of the developing world where modernity and becoming modern were synonymous with "Western-style progress and development in the contemporary world," with the emphasis on secular institutions and social organizations (Knauft 2002, 18). Despite these efforts, modernity was not uniformly achieved outside the West; rather it emerged as a different creature altogether. The different modernities outside the West have been described as "alternative," "other," or "vernacular" (Gaonkar 1999; Rofel 1999; Mitchell 2000), but all emphasize a process of "creative adaptation" that, based on their own local circumstances, individuals and states employ to become modern in their own way and on their own terms (Gaonkar 1999, 16).

Yet this replication needs to be placed within the local context of how Western modernity's aura is seen as a strategy to deal with local social and political problems at particular historical moments. The movement to protect the Old City from demolition in the late 1970s and early 1980s was taking place when the Ba'th regime was fighting the Muslim Brotherhood. The Muslim Brotherhood had attacked military establishments and cadet training centers and, in 1980, attempted to assassinate then President Hafiz al-Asad (Hinnebusch 2001, 100). Traditionally, the brotherhood had strongholds and mass supporters in the historic urban center in Syria, especially in Hama and Aleppo, which were also the site of urban unrest, as well as in Damascus, though disturbances in the capital city were contained (Hinnebusch 2001, 97).[7] In 1982, the

7. In 1982 and after a series of attacks on military centers and personnel by the Muslim Brotherhood, the state razed to the ground most of the Old City in Hama where the brotherhood was quartered. The brotherhood had declared the city liberated, and since the narrow streets of the historic quarter prevented the government forces from entering, they destroyed them (Hinnebusch 2001, 93–102). In 2011 and 2012, the same scenario was repeated in another attempt by the Ba'th regime to quell any opposition by destroying entire neighborhoods and villages.

government confiscated property around the Umayyad Mosque to build a ceremonial square wide enough for the motorcades of the president and official delegations even though by then the Old City was listed on the UNESCO World Heritage Site. Described as part of an effort to revitalize the Old City, especially for tourism (McConnell 1982), the modernization of the historic urban core was also a strategy to contain the impact of the Muslim Brotherhood by giving government forces quick access to the residential neighborhoods. Although at the time many of the displaced residents and shopkeepers protested the demolition, others welcomed it as a move to preserve the "character" of the Old City (Miller 1982). However, as several Syrians whispered to me, championing urban change demonstrated support for the government in its fight against the Muslim Brotherhood. But there is no real contradiction between these two objectives, preservation and surveillance, since they both aim to create a more accessible and easily controlled urban space. This is what the Ottomans and French did; the Ba'th regime used the same tools of power as their predecessors.

Therefore, in the late 1970s and early 1980s, the future of the Old City was also being debated within the social and political context of the Muslim Brotherhood, adding another layer to the earlier debates on the role of the past in the wake of the 1967 defeat. Not only was the brotherhood the main organized opposition to the regime, but their stronghold was in the old cities of the main urban centers of Syria.[8] Since old cities were already considered conducive to a "backward" mentality that opposed progress and led to defeat and social conservatism, it was a short step to blame the built environment for encouraging retrograde movements such as the Muslim Brotherhood. One activist who defended the Old City from

8. It is easy to reduce the conflict between the Muslim Brotherhood and regime as Sunni versus Alawite. Although there have been tensions between the two groups, especially since the latter assumed control of the state, not all Sunnis in Syria supported the brotherhood. Historically, the Muslim Brotherhood in Syria was urban based, but it did not have support among the professionals and progressive Sunnis. Activities of the brotherhood in different parts of the Middle East demonstrate that they oppose any regime they define as un-Islamic.

demolition put himself at odds with progressive and liberal elements in society who thought he was siding with the Muslim Brotherhood. Ironically, he supported the government and opposed the Muslim Brotherhood, but he had to convince his detractors that the "civilization" of the Old City he was trying to preserve did not belong to, or cause the rise of, the Muslim Brotherhood. Although the neighborhoods in the Old City of Damascus were more diverse, with Jews, Christians, and Muslims who did not support the brotherhood, because of the violence that gripped the country at the time it was easy to conflate the historical neighborhoods with Islamic fundamentalism, "backwardness," and antimodernism.

Defending "Civilization"

Nadia Khost was a Syrian preservation activist who did not reject the past but insisted that it had become maligned by "backward" and ignorant individuals that needed to be educated on the importance of the Old City. She was also a well-known novelist and journalist who used her writing to crusade for the protection of the historic areas of Damascus.[9] She was born and raised in Suq Sarujeh to which she retained a strong attachment. When she returned from studying abroad and found her childhood courtyard home bulldozed and buried under a boulevard she became active in the effort to preserve the built heritage. Her books, *Al-Hijra min al-Jinna* (1989) (*Exodus from Paradise*) and *Dimashq: Dhakirat al-Insan wa al-Hajr* (1993) (*Memories of Humans and Stone*), written in a highly polemical style, forewarn the disappearance of the Old City could lead to a loss

---

9. Most of Khost's historical novels deal with Damascus and greater Syria. She is one of several Syrian women novelists who wrote about Damascus, including but not limited to 'Ulfat Idlibi, Colette Khoury, Ghada al-Saman, Siham Tergeman, and Amal Al-Jarah. Many of these women novelists portray Damascus as a woman, a girl, and even their lover, as they see urban history, especially in the twentieth century, mirrors some of their experiences as women in a patriarchal society full of uncertainty and confusion during modernization and social change. It is worth noting these women writers developed a strong identification with Damascus and conflated their struggle as women with the problems of the Old City.

of memory and a severe national identity crisis.[10] She marshaled a vast array of resources to block the demolition of neighborhoods and buildings throughout the city and served at one point on the advisory council to the governor of Damascus. She used her column in the daily newspaper *Tishreen* to mobilize public opinion and to inform the public about historic areas in the city threatened with destruction. She was an engaging public speaker and appeared numerous times on state-run Syrian television to speak on behalf of historic Damascus. Her name is synonymous with the fight to protect history and memory in Damascus. She fought for the protection of the Old City because it is *hawiyya hadariyya* (civilizational identity). Khost was aware of the universal value of Damascus, but she maintained it was strictly a Syrian Arab national patrimony. Although it is difficult to gauge her influence, she protected houses of notable Shuwam from demolition and supported the cause of the long-term residents of Hamrawi, a neighborhood near the Umayyad Mosque threatened with destruction since the 1960s.[11] I found her perseverance in saving the Old City remarkable, especially since she dissented in some ways from the prevailing local discourse on *turath* (heritage) and modernity.

Khost believed the past was not a foreign country but where Arab and Syrian identity originated; therefore, a rupture with the past was detrimental. She was indefatigable in her efforts to remind the public that the past should be a source of pride and strength. The past not only was the

10. Women have been at the forefront to protect the historic districts of Damascus from demolition. In addition to Khost, one of the vocal defenders of Damascus has been Siham Tergeman (1969) who wrote *Ya Mal Al-Sham* (*Oh Bounty That Is* al-Sham), which included a compilation of folk songs and sayings, as well as stories from growing up in a historic neighborhood. This was one of the first of several memoirs on life in a courtyard house and a traditional quarter that helped usher in an industry that fed the nostalgia for the Old City while raising awareness for urban preservation. The memoir part was translated into English.

11. In the fall 2002, I met with several shopkeepers in Suq al-Miskiyyah, outside the Umayyad Mosque threatened with eviction. Their stores were already reduced in size from the 1982 demolitions to build the ceremonial square outside the mosque. This time, the few remaining shopkeepers were determined to fight. They told me if and when Nadia Khost knew about their plight she would do something.

legacy of earlier civilizations but also provided a moral code for social relations and being in the city. Khost had a hermeneutical approach for understanding the role of the Damascus past in its present and was exasperated by those individuals who could not see what she thought was evident about the heritage of Damascus.

I was fortunate to interview her several times and to walk with her in Damascus. In an interview, she described how some Syrians felt about the Old City:

There are people, I tell you, they do not want Damascus they say Damascus is Umayyad, yes there are backward people who still think like that. They say what is Damascus, even in [the Department of] Antiquities. Let me tell you. We were meeting in the parliament and [the speaker of the house] was very understanding and sympathetic. He would tell us to come and meet and we would go and hold meetings. He understood because he lived in the Old City for a period of time. We met with all the representatives of Damascus as well as the Minister of Culture and a representative from the Ministry of Tourism and Ministry of Information and a group from Antiquities. The Antiquities group, do you know what they told me? One of them said to me what is this Damascus? It is mud and wood, what do we want with it? The Minister of Culture, who was a woman at the time, had to reprimand them. She told them they cannot say this. You see how we have this backward mentality.

Khost defined individuals who did not care about the Old City as "backward" because they were not only ignorant of their history but also easily seduced by Western examples of modernity she considered inferior to the treasures of historic Damascus. The "backward mentality" was also mentioned by Syrian businessmen as the obstacle to economic liberalization (Selvik 2009). Young private entrepreneurs who welcomed neoliberalism worked on overcoming the social and cultural obstacles rather than institutional and state shortcomings to creating a business-friendly environment (Selvik 2009, 54–56). Therefore, progressive elements in society, whether seeking to protect the Old City from destruction or solving the country's economic problems, shared a common enemy in the backward mentality.

Blaming the "backward mentality" for economic and social woes absolves the state from any wrongdoing, especially in maintaining certain sociopolitical conditions that allow those with a "backward mentality" the power to obstruct change. It also pits social actors against one another and, in the process, reinforces hierarchies of "civilized" and "backward" that ensure social divisions instead of collaboration or cooperation. Blaming the "mentality" can also empower social actors because it allows them recourse to action, restricted as it may be nonetheless, to bring about change. The obstacle to saving the Old City is the "backward mentality," which the state insists it is helpless against; hence, it is up to those social actors who want improvement to work to change it. Khost sat in on city council meetings; she wrote about the preservation of the Old City and lectured to government workers on the importance of the built environment. If she and others like her succeeded in their efforts, then the state could appropriate their efforts. If not, then the cultural obstacles were too strong to overcome and the regime cannot be faulted. Preservation activists were able to convince the government to protect the Old City, and new policies were enacted to save the Old City and other historic district from modernization.

However, Khost opposed a shift in the local mind-set to embrace Western models of urban planning because she believed that Arab cities were older than many countries in the West and possessed more accumulated and relevant knowledge. Therefore, the shift in mentality is toward local knowledge rooted in good tradition rather than toward Western modernity. She attempted to "provincialize" the West through privileging local forms of knowledge and practices (Chakrabarty 2000). She was not seduced by the West but rather sought to undermine its authority as the point of reference for any discourse on social change. I was inspired by Khost's usage of the local past as a referent instead of the tradition–modernity binary that usually references the West as well as uses terms of discourse that do not emanate from local conditions.

Dipesh Chakrabarty (2000, 46) has called for "other narratives of human connections" in his attempt to "provincialize Europe," and his approach is useful to understanding how Syrians such as Khost defined their own debates and set the parameters of the discourse on social and urban change rather than having it set for them. Khost, as much as possible, was using local narratives that were not "hegemonized" and "homogenized" by Western discourses of modernity (Asad 1987, 603). As Chakrabarty made cogent, provencializing Europe was not to dismiss European thought but to highlight its shortcoming when understanding non-Western realities. He was also seeking new ways for "how this thought—which is now everybody's heritage and which affects us all—may be renewed from and for the margins" (16). Hence, to understand gentrification of the Old City through the dyad of "civilization" and "backwardness" rather than "modernity" and "tradition" is an attempt in this direction.

Khost critiqued the trend to imitate the West in cultural and political issues, which was dominate after 1967, specifically by the generation of Syrians raised on undermining the Arab past (Shannon 2006, 74–77). Moreover, in Khost's support for local forms of knowledge she worked against the process of modernity that broke the past into increments, where "every image of the past that [was] not recognized by the present as one of its own concerns threaten[ed] to disappear irretrievably" (Benjamin 1968b, 255). This process could fragment the Old City into Umayyad, Ayyubid, or Mameluke rather than their aggregate "civilization" and render it easier to destroy the historic core by eliminating unpopular periods.

The past in the Old City could easily be dismissed when the political rivalries of the present are imposed on the past. An Umayyad Damascus promoted a Sunni Arab hegemony that worried some non-Sunni, mainly the Shia, and non-Arabs living in Syria. An Ayyubid Damascus highlighted its Kurdish legacy. Furthermore, since the relatively prosperous merchants lived in the intramural neighborhood, many groups considered the Old City the Damascus of the bourgeoisie, the wealthy, the privileged, and the entitled. It was this image that ironically united the often warring factions: the leftist groups and the Ba'th were united with elements of the Muslim Brotherhood, if on nothing else, in supporting the demolition of the Old City because it supposedly belonged to the bourgeoisie.

The past serves different purposes (Lowenthal 1985, 1996), but in the context of the Arab world, the past as turath (heritage) insisted on its relevance to the present by demonstrating its continuity. Muhammad Al-Jabari (1991, 23) has stated that when translated as "heritage" or "patrimony" turath does not fully encompass the emotion and ideology in the Arabic usage of the term. In its current meaning and usage such as by Khost, turath represents the inherited cultural, intellectual, religious, literary, and artistic output within an ideological sentiment that units all Arabs and serves as a referent for the present not only to what has happened but also to what should have happened and did not (23–24). It is the standard by which to evaluate the present, largely because of the "ontological void of today" (Al-Azmeh 1993, 48). Hence, there is no faith in the ability of the modernity of the present to tackle society's most pressing problems, which can only be resolved through reworking the past. Both Aziz al-Azmeh and al-Jabri observed the past was important for its role in forging the future but precludes a despotic or a tyrannical hold on the future. According to al-Jabri, turath should be developed and improved to serve its purpose in meeting the demands of the present by moving from the realm of the theoretical to the practical (105). Al-Azmeh on the other hands believed the past derived its power from its inherent and unquestioned "authenticity" (56).

Turath has largely referred to an intellectual, discursive, and textual inheritance from previous civilizations (Massad 2007, 17) rather than for a vernacular and tangible tradition. As Joseph Massad (2007, 29) has observed, turath has undergone "myriad interpretations" since the late nineteenth century but remained committed "to an evolutionary temporal schema that recognizes change only within the dyad of turath and modernity." In such an interpretation turath was always posited against a western evolutional scheme of progress. The turath that concerned al-Jabri, al-Azmeh and Massad were the classical texts that have been interpreted by philosophers, historians, literary critics, and other scholars. The vernacular is of more interest to the public and has more concrete applications. There has been a bias in Arab intellectual thought against the common, vernacular, and oral tradition.

Nonetheless, the same understanding for the textual turath applies to the vernacular if we accept Khost's appreciation for the past comes from dwelling in the Old City. Yet in the current gentrification, the turath is not only used to guide and affirm the present, there are also economic opportunities with the increase in the desire for the consumption of all things old (Salamandra 2004, 3). The preservation of the traditional courtyard dwelling is an attempt to "monumentalize the vernacular." In Rethemnos, Greece, the struggle between long-term residents and the state was over "monumental" versus social time (Herzfeld 1991). Under new economic conditions in Syria, investors were choosing to imbue the vernacular turath with the qualities of classical turath. Though this should not be confused with attempts at democratizing turath, the appeal of the vernacular past is mainly in its marketability. Investors rather than intellectuals remake the authenticity of the past to suit their own purposes and have a less conflicted relationship with turath than many Arab intellectuals (see Massad 2007).

Maybe the split between classical and vernacular should not have happened in the first place because both reflect local cultural discourses on social change and continuity. Vernacular turath also poses a set of challenges similar to the classical textual turath. As the interpretation of the textual turath resulted in exegeses where the original or authentic source remained untouched, the different interpretations of the vernacular heritage is accused of destroying the material "essence" of the past. I will return to this theme in chapter 6.

Syria Modern

In his work on how the Alamo became part of the national cultural memory, Richard Flores (2002, xvii) used the term "Texas Modern" to describe the sequence of historic and political events that led to the social and economic transformations of Texas. A sequence of events in Syria beginning in the Ottoman period led to social and political transformation of urban environment of Damascus and the emergence of new neighborhoods distinct from the traditional districts of the city. It was during this time that the basis for "civilization" and "backwardness" became concentrated in ways the past configured in the debates on modernity. The making of the Old City provides insight to the cultural *"production* of difference" and otherness in Damascus (Gupta and Ferguson 1997b, 43; emphasis in original) that helps explain the role of the past in creating the dyad "civilized"–"backward."

The Ottomans in their modernization of Damascus began to locate the "other" in their Arab provinces, and instead of seeing subjects of the empire, they saw objects for their own "civilizing" mission (Makdisi 2002). At this point, Ottomans adapted the concept of secular, Western "Time" (Fabian 1983) and began to view history as the glorious past and decaying present, attributing the latter to their Arab subjects. The French, however, did not deviate from the Ottoman position and added a new vocabulary when talking about the historic city in terms of lacking health and hygiene. Hence, the idea that the Old City was unhealthy and dirty contributed to its image as a declining urban center whose role and future in a modern state was debatable. In this period, tradition was projected onto the intramural city and by extension onto the people who chose to live there. It was part of the colonial discourse to equate spatial organization with mentality, where "colonial ethnographers considered the confusing—from a European perspective—maze of narrow, winding streets and blind alleys of traditional North African cities . . . to be a direct spatial projection of the 'alogical' disorder of the 'indigenous mentality'" (Eickelman 1981, 269).

Orientalism and colonialism began the process of delinking individuals from their built environment and severing the ties of sociability that existed to create new subjects and social relations. The ruins and monuments reinforced the romanticism of a decaying, neglected past that should be preserved and conserved. However, people living in a decaying historic setting were unhealthy and "backward." Hence, the French sought to isolate the European population from the Arab population in their colonies. Isolation was also important if either group were to survive in a colonizer–colonized relationship; hence, the French erected ring roads, physical barriers between the new neighborhoods where the French lived and Old City. Many notions concerning the lifestyle of the inhabitants of the Old City remained after independence, since by then they became universal tools of power, underscoring how colonial and postcolonial powers operated in similar ways.

At the end of the Ottoman rule, Damascus was different than it was in 1516, although most of the profound changes occurred in the last few decades of their rule. Natural expansion accounted for most of the urban transformations as more neighborhoods were built outside the wall to accommodate the population increase. The center of Damascus shifted away from the intramural city, and the relationship between the Old City and the new city altered drastically. Damascus underwent major expansion outside the wall under the Ottomans when they were able to establish security and stability in the city. The expansion was accompanied by shifting the city center away from the central rectangle to Al-Marjeh Square where civic institutions were constructed. It was also during the Ottoman period that the remains of the past were considered heritage and the target of preservation efforts.

In what was considered the first recorded act of historic preservation in Damascus, Kaiser Wilhelm II who visited Syria in 1898 found the tomb of Saladin in the Old City near the Umayyad Mosque in a state of neglect and ruin, and he provided the funds for its restoration (Ball 1994, 60). This induced the Ottomans to engage in heritage preservation that focused on the monuments in the Old City. Although the last Ottoman ruler of Damascus, Jamal Pasha, held the Arabs in contempt, he was not above instilling in them an awareness of their past (Kayali 1998). During World War I, he implemented several public works, urban renewal, and cultural education programs aimed at modernizing the Arabs. The German consultants he hired pressed him to preserve monuments.[12] The "heritagization" of the built environment began by cataloging and removing monuments from their local context, a process that continued with the French and through independence. Through the designation of historical monuments and their preservation efforts, the Ottomans were reconstructing history to give legitimacy to their presence in Syria (Kayali 1998, 306).

The French continued many of the Ottoman policies in the Old City and further isolated the intramural neighborhoods from the rest of Damascus. Although Damascus was a provincial capital under the Ottomans, the city was chosen by the French as the seat of power to what became

---

12. The first survey of historical sites and monuments in Damascus was conducted by two Germans, Watzinger and Wulzinger (1921–1924).

the Syrian Arab Republic. The French understood the Syrian territories through their colonial experience in North Africa, which led to disastrous results in the attempt to develop an effective local government (Khoury 1987, 44). However, in urban planning, they were more effective and readily implemented policies and plans shortly after assuming the mandate (Gaudin 1992, 179). Moreover, several French urban planners working in Syria, such as the brothers Danger and Michel Ecochard, developed their colonial urban experience in North Africa as part of their work with the colonial administration (Abdulac 1982; Fries 1994, 312; Verdeil 2012). In the interwar period, the Dangers and Ecochard, worked with a local cadre and influenced urban policy and development for Beirut, Aleppo, and Damascus (Gaudin 1992, 179). In the 1960s, Ecochard was invited by the Syrian government to work on a new urban plan for Damascus that proved controversial.

In North Africa, the French had a longer colonial involvement and were interested in demonstrating racial and cultural superiority by juxtaposing and isolating the historic city from the modern neighborhoods (Abu Lughod 1980; Rabinow 1989; Wright 19991). French colonial urban planning was indebted to Hubert Lyautey who was interested in an urban environment that allowed coexistence of individuals from different social and cultural backgrounds but segregated the local and colonial populations—local population in the old and Europeans in modern neighborhoods (Rabinow 1989, 285–86; Wright 1991, 75–78; Celik 1997, 39). Moreover, as Shirine Hamadeh (1992, 252) has shown for the medina in Tunis, the separation between the new neighborhoods where the French lived and the medina of the locals led to the "objectification of the old city."

Lyautey was interested in the preservation of old cities, not merely out of respect for the local culture but also because of their economic value as tourist attractions (Rabinow 1989, 288; Wright 1991, 134). When the International Congress on Urbanism in the Colonies met in 1931, they adopted many of Lyautey's ideas, especially the protection of old cities and historic monuments to encourage tourism (Celik 1997, 40).

In Damascus, the French mapped the city and cataloged the heritage sites, continuing what the Germans began under the Ottomans. The French archaeologist Jean Sauvaget (1934) explored what he believed to be the Roman grid plan for Damascus and claimed it was located in the southeast and west of the city. Sauvaget believed that "old" Damascus, though it had a certain charm, was an "inextricable mess of alley ways" in which a European could easily get lost (Gaudin 1992, 198). He believed that over the course of millennia, the ordered grid disappeared, and, as Heghnar Watenpaugh (2004, 18) has indicated, he considered the Roman city plan as the ideal urban form, morally superior to anything else that followed. Therefore, what came after the Roman civilization was considered a regression. Khost (1993, 28–29) condemned Sauvaget, claiming he failed to notice the role of the built environment in creating harmony with nature and in addressing human need for sociability and privacy. She critiqued not only Sauvaget but also urban planners who considered his approach to restructuring Damascus scientific. Khost thought urban planners were ignorant and easily seduced by Sauvaget's pronouncements on the Old City (29). Naturally, she condemned the numerous urban plans that called for the destruction of wide swathes of the historic districts in Damascus, including the Old City.

The process of designating the intramural section as the traditional city ignored the organic expansions of neighborhoods inside the wall. The rupture was apparent as the distinction between traditional and modern neighborhoods came to represent a different lifestyle and worldview. In addition, the survey of the monuments under the Ottomans and the French was the first step in heritage preservation that neglected the vernacular buildings. Even Ecochard, as a planner in the Department of Antiquities, was charged with surveying the monuments of Damascus to preserve their unique qualities from neglect (Gaudin 1992, 199–200). The French emphasis on hygiene and transportation in urban planning meant demolishing houses to create open spaces and widening roads to improve traffic in the Old City. Yet the French interest in the Old City inspired Syrians such as Khaled Maoz, who worked with Sauvaget on documenting Damascus, to advocate for the preservation of the Old City.

By the time the French left Syria in 1946, the intramural city was widely seen as old, traditional, and incompatible with modernity, although it had some prestige as the locus of resistance against the French. The detailed mapping and cataloging of the heritage sites in the Old City reinforced the division between historic and modern neighborhoods. The monuments were considered turath, but the vernacular buildings became the site of "backwardness." An international UNESCO committee visited Syria in the summer of 1953 and issued a report the same year calling for the preservation of the Old City because of its unique concentration of monuments and heritage sites in the central rectangle, a relatively small area. There was no mention of the vernacular buildings or residents. The committee cautioned that preservation did not entail condoning urban decay: "It is with no doubt that there are many elements that have no value and are parasitic establishments and unhealthy in the old neighborhoods. This condition is only natural because the Old City has its diseases and ailments like any living being. However, the elimination of these harmful elements requires detailed care and proper assessment of all that needs to be amended or eliminated" (UNESCO 1953, 38).

The anthropomorphical intramural neighborhood created a gap between the built environment and its social users. The preservation of the Old City was privileged over the needs of the long-term residents and the disease of the Old City was implied to be its long-term residents. This choice of seeing the built environment and not social users ignored the sociopolitical conditions in Syria that led to the neglect of the long-term residents.

The Return of Ecochard

As we saw earlier the rise of the Ba'th regime in 1963 came in the midst of the debate on modernity and tradition and the future of the Old City. The progressive agenda of the early Ba'th party encouraged modernization of society on all levels, and the government hired French urban planner Michel Ecochard, who worked in Damascus during the mandate, to modernize the city.[13] Along with his partner, Banshoya of Japan, he submitted a master plan for Damascus in 1968 that recommended demolishing wide swaths of the Old City to increase vehicular traffic in the Old City and

---

13. For more on the role of Ecochard in the urbanization of Damascus, see Abdulac (1982).

create parking lots around the major monuments. Ecochard had been vilified by many Syrians for suggesting the demolition of the traditional built environment. Many activists such as Khost and Siham Tergeman considered his plan an imperialist plot against the historic urban. Both women rallied against the European architect who they claimed could not understand nor fathom the Arab city (Tergeman 1969, 34–35; Khost 1993, 239). Khost (1993, 241–42) saw in his plan an insidious plot to erase the Arab city made worst by the support of government officials. Ecochard's plan generated much debate over the role and place of the Old City in greater Damascus since he valued roads and cars over the alleys and walking. He did not consider the difference between the intramural and new neighborhoods outside the wall (Bianca 1986, 12–13). Some of his recommendations were eventually implemented in the 1970s and 1980s, including the construction of highways that crisscrossed the city and encircled the Old City, further isolating it from its surroundings.

Ecochard was more interested in monuments, since he was in charge of their preservation during the mandate, than in the vernacular architecture, and this bias came through in his plan (Gaudin 1992, 199–200; Verdeil 2012, 252). Although many Syrians attribute sinister political and imperial motives for his plan to destroy the Old City and erase its Arab identity, they ignored or did not recognize that he was the student of Le Corbusier who believed that old cities and historic districts were unhealthy, "simplistic and outdated" (Rodwell 2007, 34) and preferred to rebuild them in modernist and functionalist modes (Rabinow 1989, 2; Verdeil 2012). Cities according to Le Corbusier were "machines for living in" (Harvey 1990, 32), and in modernism, "human needs are universal"; therefore, there is no need to pay attention to local conditions (Rabinow 1989, 3). Cities were to be revitalized and organized to run efficiently and effectively through organized transportation systems, hence the opening of roads that cut through densely populated neighborhoods in Damascus. Therefore, we see how driving was privileged over walking, and with the downgrading of walking, many Syrians lost interest in the Old City.

Eric Verdeil (2012, 250) suggested Ecochard did not deviate from his colonial training in urban planning from the period during the mandate, maintaining much of the approach to urban issues as during the colonial

years. Furthermore, he was invited by the independent and national government of Syria based on his earlier experience in Syria. Nonetheless,
his plan caused a huge public uproar and was greatly modified, although
it keeps reappearing in different forms to address urban planning issues
(Verdeil 2012, 258). To ward off the threat of demolishing the Old City in
the name of modernization, a grassroots movement, consisting mainly of
residents, scholars, historians, artists, and writers, coordinated efforts to
save the Old City from demolition. Khost (1993, 242) gave some details
about a group of intellectuals meeting with government officials in an
attempt to convince them to save the Arab city. Writers became the leading activists in calling for the protection of the Old City (Salamandra
2004, 135). Individual efforts combined with the work of the commission
organized by the Department of Antiquities to supervise the Old City
(McConnell 1982) led to the designation of a UNESCO's World Heritage
Site in 1979. It was among the first historic urban cores to be listed in the
UNESCO registry of universal patrimony. However, the designation did
not include a management plan but allowed nations to devise their own
plan for heritage preservation (Rodwell 2007, 133).

The timing of Ecochard and Banshoya's plan was also significant
because it was published in the wake of the Arab defeat in 1967. Several
activists working on behalf of protecting the Old City from destruction
came to its defense and wrote memoirs and treatises highlighting its civilization and heritage. Siham Tergeman published one of the first memoirs
in 1969 about living in a bayt 'arabi in a traditional quarter. It exploited
the growing nostalgia for the comfort of courtyard houses increasingly
felt in the wake of the defeat in 1967 by many people who were raised in
one but no longer lived there. The courtyard evoked a golden past not
associated with humiliation and defeat. Tergeman spoke longingly about
her childhood home and recounted stories, recipes, childhood games,
and riddles as well as trips to the *hammam*. In the first chapter titled
"ana raj'iyyeh" (I am returning, or I am reactionary), she played on the
meaning of return as a reaction to the current conditions facing Syria and
the Arab world. Not unlike Khost, she argued for progress that was not
defined by Western models.

Abdul Qadir Al-Rihawi (1969, 86), who worked in the Department of Antiquities during the French Mandate, had to defend his intention for preserving the Old City: "I do not want the reader to understand my concern for the protection of Old Damascus and my opposition to those who want to modernize it, that I want it to remain in this state of neglect, banned from all development and rehabilitation. I want it to have its share of all the services necessary for the existence of its population on the condition that this does not lead to its eradication or affect its historical appearance and original nature." He may have been thinking about the defeat of 1967 as he assured his readers his support for the Old City was not simply reactionary.

Therefore, as a result of social and political transformations along with the defeat in 1967, the Old City was considered an unsanitary and dirty place, unsuitable for living, though some of the monuments merited preservation. Others did not believe the monuments should be separated from the vernacular because their sum makes the Old City. Yet al-Rihawi's appeal was to stress the "historical appearance and original nature" of the Old City that privileged the time when Shuwam lived there but ignored the current rural migrant inhabitants. He also cautioned that the period of rapid modernization and political defeat should not result in preferring new neighborhoods over the Old City. According to al-Rihawi and other activists who labored to protect the Old City from demolition, the neighborhoods outside the wall were not the true Sham and could not become a substitute for the historic districts. Several interviews I conducted with Nadia Khost reiterated that the al-Sham is not Abu Rummaneh and Malki (two elite modern neighborhoods) but the historic districts, including the Old City. The modern neighborhoods were designed by urban planners and built by architects and lacked any individuality. As Hakki also noticed, to live in one modern neighborhood in Damascus is the same as living elsewhere in the country. Moreover, without the historic districts, especially the Old City, there would not be the contrast in embodied experience that brings about the cultural dynamics of "civilized" and "backward." Although there would be another embodied experience, the essence of what it means to be Shami remains rooted in the Old City.

Some Syrians, especially the Shuwam, took exception to the state's "monumental conception of history" (Herzfeld 1991) since it diluted their own claim to the Old City. They also suspected the motive of the predominantly Alawite regime supporting the protection of the Old City and the role of government agencies such as the CPOC (Salamandra 2004, 82–89). Although these suspicions are an extension of the animosity of local anti-Ba'th and anti-Alawite entities for anything initiated by the regime and though sometimes they are justified, they do not necessarily refer to actual plots against the Old City. The Old City was abandoned by the Shuwam who pursued modernity outside the wall, and the heritagization of the historic center began during the Ottoman period. There is nothing significant about the process of heritagization and gentrification of the Old City that does not echo the same concerns of residents of other cities around the world (see Herzfeld 2009, 1991). This is not an attempt to downplay local concerns and dismiss the social conflicts in Damascus, but rather to recast the events in Syria as part of the politics of heritage where the state, any state, uses the past as means of "political control through temporal as well as spatial marginalization" (Herzfeld 2005b, 370).

Return to Civilization

The Old City remained at the center of the debates on urban and national modernization even after it was declared a heritage site. In 1982, a colloquium called for the protection, maintenance, restoration, and documentation of the Old City, as well as the establishment of tourism in certain areas (Hasan 1985, 443). The conference proceedings recommended tourism as a "civilized form of investment" over "industrial investment," a reference to such industries in the Old City as tanning, which created pollution and endangered the built environment. A decade later this became government policy. Investment in tourism is supported from the highest levels, starting with the president's office. One official in the Ministry of Culture that oversees the Old City told me the Minister of Tourism stressed the role of tourism in economic growth and called for fewer restrictions on investments in the Old City. According to the official someone at the meeting quipped whether this would lead to *taswih* or *tasyih* (touristification or dissolution) of the city.[14] The pun on the Arabic word for tourism (*siyaha*) underscores the anxieties many feel about the rapid gentrification of the Old City that does not allow for understanding its ramifications on the fragile built environment and on the people who live there. It also demonstrates the competing interests of government ministries and private investors under economic liberalization. Currently, the promotion of tourism is far from the mind of the regime as it battles insurgents in several cities throughout the country, halting the *taswih* or *tasyih* of the Old City for the foreseeable future.

The new restaurants attracted local customers who came to the Old City to experience the past. This movement was described as ʿawda (return) in the figurative sense to "civilization" since many do not move back (Salamandra 2004, 77). Yet ʿawda is an important commentary on social differences and is associated with the middle and upper classes. The poor are not encouraged to come to the Old City, and the less privileged in the Old City are encouraged to relocate because their presence is deemed harmful to the heritage site.

As early as 1982, when efforts to revitalize the Old City were under way, the director general of the Department of Antiquities, Dr. Affi Bahn-assi, wanted to bring back residents who had moved away (McConnell 1982). For more than twenty-five years, there has been a growing trend to buy houses in the Old City to live in, though seldom by descendants of the former residents who left in the middle of the last century. Throughout the past several decades, while the future of the Old City was being debated, it remained a viable and vital urban center with schools, clinics, workshops, small factories, businesses, and other services and activities. Gentrification will undoubtedly impact urban vitality.

I began this chapter with a walk from the new neighborhoods to the Old City to provide the reader with a temporal and spatial image of the city

---

14. In the past few years, there have been several travel articles in Western newspapers and magazines about tourism in the Old City. See, for example, http://www.thenational.ae/article/20090131/TRAVEL/803494536/0/NEWS, *New York Times*, http://query.nytimes.com/gst/fullpage.html?res=9A00E7DE163DF931A25755C0A9639C8B63 and *Guardian*, http://www.guardian.co.uk/travel/2008/dec/20/damascus-syria-shopping.

and how the contrast between the new and old neighborhoods brought about the dialectical relationship between "civilization" and "backwardness." Yet the tension between the images of the new and old city were the result of how the "neutral grid" of space was inscribed with notions of "civilization" and "backwardness." The Old City remains an important forum for negotiating social change and identity constructions under new conditions.

These different interpretations of history and heritage remain relevant in the current gentrification since they are finding new expressions in the gentrification of the Old City and in the renovation of the bayt 'arabi into new sites for cultural consumption. Before we discuss how the courtyard house emerged as the new site for the debates on "civilized" and "backward," we must first understand the social categories that have developed in the process of making the Old City. Houses only make sense when we see how social actors lived in them. Therefore, the next chapter continues the discussion begun in this chapter on the making of the Old City and looks at how social actors were defined in the process. We will explore the development of the Shami–rural binary as well as how this division became associated with notions of "civilized" and "backward" social actors.

2

"Villagers Do Not Become Shuwam"

I return to the series *Dhikryat* for a specific scene that illustrates the impact of the Old City on new rural immigrants, and that will set the theme for the discussion to follow on the Shami–rural binary that has long defined social hierarchies in the city. In this scene, a young female migrant narrates her introduction to Damascus. Born in a village to ignorant and "backward" parents she realized at an early age she wanted more of life then the limited opportunities of the village. She did well enough in school to graduate and enter the university in Damascus to study law. On her way to the city, she vowed never to go back to the village but to make al-Sham her new home. But the city was not hospitable; instead, she was met with Shami snobbery toward rural migrants. One day, on her way to the court to sit in on hearings, she slipped and fell. Only one young man came to her aid who, she found out, lived in the Old City. She asked him whether there were any rooms for rent in his neighborhood, because she believed that if she lived in the Old City, the heart of Damascus, "she will understand the city and it will understand her." Hence, to overcome social alienation and ostracism in Damascus, she had to unlock the key to the city, which was only possible by dwelling in the Old City.

Although a dramatized narrative, several elements resonate with many rural migrants to Damascus, especially for people seeking to improve their social standing. Upward social mobility was mediated through the urban setting because opportunities existed in the city, but more importantly, urban dwellers ranked higher than residents of villages. The fictional lawyer already assumed that her presence in Damascus would be transformative. No longer will she be a country "hick" but will become a sophisticated urban dweller. However, this transformation could not occur without living in the Old City because that is where the "essence" of being a Damascus dweller, a Shami, originates. It is assumed rural migrants transform into urbanites by embodying the Old City. The young man who came to her assistance lived in the Old City and demonstrated Shami civility, and though it is not clear whether he was Shami, he at least was "Shamified," or had undergone the process of becoming a "civilized" urban subject. Moreover, the marginalization she experienced outside the wall could be mitigated in the Old City because she will be embedded in the daily practices of the neighborhood. By dwelling there and by being seen in the alleys, she will be less unfamiliar to the city. At the same time, the city and its ways will become familiar to her. However, the Old City is where cheap accommodations are found; therefore, it makes sense for recent arrivals to Damascus to live there.

In this chapter, I examine the evolution of the Shami identity as a distinct social category with the "other" located in the rural migrant. This examination entails an analysis of how being Shami came to stand not only for people of a certain origin but also for a civility and sense of aesthetics associated with living in the Old City and the bayt 'arabi. In the next chapter, I discuss how being Shami evolved through dwelling in the courtyard house, while in this chapter, I focus on the often contentious relationship between the city and the country in its historical context. What further complicates the urban–rural binary in Damascus is the rise of the Ba'th party, with its predominantly rural membership and leadership. When Hafiz al-Asad became president in 1970, the presence of Alawites was noticed in state institutions, and many Shuwam believed they dominated the local bureaucracy. Hence, a new subset of the urban–rural binary arose, the Shami–Alawite division, and some Shuwam worried the regime's urban policies endangered the Old City and Damascus (Salamandra 2004, 33).

What is fascinating in the narrative of urban–rural relations in Damascus is even though the city has always been a magnet for rural migrants throughout its long history the political transformations of the previous century altered the relationship between the city and the countryside. Before the rise of the Ba'th party, rural migrants eventually assimilated and adopted the urban way of life, and many prominent Shami families are recognized as having migrated to the city at some point.[1] However, since the 1960s, moving to the city was less about assimilation and adapting an urban lifestyle and more about becoming better villagers. Though the rise of the socialist regime marks the beginning of the transformation in urban–rural relations, the shift is the result of not just political change but also social and economic factors. As Tahire Erman (1998) observed in rural migration to Ankara, migrants have a different approach to assimilation and choose the extent they want to integrate into urban society. Erman calls attention to the different experiences among rural migrants that is elided in the binary urban–rural, especially in the ways rural migrants define their place in the city in different ways.

Syrians from other cities, including the second largest Aleppo, as well as from smaller cities, such as Hama and Homs, have also migrated to Damascus. However, urban migrants have not had the same contentious relationship with the Shuwam as rural migrants perhaps because their numbers are not as large. Besides, they come from established urban areas and had a certain urbanity that did not visibly clash with that of the Shuwam. The Shami identity remains largely defined through its opposition to rural rather than to urban migrants.

In this chapter, I begin to analyze "spatializing culture," the term Setha Low (1996, 2000) used "to locate—physically, historically, and conceptually—social relations and social practice in space," and which I will continue to examine in the next chapter. Building on the preceding chapter where we saw how the Old City emerged as a distinct physical urban neighborhood in greater Damascus that juxtaposed monumental "civilization" with vernacular "backwardness," I address how the social categories "civilized" and "backward" developed to correspond to the ways the city was not only imagined and experienced but also lived.

1. Prominent families in Damascus such as *al-'Azm* were posted to the city by the Ottoman sultan in the seventeenth century and eventually became leaders and notables of the city. Their first ancestor came from a village outside of Hama. By all accounts, they were considered to be *Shuwam*, but perhaps because of their prominent role in the history of the city, the family's move to Damascus is still recognized.

I will conclude with a discussion of how the neoliberal economic policies led to the emergence of *al-tabaqah al-jadida* (new class) (Perthes 1991,
31) who are able to forsake the concept of origin ('asl) as they identify
themselves as private entrepreneurs. They are criticized for being beholden
to profit over social ties. Many members of the new class are involved in
the gentrification of the Old City either as producers or consumers of
Shami identity. As a result the "Shamification" process under new economic conditions is about attaining what I call "cultural affinity" for the
Old City through mediated experiences with the renovated bayt 'arabi.
Although I define cultural affinity as an appreciation of Shami vernacular turath (heritage) and assuming its stewardship, it also underscores the
primacy of the urban culture in the new identity formation though one
shorn of any political and historical significance as it is reconstructed for
consumption rather than for social or political purposes. Cultural affinity
as we will see in the next chapter allows investors to relocate long-term
residents in the gentrification of the Old City.

The City and the Village

Urban space as Darrow Zenlund (1991, 7) indicated for Aleppo becomes
important as a "classifying device." The same process applies to Damascus where the Old City becomes the site for an "authentic" Shami identity
unlike other neighborhoods in the city. Hence, according to social actors
in Syria a clear binary exists between the Shuwam who locate their 'asl
in the historic quarters of the city and rural migrants not only over the
meaning of urban space but also in the "spatialization" of culture.

In Damascus, not unlike other cities in the Mediterranean, there is a
rural–urban divide that depicts the "separation of space and society" (Ossman 1994, 22) and becomes necessary for understanding the ways social
actors construct their identity. Although in Syria the countryside has been
depicted as the site of "cultural authenticity" and nostalgia for a simpler
purer life (Shannon 2005), such representations of rural areas are important for what they inform us about how urban dwellers navigate social and
economic changes (Williams 1973; Ferguson 1992; Harms 2011). As Erik
Harms (2011, 5) has shown in Vietnam, the binary between the city and

the countryside is useful in the ways social actors "deploy" the difference in everyday life to comment on their own situation. The difference is also important for understanding social fears during times of crisis or change. The countryside became a source of anxiety for elite Damascenes who worried about their own power and authority in the city with the influx of people from villages to city (Shannon 2005, 376; Salamandra 2004). In Zambia, the "wholesomeness" of the countryside was becoming difficult to maintain among urban dwellers with the rise of "actual and antagonistic social relations" between the city and the country (Ferguson 1992, 90).

Moreover, in many cities around the Mediterranean, the "ruralization" of the historic city center facilitated gentrification. In Fez, the middle-class Fassis considered the historic city center poor, dirty, and populated by rural migrants. Although many of the Fassi homeowners rent to the rural poor, they prefer to sell to foreigners who will undertake the necessary renovations (Newcomb 2009, 17). In Istanbul, gentrification was mainly located in neighborhoods vacated by ethnic and religious minorities but became populated by rural migrants (Islam 2005). Therefore, the displacement of rural migrants was not an issue for government officials and gentrifiers because they were not considered the owners of urban space but rather squatters or recent arrivals who contributed to the decay and decline of the historic site. Rural migrants displaced the "true" residents; hence, gentrification is about reclaiming this tarnished history.

Whereas cities in the West grew as a result of industrialization and became urban centers that attracted rural migrants, cities in the East were always the center of political, economic, and religious power.[2] Despite this difference in historical evolution, there are certain observations on Western cities that can apply to Damascus. According to Raymond Williams (1973, 289) the difference between the city and countryside in England "is one of the major forms in which we become conscious of a central part of our experience and of the crises of our society." The problematic relationship between Damascus and the countryside, which predates the modern

---

2. For the role of cities in Arab and Islamic history, see Andre Raymond (1984) as well as Ira Lapidus (1969).

period, is necessary for understanding how the residents of Damascus tend to negotiate crises and social change.[3]

The evolution of Damascus as an important economic and political hub was in part due to its ability to siphon resources from the countryside and not reciprocate in any meaningful way (Petran 1972, 25; Batatu 1981, 336). Beginning in the Ottoman period, "urban notables" in Damascus as well as Aleppo, Hama, and Homs were awarded entire villages for their service to the Ottoman sultan (Khoury 1983, 15, 28; see also Batatu 1999). Hence, a geographical and social hierarchy was already in place with the demise of the Ottoman Empire that continues to inform social relations in Syria. This feudal system did not encourage rural to urban migration, though at times of famine and crisis peasants fled their village for the city (Khoury 1983, 82). It even included modern-day forms of slavery; girls from the villages, especially from Alawite families, were sold or sent to work as servants in the homes of rich city dwellers during times of crisis in the village (Batatu 1981, 334). The entrenched symbiotic relation between countryside and city continued into the modern period; the hinterland fed the city while urban notables owned surrounding villages; in times of crisis peasants migrated to the city.

Until the middle of the twentieth century, peasants were marginalized and subservient to urban notables. The social division placed peasants below city dwellers but above Bedouins, and in the early years of independence, the countryside was considered backward when compared to the "civilized" urban centers (Devlin 1983, 23). Many urban dwellers believed peasants were cunning and deceitful and therefore not to be trusted to act like the proud and honorable men who lived in cities (Batatu 1999, 95). In contrast, Ibn Khaldun (n.d., 151) thought peasants were purer and not corrupted with their desire for luxuries but lived closer to nature than the "soft" urban dwellers. However, peasants lived in a primitive state and for

3. For an overview of peasants in greater Syria during the mandate period, see Jacques Weulersse (1946). Although he gave a detailed historical account of the countryside's relationship to urban areas as well as information on social organization, religion, land tenure, and agricultural practices, he ignored the impact of the French Mandate on Syrian peasants.

them to improve their living conditions they had to move to the city where they were socialized into urban life (Mahdi 1964, 212). In Syria, the city is the site of "civilization," whereas the village is "backwardness," and the force of these images remains undiminished even as the city became home to rural migrants.

French Mandate

In Damascus, an extensive network of notables formed a political rather than social category. Composed mainly of Sunni–Muslims, the notables shared the same ethnic and religious background with most of the country, a quality that facilitated their political activities (Hourani 1968, 48; Khoury 1983, 5). The network included wealthy landowners, rich merchants, and religious leaders connected either through family ties or economic and political interests. This leader-class was vested in maintaining order and stability in the city, since it allowed notables to establish themselves as mediators between the Ottoman regime, the local urban population, and the rural hinterland (Hourani 1966, 45; Khoury 1983, 81). The notables included the *'ulama* or the religious establishment from the local families who conferred legitimacy on the Ottoman rulers. The upper echelons of power also integrated local military leaders and "secular notables" who derived their power from family genealogies and linkages (Hourani 1966, 49). At the bottom of the social order were the merchants and traders as well as the rural migrants (Khoury 1983; Schilcher 1985). Many of these social categories lost their significance with the modernization of the Ottoman province and establishment of the French Mandate, though individual members of the notables became prominent in the nation-building process. However, merchants as a social category were able to adapt to social and political change and emerge as an important Shami group unlike other elite urban groups.

According to the Syrian historian Abdullah Hanna (1985, 14), the merchants of the eighteenth and nineteenth centuries were the link between the populace from which they came and the elites with whom they supplied goods. Powerful merchants were not restricted to the Sunnis but included some members of the local minorities, Jews, and Christians, especially when trade in Damascus expanded to include imports from Europe (see Hourani 1966; Khoury 1983, 6). As we will see in chapter 4, the bayt 'arabi is rehabilitated to represent the wealthy Shami merchant home of this period. The trope of the merchant came to stand for an idealized local identity since it was the only social group that was able to survive from premodern times and therefore possessed a certain "authenticity" from its connection to an idealized past that appeals to investors in the current gentrification.

Although urban notables began to see their political influence recede with the Ottoman reforms, it was under the French they became marginalized. The French focused on cultivating a local intermediary class from the rural population.[4] They were especially interested in the historically marginalized minority rural groups of the mountainous villages in central Syria such as the Maronites and Alawites (Batatu 1999; Khoury 1987, 53).[5] The ruralization of Syrian politics occurred during the mandate period, although it was not until the rise of the Ba'th movement, and its assumption of power in 1963, that rural elements became national leaders as well (Batatu 1999, 134; Khoury 1987, 60).

During the Ottoman period, the political leadership resided in the traditional quarters among their supporters in the Old City, but during the French Mandate, as patronage was no longer feasible, they began to move outside the wall (Khoury 1983, 295). Moreover, a distinction arose between the western-educated leadership and the more "tradition-bound masses" that was also expressed spatially by leaving the traditional quarters to the traditional masses (Khoury 1983, 296; see also Hinnebusch 2001, 26). Hence, the social order of the Old City was being challenged by colonialism when many of the westernized Shami leadership began moving outside of the Old City during the 1930s (Khoury 1983, 298). Yet many

4. For a detailed account on the role of the urban notables during the French Mandate, see Khoury (1987).

5. However, the French had mixed results with minority rural populations. Some members of minority groups fought against the French as in the Alawite community. Nonetheless, the French emphasis on minorities, such as the Maronites and Alawites, allowed for today's Lebanese and Syrian sociopolitical structure.

of my interlocutors did not mention this movement as abandonment or exodus, if at all. Rather, according to many of the Shuwam I talked to, they believed the elite left their homes in the Old City only after independence in 1946 and in increasing numbers when the Ba'th came to power.

Nonetheless, remaining in the traditional neighborhoods and forsaking the conveniences of modern apartments was an act of patriotism and an expression of Syrian national distinction from the French who lived outside the Old City. Adopting what Chatterjee (1993) called the "inner domain of national culture" (1993, 9) some elite Shuwam associated their national identity with the traditional quarter and the bayt 'arabi. Therefore, there were deep Shami division not only between classes but also among the elite that tend to be ignored in the idealized past of the Old City. After independence, the national cultural difference between colonized and colonizer was no longer an issue, and therefore, it was no longer considered unpatriotic to move outside the wall. Rather it became "fashionable" to leave the bayt 'arabi for a modern apartment. As we will see in the next chapter, the courtyard house was becoming "backward" because it lacked the amenities found in apartments such as running water and electricity. Furthermore, it was designed for extended families, a concept declining in importance among the upper classes (Khoury 1983, 296). Of course, many of the amenities could be added to the bayt 'arabi, and as for size, not all of the courtyard houses were built to accommodate large extended families; some were designed for smaller families. However, the bayt had lost its appeal for the postindependence generation desiring a modern lifestyle.

On 'Asl of the Shami Identity

Before, I discuss the spatialization of the Shami identity, it is important to explain a few things about 'asl, which I have been attributing much of the social categorization in Damascus. This section will unpack the concept of 'asl and how social actors deploy it in daily practices to negotiate social hierarchies and power relations. Although many Shami families left their ancestral homes for the plush modern neighborhoods their 'asl continued to be documented in the historic districts they came from and based on the Ottoman census of the late nineteenth century. Hence, Shami origins in the historic quarters is officially recognized and legally documented.

'Asl, largely conceived, is genealogical descent located in place and which informs a person's social background and moral character. It is widely believed, by Syrians as with other Arabs, that geography molds disposition (Rosen 1979, 92; L. Abu Lughod 1986, 45). 'Asl is not just about "locality" (Rosen 1979, 92) but how blood, time, and geography come together to produce individuals with characteristics, attributes, and morals different from individuals of another locality. The authority of 'asl is derived from the past, the "context from which the individual stems, the situation that contributed to his distinctive antecedents" (Rosen 1979, 92). Time and place are important in the definition of 'asl; therefore, the new neighborhoods where the majority of the Shuwam in Damascus currently reside have not replaced the Old City as the site for the production of the Shami identity since they lack the pastness of intramural neighborhoods. In addition, 'asl remains strongly patriarchal and descent from the male line carries more authority than the female line. In Syria and in other parts of the region, a person's 'asl could be determined from the surname since some names are closely associated with certain neighborhoods, villages, and cities, or indexes a family descended from the Prophet or one of his companions.

'Asl that began as local cultural practice became an official administrative category listed on Syrian government-issued identification cards. For many Syrians this includes the village they descended from regardless where they currently reside. Identity cards issued for Shuwam indicate their place of origin in one of the eight intramural and extramural quarters that composed the city during the late nineteenth century. The Ottomans were the first to link identity to place in an attempt to control the city "by regularizing its subdivisions" (Hudson 2008, 41).[6] Therefore, what began in

6. Al-'Allaf (n.d., 43) and Qasatili (1879, 191–92) list different eight districts. As Rabbat noted, many of these names coincided with Ottoman administrative units based on geography and ethnic composition (2002, 205 and see note 15). To institutionalize these geographical division, they were following accepted customs so that the city can be

the late nineteenth as Ottoman attempts to standardize and control neighborhoods sanctioned 'asl as an institutionalized marker of identity.

The neighborhood was "a central element of personal and even political identity of men in Damascus for a very long time, but its inclusion in religious/legal documents represents recognition of that component of identity as administratively important" (Hudson 2008, 41). Therefore, to be Shami regardless of religion or ethnic affiliation could be proved if an identity card reflected one of the eight neighborhoods. By the same token, those who lived in the Old City for decades remained officially registered in their village unless they officially changed their place of residence on their card. When investors claim that those who live in the Old City do not belong there, they may have a legal precedent.

I became aware of how identity cards were important for spatializing identity when I met Radwan. He was dating one of my American acquaintances in Syria, and I saw him at social occasions. He showed interest in my research and offered to help by taking me on walks or by introducing me to his relatives who lived or worked in the Old City. When I asked if he was from Damascus, he replied with evident pride, "I am a Shami from Qanawat, *khanah 'idash*" (household eleven). Though he did not live there, and the family home was razed and paved over when a major street cut through the neighborhood, he still saw himself in the Ottoman configuration of the city, as coming from one of the wealthiest neighborhoods outside the Old City. Qanawat becomes a place-name illustrating not only his family's Shami roots but also socioeconomic status as well. The significance of the number eleven means his family was there during the Ottoman census and although he did not live in Qanawat, he could lay claim to the extramural neighborhood. His identification card and the cards of his descendants, barring a new administrative category, will continue to reflect Qanawat and khanah 'idash, regardless of where they will be born or live, and as long as Radwan registers his children in Syria. Therefore, the old neighborhoods were firmly etched in the imagination of the Shuwam with

---

organized similar to European quarters and to simplify and contain a "complex, organic urban area" (Hudson 2008, 41).

identification cards and the Ottoman spatialization of the Damascus where neighborhoods were conflated with social status remained important for how the Shuwam saw their ownership of city (Salamandra 2004, 41).

The spatial social arrangement of Damascus is not always obvious from identity cards because they show the ancestral place of residence rather than the current residence. Tariq, one of the shopkeepers in Harat Hananya, had an interview applying to enroll in a computer program and was asked about his 'asl. Tariq replied Midan. The interviewer looked at Tariq who was dressed in a suit and tie carrying a briefcase and asked to see his identification card. Midan was the traditional extramural quarter, known for extreme religiosity, with a large rural population, and Tariq did not seem to fit the image of someone from there. Rather, his sophisticated appearance marked him from one of the modern neighborhoods. He actually lived in Qasaʻ; nonetheless, he was proud to be from Midan because it was his 'asl and Qasaʻ did not have the same prestige as the more established extramural neighborhood. Tariq never lived in Midan, and his parents were raised in the intramural neighborhoods before they moved outside the wall as many other families have done.

Yet the origin for Shuwam remains relevant. Thus, when talking about 'asl, it becomes clear that "the origin is never at the origin, it emerges as such only through its displacement" (Ivy 1995, 22). The displacement for many Shuwam is from the center of events in their own city. Though they live in their city close to the neighborhoods of their origin, many do not feel it is their city. In addition, many of the homes and neighborhoods have been destroyed or severely altered, which makes it harder to find memory triggers in the cityscape; therefore, identity cards are all the more important. They represent what remains of neighborhoods and communities that no longer exist. The identification cards "evoke the past of families, the geographical location of their belongings, their personal relations with other . . . families" and provide the Shuwam with their right to the city (Halbwachs 1992, 123).

People in Syria, not unlike in other parts of the world, were very astute about one another's 'asl as an attempt to gain insight into moral character that would assist in calculating forms and course of social interactions. In Damascus, there were various ways to deduce a person's 'asl without asking them directly. The ability to know by seeing had to do with a highly attuned sense of attention to physical appearance and behavior as in the case of Tariq and his interviewer. These differences were detected in skin tone, eye color, fashion sense, dialect, inflection of speech, and dialect. Alia, who I met at Damascus University, came to visit me in Harat Hananya and met George, one of my Shami friends in the neighborhoods. During our conversation, I told her George is Shami, and she replied, "Of course you could tell by looking at him." I, of course, could not, but as a resident of Damascus, Alia was well-versed in the game of 'asl and was able to guess whether a person was Shami. She was from a rural background and could detect a Shami just as easily as a Shami could notice her rural roots. I was disturbed by this essentialism and stereotyping of many people in Syria, which became "a substitute for thinking" and a "matter of convenience" (Herzfeld 2005a, 211). However, for my Syrian interlocutor, it was normalized in social interactions.

'Asl as an essentialized discourse is fraught with stereotypes and bigotry and stereotypes are "discursive weapons of power," with "the possibility of subversion" (Herzfeld 2005a, 202). Moreover, stereotypes are about "placing people" by "sifting through signs of identity" where these signs are "not of a fixed social order but of social imaginary immanent in *ways*" (K. Steward 1996, 201; emphasis in original). Placing people allows social relations to remain fluid while maintaining the social hierarchy. Although the Shuwam do not have political power, they have cultural power by virtue of being *from* and *of* the city that has a long history and civilizational aspects. Even when the Ba'th came to power they maintained Damascus as the capital, which vindicated the Shuwam and their belief in the superiority of their city. Damascus with its longevity, history, and powerful resonance among Syrians and Arab conferred legitimacy that would have been impossible to duplicate in a new location. Although the regime may be ambivalent about Damascus and what it represents (Salamandra 2004, 33), it is impossible to maintain political legitimacy in Syria without the city under their control. Much to the chagrin of many Shuwam, street signs in the city even proclaim "Dimashq al-Asad."

Neoliberalism made many of these subtle differences between the Shuwam and rural migrants less distinct, especially among the younger generation that were adopting habits and manners more in line with cultural consumption and who saw such notions of 'asl as cumbersome in the global market of culture and ethnicity. Nonetheless, it is easy to see how 'asl becomes an "*intermittent* phenomenon," the description Rogers Brubaker (2006, 208; emphasis in original) used for ethnicity and which could certainly apply to 'asl because it "*happens* at particular moments, and in particular contexts." Most of the discourse surrounding the decay and neglect of the intramural quarters began to circulate when the "original" inhabitants, the Shuwam, left the neighborhoods, taking their supposedly "civilized" ways with them; therefore, the historic quarters remained a site of civilization but lost its "civilizing" role. Since rural migrants were not from the historic city, they could not become civilized just by living there and without the tutelage of the Shuwam into city ways. This brings us to the era of the Ba'th regime when the urban–rural binary was simultaneously challenged and maintained and which will serve as the immediate context for the current situation in Syria.

Ba'th and Damascus

The Ba'th party instigated a coup in 1963, and for the rest of the decade worked on consolidating its power over other political factions. It also introduced a progressive social agenda aimed at undermining regional and sectarian difference in Syrian society. Article 15 of the Ba'th constitution stated that national affiliation should supersede all other ties (Devlin 1976, 348). It is debatable to what extent this was accomplished and whether any attempt was made to forge a national identity that undermined regional, sectarian, and ethnic attachment. What has been established is that the party succeeded in creating acrimony between the regime and urban dwellers. As a party composed primarily of a rural leadership, the Ba'th regime attracted other rural migrants to Damascus to work in government positions and to fill military slots. Damascus, the capital city, witnessed a massive demographic transformation as the population swelled from half a million in 1960 to more than 1 million in 1981, making the Shuwam a minority in their city (Batatu 1999, 160). Employment in the state bureaucracy was offered to relatives and supporters of the regime. Many were unqualified for these positions, further alienating the Damascenes. Shami merchants found it difficult to conduct their business when they had to deal with new rural bureaucrats, who were not only unsympathetic to their needs but also lacked understanding of how commerce functioned (Batatu 1999, 160; Hinnebusch 2001, 53). Sami al-Jundi (1969, 39) one of the early members of the Ba'th movement, wrote a memoir of these years, describing how the party snubbed the Shuwam and created a "wall of impossibility" in their dealings with them.[7] At the time, he was thoroughly disgruntled with the party and exiled from its ranks. His scathing critique offered insight into the early relations between the Ba'th leadership and Shuwam. He emphasized the lack of respect and appreciation by the Ba'th cadre for city, its longevity and role in Arab and Islamic history. Granted, there was never much support in Damascus for the Ba'th party and its ideology during this time (Batatu 1981, 339). Because of the historical asymmetrical power relation between the city and the countryside there was also not much admiration by rural migrants for urban dwellers.

As indicated throughout Syria's long history, the city oppressed the countryside. The reversal of the usual order did not sit well with many urban dwellers, which was compounded when rural immigrants came to the city to rule, rejecting "Shamification." In addition to the shift in the power hierarchy, new infrastructure and technology facilitated communication with the village where many of the new regime's supporters still lived. Even for those rural migrants not in power, leaving the village at this stage was not seen as abandoning the ancestral home. New highways and means of transportation allowed many members of the regime leadership to shuttle between the city and their village. They did not develop strong attachments to the city and they were able to maintain contact with their political supporters in the village. This circular movement explains why many rural migrants did not assimilate into urban life, although the memory of discrimination and centuries of exploitation by the city were also a factor.

7. Most of the Ba'th leadership had rural origins, and the movement had few leaders from the main urban centers (Hinnebusch 2001, 31).

Nonetheless, Hafiz al-Asad who came to power in 1970, sought to appease the urban elite, especially merchants in Damascus, by courting their political support through favorable economic policies (Petran 1972, 244–51; Batatu 1999, 208–16). In the process, he was able to co-opt many leading Shami notables who shared common economic, if not political, interests (Hinnebusch 2001, 67, 91), but this did not always translate into smoother relations between the two groups.

Qusay is a Shami from a notable family whose father and grandfather played an important role in the economic and political life of Syria from the late Ottoman period until the advent of the Ba'th regime. He still lived in his ancestral home in the Old City, which was closely intertwined with his identity as a Shami. He was in his thirties when I interviewed him; yet, he recalled a time when everyone wanted to sell courtyard houses and move to the new residential areas. But the pull was due to "fashion" rather than politics. He observed, "The Shuwam wanted to exchange the neighborhoods in the Old City for something fancy," and living in an old house meant "being poor or old-fashioned." But Qusay always loved his courtyard home. Although he visited friends and relatives in Malki, he did not feel comfortable in the modern apartments and neighborhoods. Moreover, the house was very much the life of his father and grandfather. He said, "My father didn't want to sell. He saw his own father in the house and believed that much died when the owner of the house died. The house has its own character and life and so he kept it as his cousins and brothers sold their inheritance and moved."

Yet the steadfastness of Qusay in his ancestral home is also political, a Shami stance against the regime. He described the relationship between the urban notables of Damascus and the new rural powerbrokers as *harb tabaqiyya* (class warfare). Families that belonged to a certain class before the 1960s were considered enemies of the new regime. Even today, whispers of this animosity surface. One of my informants, while discussing urban planning in the Old City during the 1960s, insisted that politics dictated many of the decisions when he said, "the political leadership in Syria does not like Damascus all that much." Resentments between the Shuwam and the Ba'th regime remain potent because they have never been nationally addressed, and reconciliation has not been attempted but rather suppressed. The Ba'th's attempts at national solidarity not only fell flat but also reinforced ethnic, sectarian, and urban–rural divisions that ironically included new forms of alliance among the elites regardless of sect. Social actors "misrecognize" the blurring of binaries since it disrupts their own sense of identity. Although sectarianism is not new in Syria it was redefined by the Alawites when they displaced the Sunnis in the political hierarchy (Petran 1972, 36).

Ibn Khaldun believed peasants were simple in their lifestyle and as a result possessed a pure moral character when compared with urban dwellers. He believed urban dwellers to be deceitful and artificial in their social interaction (Mahdi 1964, 195). Therefore, the civility in the city is about forms of politeness that disguise the true intent of social actors for maintaining the existing social order (Sennett 1990, 84). However, for the Shuwam and other Damascene, they consider the rural migrants to be deceitful and do not belong in the city. In the gentrification of the Old City, investors effectively used these stereotype to relocate long-term residents.

In this section, we have seen the historical context for the evolution of the urban–rural binary to encompass the Shami-Alawite/Ba'th rivalry. The next section will explore how social actors use these categories to spatialize difference in the Old City.

Out of Place

Malik, a young restaurant owner in the Old City I had gotten to know, used to sit on the street outside his restaurant greeting customers and people walking by, and after numerous times of passing him during my walks we struck a conversation beyond exchanging pleasantries. I later interviewed him in his restaurant, and like many of his fellow investors, he had little regard for long-term residents. He addressed the difference between the Shuwam and rural migrants in concrete terms: "Villagers are tough; they have different behaviors. In Damascus it is important to keep peace, keep relations going, and bring hearts closer together. Villagers do not become Shuwam, they don't have the love of the Shuwam. They might pick up some habits but they remain different."

According to Malik, rural migrants are unable to assimilate to the urban way of life because of their 'asl, or essence, as villagers that renders them immune to socialization into a Shami lifestyle. Rural migrants are rough because of the harsher lifestyle that exists in the villages. The harsh lifestyle could also have rendered villagers resilient or immune to urban qualities. However, Malik's narrow view of villagers' behavior is how it sharply contrasts with the Shuwam. Hence, the "contrastive place" between village and city not only linked human behavior with place but "singled out part of the whole of another place to stand for the whole of that place because that part best contrasts to our own place" (Fernandez 1988, 32). Therefore, Malik blames rural migrants and not the urban setting for the difference between the Shuwam and rural inhabitants. He does not consider that the city perhaps has lost its "civilizing," role and the process of integrating villagers into the city has been disrupted. Moreover, by claiming villagers remain different and do not belong in the Old City, Malik is stressing his distinction from long-term residents. Hence, his being in the Old City is due to his involvement in gentrification and the preservation of heritage and not as a long-term resident. He belongs in the Old City because he is more "Shamified" than are long-term residents.

In addition to the inability of rural migrants to assimilate by choosing to remain "rough," they also brought filth and decay to the city. According to Pierre, an architect who worked in the Old City during the 1960s, it was the "pollution *sukani*" (residential; he used the word pollution with the Arabic for residential) that pushed many of the Shami families from their ancestral homes in the Old City.

> Once I was in old Damascus visiting people and there were two families here and two families there fighting among themselves. You are at this evening gathering and you hear everything; the cussing everything, very *haqarah* (vulgar). In the past you would not hear this, you would not hear this; if Shuwam were sitting you would not hear this. Shuwam speak in a low voice they do not fight much. The *degout*. [He used the French word for disgust-or, repugnance]. They have very loud voices. And the cussing, it is a way of life that is different. And there is one toilet or one bathroom in the house that created lots of problems. Then there is their personal hygiene which they don't have and they produce a lot of *waskh* (filth).

I almost thought that Pierre was going to excuse himself and go wash his hands as his reaction was very visceral. He insisted that the Shuwam lived differently in the Old City. They were more civil, especially since cussing was not a way of life for them. In addition to their "vulgar" behavior, rural migrants were dirty and the filth was not confined to their homes and person but spilled over into the alleys and streets of the Old City. Whereas vulgar behavior can be confined to the homes of the rural migrants, filth could not and it contaminated the Shuwam. I lived with a family from a village in the Old City, and they were very clean in their home and person, but I could not argue with Pierre. He was much older, and I felt obligated to be deferential to the age and gender difference according to local social norms. Both Malik and Pierre maintained the local discourses that rural migrants destroyed the city to distinguish themselves from the rural migrants. The chauvinism in both men's statements demonstrates how "pollution beliefs can be used in a dialogue of claims and counter-claims to status" (Douglas 1966, 13) where rural migrants are accorded a "marginal state" in the Old City that continues to be associated with the Shuwam even when they no longer live there. Although the Shuwam left to seek modern conveniences, in the narrative of Pierre, the push factors figured more prominently than the pull factors. Lack of status for rural migrants continued to inform the recent gentrification, especially when it came to the displacement of long-term residents, many of whom were of rural origin.

Hence, the Shuwam were not only clean in person, behavior, and living conditions but also knew how to cooperate and collaborate with others and "kept the peace" because of the "love" they had for one another. Despite the vast age difference, almost thirty years between Pierre and Malik, and socioeconomic and religious backgrounds, they both agreed that rural migrants did not assimilate to the civility of the city nor did they adopt its "hadarah." As a result of the sociopolitical changes in Damascus, many Shuwam define their belonging to the Old City through their spatial behavior that not only distinguishes them from rural migrants but also gives them symbolic power. Therefore, they "do" 'asl to borrow the term used by John Jackson Jr. (2002, 228) to describe how African American residents of Harlem determine "racial authenticity and inauthenticity" through behavior, which in turn supports racial and class identity in Harlem. But Harlem is more than just a geographical location, and Jackson uses Harmlemworld to illustrate how Harlem stands for a "multiplicitous location seen by so many people as so much more than the literal place itself" (10). Harlem becomes a black space, not because it is the origin for the development of a black identity but as a result of "historical connections between racial and class-based interests" (54). Whereas Harlem becomes a contested "black" space, the Old City is firmly established as a Shami city whether or not the Shuwam live there. The Shuwam cannot be Shuwam or do Shami identity without the Old City, and the new neighborhoods outside the world are no substitute for the construction of social distinction by the Shuwam.

Although I am not dealing with racial categories in Damascus and I do not imply that the differences between the Shuwam and rural migrants are racialized, what is fascinating is that social binaries and differences, when deployed by social actors, tend to be about behavior that reflects mainly 'asl and sometimes social class. As we will see in the next chapter, "doing Shami" is in place, and the place is not only the Old City but also the bayt 'arabi.

Shami Merchants

The preceding discussion on the rural–urban binary in Damascus has been general in its contours and delineations, especially when discussing Shami behavior. The Shami merchant as a social category not only survived from premodern social stratification in the city but also stands for the model Shami identity today. Therefore, to be Shami is to do like a Shami tajr (merchant). However, not all Shuwam are Sunni, wealthy, or merchants, but the trope of the tajr became a romantic figure associated with the idealized past, reinforcing the civility of intramural neighborhoods.[8] The Shami merchant has a physical trace in the Old City in

---

8. See Schilcher (1985) for more information on the other social categories in Damascus before the end of Ottoman rule. Damascene notables as *aghas* relied on trade as a source of income but did not necessarily see themselves as merchants.

the numerous "treasure" houses in the Old City targeted in the current gentrification. Moreover, numerous television dramas that valorize life in the historic neighborhoods have merchants as protagonists. They hold their neighborhood together in times of crisis and protect the weak from bullying. Therefore, any discussion of social categories in contemporary Damascus must focus on merchants and the role of commercial interactions in social interactions.[9]

Al-Jundi (1969, 39), who I mentioned earlier, did not conceal his admiration for the Shami merchants: "The making of this mercantile city is a spontaneous tribalism and a moral standard that makes relations between individuals semi-sacred: If they are gone, gone is the meaning of Damascus." Al-Jundi's romantic description of Damascus elevates the merchant over other occupations since trade has long been associated with the city. Merchant transcends vocation; it becomes a way of life. The suq has long been the focus of researchers in the Middle East for what it could inform us about the social relations in society at large (Geertz 1979; Zenlund 1991; Ossman 1994, 42; Kapchan 1996). Merchants by the nature of commercial activity are swindlers; trade is based on bargaining, which includes an element of deception and trickery. The "merchant as trickster" has long been suspected of moral shortcomings (Zenlund 1991, 7–9; Kapchan 1996, 41). In Damascus, as we have seen in Jundi's account written in the 1960s, they have become more exalted. They set the moral and religious standards for society. Their interaction with one another and with customers has become the basis of Shami identity.

According to al-Jundi, the people of Damascus had perfected these social relations because they were savvy traders and in turn were able to create a city in which they could develop their trade and their identity. In these relations, we see sociability based on a religious and moral code that maintained social harmony, even among supposedly competing merchants, whose behavior became the paradigm for all that is civilized in Damascus. Again Nadia Khost summed it up:

9. In her discussion of elite marriages in Damascus, Salamandra (2004, 2006) examines the role of "chastity capital" in the marriage market.

There is a type of Damascene merchant that has highly refined social relations. The merchants believed that because they were rich, they had to give to the poor. They were raised on the values of *rahma* (compassion), sympathy and responsibility. For example, they would take bags of rice, and maybe also as a religious duty zakat, and place them at the doors of the needy at night so that no one would know they did this. They protected the dignity of poor people. They would put the bags of rice in front of the door. The old merchants for example gave a promise; there were no documents exchanged. But the promise was binding. For example I sold you fifty of something at this price and you will pay me in the morning. The next morning the price goes up, but I cannot change. They never changed the price because they gave their word. Word of honor.

Historically, the "business of the suqs was not always a cash-and-carry affair between buyers and sellers. Each shop had a clientele formed as much by factors of kinship, neighborhood ties, ethnic or religious solidarity as by competition in the selection, quality, or prices of the goods offered" (Schilcher 1985, 64). And this is where Khost's "word of honor" among merchants became binding. Khost's recollection is a form of "structural nostalgia" where "people attribute the superior qualities of the past to its more perfect adherence to a set of structured rules and principles for the conduct of social life" (Herzfeld 1991, 75; see also 2005, 173). Yet in this nostalgia the concept of 'asl remained entrenched in the social exchange. The ideal type of merchant and the rahma in their social interactions undermine social and class differences and recast them into relations of reciprocity; the wealthy merchants do their duty to poorer neighbors, and the poor in turn accept the generosity of the merchants. But the merchants were also improving their "symbolic capital" where such acts of generosity are satisfying expectations not clearly stated but rather "misrecognized" (Bourdieu 1977, 171–72). The merchants involved in the "good faith economy" expend much energy in disguising their true intent and the actual workings of the mechanism of the economic exchange. It is this "misrecognition" that allows for smooth social interaction when the true intent is concealed.

Furthermore, merchants become an important social category because they were replicable from one generation to another and have endured the political and economic transformations in Damascus. The rise of the professional class under the French Mandate did not erode their power and the elite merchants became the allies of the Ba'th regime. Farid, who lived in the Old City, would sometimes take me on walks in his neighborhood of Shaghur. He told me about the ideal Shami merchants who worked to maintain the social order in their favor, through creating harmony among one another instead of encouraging competition. Merchants were neighbors and competitors in the suq, especially when they were selling the same commodity; therefore, they had a good sense of how much other merchants were selling and at what price. Among the older generation of merchants, if one store had customers in the morning, it was not unheard of for the owner to tell a new customer to go to the neighboring store, which had yet to sell anything. Beyond profit, merchants were careful to maintain a situation in the suq where all merchants were doing well, not just some. This form of business operation, "encompassing rather than competitive" supported smaller merchants by sharing customers, rather than driving them out of the market (Faneslow 1990, 257). This practice was an important part of the civility in the Old City because a competitor could be a kin or neighbor who if they fell on hard times became the responsibility of the better-off merchants. Hence, the encompassing model of business allowed for concealed charity that saved face for all those involved.

Farid explained this was more common among older merchants; the younger generation adopted more competitive practices to suit the current economic environment. Among the younger merchants the "misrecognition" of social interaction disappeared under new economic conditions. The older-generation merchant and their idealized practices become the "object of rhetorical longing" for "a mutuality that has been, perhaps irreversibly, ruptured by the self-interest of modern times" (Herzfeld 2005a, 149). In this commentary on the present, Farid, Khost, and others see the preservation of the Old City as an attempt to conserve the built environment that engenders such forms of social interactions among people. It is hoped that traces of social harmony and sociability will remain in the preserved environment and soften the harshness of social interaction in the present.

However, this ideal Shami merchant was not above criticism. Rural migrants remember unscrupulous business dealings with merchants that left them heavy in debt. The highly sophisticated social interactions of merchants were considered to be calculating and conniving by many people who were not Shami. Since the rural migrants were not part of the social network of Shami merchants, they were not subjected to the good faith of economic exchange. At one point, I told my friend Basma, who was from a rural background, about the kind and generous Shami family I had gotten to know when I was living in Sha'lan. She was skeptical of their civility toward me and told me that my neighbors have the mentality of a tajr; they do nothing without calculating how it could be in their interest. I argued with her and said that there was no profit to be gained from me. She replied, "The Shuwam do not do anything for nothing." What she missed in this instance is that I had become part of the social exchange in the neighborhood and was implicated in the "sincere fiction of a disinterested exchange" (Bourdieu 1977, 171).

Who Is a Shami?

I concur with Christa Salamandra (2004, 14–15) that it is difficult to ascertain who is a Shami today, although social actors in Syria are more adamant in their ability to categorize, document, and classify. Nonetheless, social actors deploy the Shami identity to navigate the social, political, and economic change in Damascus. Unlike Salamandra, I do not focus on the elite Shuwam (she calls them Damascene) who, as she accurately notes, have dispersed and as a class have become diluted as result of social and political change (14). However, I am intrigued by how the Shami identity is applied and ascribed by the "ordinary practitioners of the city," to return to de Certeau's term, in everyday life and situations. Being a Shami becomes a series of cultural manners, behaviors, moral code, and civility that distinguishes the Shuwam from individuals with a rural 'asl. Since their genealogical lineage was located outside of Damascus, it was associated with certain manners and practices that many Shuwam claimed were alien and incompatible to their urban ways.

When I described my exchange with Malik to George, he laughed and said, "Malik is not Shami. He might have lived in the Old City but his family is from a village near the Lebanese border. *Khurafik* (He pulled your leg)." Possibly, I was new at this 'asl game, but what else was I to think when Malik spoke about the "love" Shuwam had for one another and how that love was lacking in the "rough" rural migrants. Why would he mislead me into thinking he was a Shami? Did he think that even though he was a villager he was superior to the long-term residents in the neighborhood where he had his restaurant? Probably since even rural migrants in Damascus are ranked based on the region they come from. Although Malik was probably commenting on his presence in the Old City, he was distinguishing between rural migrants that moved to the Old City and adopted its ways and those who did not. The Old City was still considered a backward neighborhood in Damascus when he started his investment. He could have been thinking that he had a right to invest in the Old City because he was raised in a Shami environment and accepted the "civilizing" ways of the Old City. At the very least, he perfected the Shami language and was able to speak it fluently.

He insisted he was a Shami "dwelling" in the Old City even though he owned a business instead of a home. He told me how he usually attended funerals and weddings when he was invited. When a neighbor's daughter got married, he opened a bottle of champagne to toast her. He spread the red carpet, reserved for dignitaries visiting his restaurant, for her to walk on as she exited her father's house to go to the church. When he saw a woman coming home from a trip carrying a bulky suitcase, he sent one of his employees to help her with her load. He stood outside his restaurant greeting passersby, which was how I met him. For neighbors who dined in his restaurant he offered a discount. He explained that to be a Shami means demonstrating Shami ways among non-Shuwam—he was smoothing relations with his neighbors.

The Shami civility, not unlike the Italian concept, has "deep roots in the idea of the city and its manners as the ideal model for good living" (Herzfeld 2009, 182). Malik opted for maintaining the peace and sociability with his neighbors through practicing Shami civility. Yet civility is a "kind of urbanity that disguises (but also communicates) arrogance, power, and hierarchy" (Herzfeld 2009, 182). Malik was demonstrating not only his belonging in and to the Old City but also how a "Shamified" way of belonging had a higher status than villagers. Civility also resulted in the snobbery many rural migrants encounter when they interact with the Shuwam as with the lawyer in *Dhikryat*.

I did not think he was doing anything that his rural neighbors would not do, and I was trying to understand what in his behavior was exclusively Shami. It later transpired that he was met with resistance when he first proposed to convert the bayt 'arabi he purchased into a restaurant. His attempt to integrate into the neighborhood by performing neighborly duties was perhaps his way of smoothing differences and avoiding future altercations with neighbors. Hence, his Shami civility was his skill at avoiding conflict and creating harmony in the neighborhood, which would ultimately benefit his business when customers felt comfortable patronizing his restaurant. It is not the performance that defined him as Shami but how the performance of civility and sociability were deployed to ensure a specific outcome in the interest of the performer. Therefore, there is some of the merchant mentality in his social interactions.

Nadia Khost explained the "civilizing" process of the Old City differently. She told me,

> I am the daughter of this civilization. It does not matter that my grandfather was Circassian from the Caucasus. This does not deny the education and culture that I had. I was raised in Damascus. My teachers. Who were my teachers? I studied in schools, good schools, government schools, but good schools. I remember for example that my teacher of religion turned out later to be an important sheik and was one of the best teachers. We never put on a veil in class and we would listen. Religion for him, for us, was a language of eloquent poetry and mercy and human values. He did not tell us you have to pray or you will burn in hell. There were no threats. Now those are the Shuwam that made an impression upon me naturally.

Thus, by being born and raised in the milieu of the Shuwam, with their distinct ways and superior taste, she appropriated their civilization where environment triumphed at least in this instance over 'asl. Through education, and by being in a dominantly Shami environment, the civilizing impulse naturally occurs. She described this process of enculturation as *tashabuʻ* (satiation), the embodiment of Shami ways that eventually become her ways. For Malik and Khost, becoming Shami was voluntary, almost too voluntary, because they both seemed to insinuate that once exposed to this refined civilization one could hardly refuse to become a part of it. It was the highest level of refinement that they assumed all people aspired to attain.

According to Ibn Khaldun, "civilization" could exist only in cities: "the natural completion of the life begun in primitive culture and the end to which human nature has been moving ever since the creation of the most simple forms of communal life" (Mahdi 1964, 201). This remains one of the strongest images of Damascus, a city that has attained the highest levels of refined living and where humans can fulfill their utmost desires beyond the need for survival. Cities require a high concentration of humans living together. Social interaction based on economic and political interests replaces blood relations (Mahdi 1964, 214). The sociability in the city ensures that the interaction among individuals keeps these interests strong.

Furthermore, the sociability among Damascenes can be condensed in the behavior of merchants toward one another and is easily appropriated by investors such as Malik. He not only overcame his neighbors' objections to his presence in the neighborhood by overwhelming them with Shami sociability but also used his appropriation of the Shami identity to claim ownership and belonging to the Old City over the long-term residents. His restaurant business, a manifestation of the best Sham ways, was a broker of tangible heritage in the former courtyard house and of an intangible heritage, the Shami mystique. Thus, the social categories of "civilized" and "backward" continue to exist but are no longer confined to Shuwam and rural migrants or refugees. As Arlene Davila (2004, 211) observed in the gentrification of East Harlem, "not all type and manifestation of 'culture' are profitably or economically viable." In search of the "authentic experience" of place (Zukin 2010), investors reinvent the binary of rural–urban that has defined Damascus through much of its modern history. Furthermore, what is emerging in this marketing of identity is a difference among social actors no longer confined to 'asl but based on an appreciation for the Shami heritage as determined through commodification, a process made possible by neoliberal economic policies and the rise of Western-educated entrepreneurs. The investors possessed this affinity that made them and their enterprises belong in and to the intramural neighborhoods more than long-term residents.

Social actors can reject "Shamification," and this rejection becomes part of the contestation over the gentrification of the Old City. The rural migration that accompanied the political and economic transformation in Syria with the rise of the Ba'th regime are considered to be impervious to "Shamification" and form the biggest threat in the minds of many Shuwam and "Shamified" Damascenes to the "civilization" of the Old City. As we saw in the last chapter, the contestation over the role and meaning of the Old City in a modernizing nation-state was resolved once preservationists proved the significance of the Shami city for the nation and for the world. The current gentrification of the Old City continues the conflict over the meaning of space, appropriate behavior, and social order. Gentrification and new economic conditions are privileging a new form of "Shamification" based on the consumption of a Shami city, albeit idealized and depoliticized. Therefore, belonging and being in the heritage site has diluted the concept of the Shami 'asl to include social actors who lack the origin but who "do" Shami. Any rejection of Shami cultural identity results in social ostracism, especially for ambitious individuals who aspire to higher social status in Syrian society. Moreover, it was only within the past fifty years that 'asl became a rigid category and that cultural differences between the Shuwam and rural migrants became fixed in place and time. The current gentrification is challenging this rigidity.

This chapter investigated the historical and social reasons that led for the current understanding of the social Shami–rural binary. These social categories were mediate through the Old City but have a long history in the relations between the city and the countryside. The concept of 'asl takes an added significance as the gentrification of the Old City promotes an idealized Shami city for consumption by new social users from outside the wall. The Shami tajr becomes a trope in understanding the civility in the historic neighborhoods where social interactions are defined through a series of exchange that "misrecognize" the asymmetrical power relations. Investors are able to employ these social interactions in the gentrification of the Old City whether to overcome opposition to their investment or demonstrate the authenticity of their venue in depicting Shami ways.

In the next chapter, I continue my discussion of how Shami cultural behaviors developed through the dwelling in the bayt 'arabi. If the Old City is the site of an authentic Shami identity, then its formation came through the ways the traditional vernacular courtyard dwelling was navigated by the Shuwam who lived in it. Therefore, it is only natural that the courtyard house becomes the target of gentrification because it embodies what it means to be Shami. I will further probe the social and cultural reasons why the ideal abode was abandoned by the Shuwam. Understanding the reasons for the abandonment of the Old City and the courtyard houses then allows us to appreciate the "return" in chapters 4 and 5.

3

"I Am King in My Home"

I was invited to a party at an art gallery in a refurbished bayt 'arabi where the owner had done little to modify the layout of the house. The main elements including the 'iwan or liwan (three-walled room) was flanked by two rooms modestly decorated with stone inlay provided an elegant backdrop for the artist's work on display. Across from the 'iwan, rooms converted into workshops opened onto the courtyard. Other rooms on the ground level were refurbished as office space. The second level was still being renovated as living quarters for visitors to the gallery who would like to spend a few days in the Old City. In the middle of the courtyard was a gurgling fountain shaded by a pomegranate tree, surrounded by flowers and rose bushes. In the still of the night, the tinkling fountain and the scent of the flowers were intoxicating.

I was sitting with some of the guests in the courtyard around the fountain, enjoying the breezy Damascus summer night when one guest, visibly enthralled by the ambience of the courtyard, turned to me and excitedly asked, "Do you live in a house like this?" I thought of my room that was converted into a very comfortable efficiency on the second floor of a modest bayt 'arabi owned by rural migrants. Perhaps at one point the house was larger, but now it was two rooms opening onto the narrow and irregular-shaped courtyard with three other rooms on the second level. It was a simple basic home in the Old City, with no fountain, 'iwan, or decorations of any sort, and the courtyard was covered and transformed into the family sitting room. I replied, "No I don't." However, as soon as I uttered these words, I realized I had internalized the prevailing perception of the bayt 'arabi among investors, government officials, and visitors to the Old City and started to "see" the local courtyard in terms of the idealized Shami form perpetuated by the art gallery and restaurants such as Opalin. In this chapter I deconstruct the vernacular courtyard house and examine how traditional architecture became the site of an idealized Shami culture.

Traditional dwellings not only provide shelter but also are fundamental for understanding local culture, social behaviors, and practices (Humphrey 1988; Lawrence and Low 1990; Rapoport 1990, 1969; Bourdieu 2003; Vellinga 2007; Bertram 2008). According to Amos Rapoport (1969, 48), the "house is an institution, not just a structure, created for a complex set of issues" that address social, cultural, environmental, and ecological needs. In his influential work on the Kabyle house, Pierre Bourdieu (2003) illustrated how the gendered division of domestic space allowed for an understanding of wider societal organization and worldview. In Turkey, the wooden Ottoman house has become the site of nostalgia among modern Turks for an idealized past, although such structures are nearly extinct (Bertram 2008). Nonetheless, as Carel Bertram illustrated, the proliferation of the wooden house in literature and art ensures that the traditional dwelling remains in the collective memory of present-day Turks and informs how they construct their modern Turkish identity (9). In Egypt, the tension between official and vernacular modernity was manifest in how inhabitants of a government housing project embodied their new living space (Ghannam 2002).

Unlike the vanishing Turkish house, the bayt 'arabi is ubiquitous in the Old City and in other historic neighborhoods outside the wall. As we saw in chapter 1, the courtyard house was at the forefront of the debates on modernity and tradition. In the current gentrification, it has become the site of an ideal Shami past and where cultural as well as social difference between the Shuwam and rural migrants is constructed. In the gap between imagined and actual bayt 'arabi, social actors in Damascus negotiate "backwardness" and "civilization" under new economic conditions. Although maintaining the residential function of the bayt 'arabi is not a priority in the gentrification of the Old City, new uses for the courtyard house promote the civilizational aspects that are associated with dwelling in the Old City. In this chapter, I address the "civilizing" as well as "backward" features of the courtyard house by illustrating how architectural features and design came to represent the essence of Shami identity. These

qualities are what gentrifiers strive to replicate in their renovated courtyard houses to evoke in visitors a sense of the idealized past and an appreciation for the cultural heritage of the Old City. In addition, the changes in
the form and function of the bayt ʿarabi provide insight to the ways Shami
identity was redefined for cultural consumption, which will be the topic
of chapter 5.

This chapter begins with a description of the main architectural elements in a bayt ʿarabi reified by investors who seek to restore the bayt
to its Shami ʾasl and, in the process, erase the traces of rural migrants.
Although other forms of traditional dwellings exist in the intramural
and extramural neighborhoods, the courtyard style common among the
Shami merchant class during the later part of the nineteenth century has
become the prototypical Damascene habitat sought by current investors,
not only for their aesthetic value but also for the civility that these houses
purportedly engendered in the Shuwam.[1] Therefore, I once again return
to the trope of the Shami tajr, but in this chapter, I focus on how the
courtyard house they lived in purportedly made them. Many of these
dwellings were greatly modified and modernized as the city transformed
during the Ottoman period, but today, they stand for a timeless, authentic, tradition of vernacular architecture that engendered social cohesion.[2]
I will also interject in this discussion the experience of long-term residents in the courtyard house, this will include the difference between
owners and renters. I will end with how investors are able to use these

1. See Rabbat (2002) and Abdul Nour (1982) for a description of different types of
dwellings that existed in Damascus. Moreno (2000) includes a detailed analysis of different types of houses in Midan during the late Ottoman period.

2. During the late nineteenth century, residents of both the intramural and extramural quarters and neighborhoods of Damascus, were renovating their houses to reflect
the changing tastes in furniture and interior decoration, based on what it meant to be
modern (Reilly 1991; Weber 1997–1998, 2002, 2004). Qasatili (1879) also included a
depiction of new architectural elements introduced into houses during the same period.
For an overview of houses in Damascus during the nineteenth century see the comprehensive study by Dorothee Sack (2005).

differences to undermine long-term residents' claim to the Old City and support their relocation.

A Vernacular Dwelling

I take my understanding of the vernacular from Amos Rapoport (1969) to mean buildings of similar form built by anonymous tradesmen for people in their community to address shelter, social, and cosmological needs. As for "dwelling," I find Caroline Humphrey's definition (1988, 17) most useful. In addition to the organic quality of houses, dwellings are also "both process and artifact." The vernacular dwelling in Damascus has been constructed by anonymous builders from locally and readily available material using building techniques that have been passed down for generations and although the courtyard house is common throughout the region, in Damascus, it has come to reflect the local social order and worldview.

Built mainly from readily available materials—stone, mud, straw, and wood—the fragile nature of building material usually limited the vernacular dwelling to two stories, although in some cases, a room could be built on the third level. In addition, houses had a short life span and had to be annually maintained, and the nature of the building material made it easier to recycle one house into the next. The courtyard house found its earliest antecedents in the dwellings of the Aramaeans. Although there have been changes to form and function of the house, the courtyard remained an essential element in the local vernacular dwelling until the introduction of modern building material such as cement and steel in the nineteenth century, which allowed for multistory apartment complexes that lacked the open interior space (Burns 2005, 15). During the mandate, the French promoted and created a demand for "modern" cement over traditional building materials, which resulted in social denunciation of traditional materials as "backward." Now mud, straw, and wood are back in favor, not only because they are required in the reconstruction efforts, as outlined in the official preservation guidelines, but they allow investors to demonstrate their vast knowledge of traditional architecture and lend their renovation projects an aura of "authenticity."

Courtyard houses are common in numerous cultures around the world, in different climates and topographies built to underscore the relationship between social and spatial organization (Tuan 1977, 107; Rapoport 2007, 58). In Damascus, the courtyard was a common feature used not only for constructing homes but also for places of worship and business, such as mosques, schools, and khans. The Damascene courtyard houses in the recent gentrification have survived from the nineteenth century, though some houses might contain features from an earlier period (Sack 2005, 52, 92). In his history of Damascus, Nuʿman Qasatili (1879, 166) described dwellings during the late 1800s that were the predecessors of dwellings in the Old City today: "As for the interior arrangement of houses these days they most likely include an ʾiwan flanked by a *hujra* [room] with the rest of the rooms facing one another. They all have many glass-paned windows called *frankat*. Each house must have a *sahn* [courtyard] and some have ʾakbiya [cellars] where they store vittles."

It is significant that Qasatili began his description with "these days," indicating that he was aware of the modifications in the courtyard house within his lifetime, especially as he wrote that such elements like the frankat and even the ʾiwan were more common than in earlier periods. The house as process is apparent in his description of the new architectural features that became popular, which addressed the importation of new building features and styles such as the frankat. But he also wrote that each house *la bud* (must) have a sahn (courtyard), which naturally is the main element of a bayt ʿarabi and serves a social, cultural, and aesthetic function.

The architectural elements of the courtyard house coupled with the heritagization of the bayt ʿarabi are significant in the construction of the Shami identity; as the Shuwam built their houses, the houses built them. Not unlike the Turkish house, as described by Bertram (2008, 148), the bayt ʿarabi also becomes the "appropriate space" but, in this instance, for the representation and the imagining of a unique Shami identity from the standpoint of those on the "inside." The courtyard is not the architectural feat of Shami ancestors, but in the creation of a Shami sense of aesthetics that in turn informs the Shami sociability and civility and sets them apart from rural migrants. Hence, the difference between rural migrants and the Shuwam is how they embody the courtyard house.

Deconstructing Courtyards

The courtyard has several names in Arabic, *'ard al-diyar*, *fusha*, sahn, *baha al-samawiyya*, or just *baha,* that attest to its functional and social importance. The centrally located courtyard is an interior rectangular space open to the sky. Usually, a house has one courtyard; however, large homes belonging to officials and wealthy merchants have several internal openings of various sizes and purposes. The courtyard facilitated movement inside the house and between the inside and outside worlds. All rooms on the first floor of the house open directly onto the courtyard. Because the rooms are not internally connected, they can be only accessed through the courtyard, a quality that made courtyards popular rental properties. It was easy to rent out rooms, and several families could live in one house. The second floor is reached through the staircase tucked in one of the corners of the courtyard.

A *dihliz* (corridor) connects the courtyard with the street, but the link is not just about facilitating movement between the inside and outside world; it enforces the power of aesthetics in the bayt 'arabi. Users pass the blank exterior of the house and the drab dusty street through the door that leads to a dark, narrow corridor before arriving in the colorful, fragrant courtyard garden that according to one local observer "enthralls the soul" (Al-'Ash 1953, 49). The dusty street provides little, if any, shelter from the hot sun, but once inside, the cool and dark corridor leads to a welcoming garden courtyard. Movement is also heightened by a sense of mystery, especially for first-time visitors who do not know what to expect in the courtyard. The dialectical relationship between the two modes of embodied experience, especially in the Damascene summer, outside–inside of the bayt 'arabi is one of the many ways for the Shami culture to become. The plain exteriors of the houses face the street and betray nothing about the inside. This is a common feature of courtyard houses that emphasizes discretion, which is important for maintaining smooth social relations

7. A glimpse of a courtyard from the street, ca. 2004.

with neighbors though it extenuates the interactions among members of the same household (Tuan 1977, 107).

The garden courtyard is an important feature of the traditional Shami home, where the trees, flowers, and fountain beautify the lifestyle in the bayt. Citrus, especially lemon and bitter orange, or loquat and pomegranate are the typical trees found in the garden courtyard. Many houses have grapevines. No internal garden could be complete without the ubiquitous white fragrant jasmine, the flower of Damascus. Nizar Qabbani (1995, n.p.), the consummate poet, averred that he could not write about Damascus without jasmine "trellised" on his fingers.

Many of the architects I interviewed described how responsive the traditional bayt ʿarabi was to the fluctuation in temperature, before the advent of electricity and air conditioners. This is where we see the dwelling as a "process" (Humphrey 1988, 17), as social actors embody the space to mollify the impact of extreme weather. With its short winter and long, hot, dry summer, the open courtyard was considered ecologically compatible to the climate of Damascus (al-Nahawi 2000, 249).[3] The fountain and trees buffer the hot dry air in the summer. However, the winter cold made living in the courtyard dreary since movement inside and outside as well as within the house exposed people to the elements. Many families huddled in the upper rooms considered to be warmer than the ones on the ground level. Therefore, the house became familiar to its inhabitants, through their activities according to the season.

On the ground level, the main room that oriented the dwelling was the ʾiwan,[4] a room with three walls, with the fourth wall opening onto the courtyard and always facing north. Because of this orientation, the ʾiwan is designated as the summer sitting room because it is never directly hit by the sun. Water from the fountain, vegetation, and the black and white tile pattern of the courtyard flagstones contributed to cooling effects during the summer.[5] In many single-family homes, occupants dwelled on the first floor during the summer to make the most of the soothing aspects of the courtyard during the hot months. However, the family moved to the second story during the winter and lived in one room that they kept warm

3. Manuela Römer provided the translation from German for parts of this article.

4. For more information on the historic uses of ʾiwan in Arab-Islamic architecture, see Rabbat (1997).

5. The courtyard becomes a microclimate with the fountain and vegetation (Rabbat 2002).

8. An 'iwan, ca. 2004.

with braziers or wood or diesel stoves, though they still used the ground floor where the amenities were located.[6]

Piece of Heaven on Earth

The garden courtyard becomes a major incentive for many long-term residents to remain in the Old City. Abu Sami, a long-term resident in Harat Hananya, explained, "At night I sit out here and turn on the fountain. The sound of water, the sky above my head. This is heaven. I am king in my home." Abu George also from Harat Hananya added, "There is nothing like a bayt 'arabi. It is freedom. It is a man's castle. I don't have to worry

6. The fictional account by 'Ulfat Idlibi (1980) offers an accurate description of life in a courtyard house and how the seasons lead to movement between the lower and upper levels in the house.

about my neighbors. In a tabiq, I do not own the roof, or floor, only the four walls and just barely. No you cannot compare a tabiq to a bayt 'arabi. In some apartments they do not get sunshine." Although an apartment indexes a modern lifestyle, it comes with the loss of privacy and control over living space. This loss of privacy is acutely felt more by men than by women, which as we will see below brings to the forefront the gendered aspects of the courtyard house.

Shadi, one of the few Shuwam to return to the Old City to live, said he moved back because the apartment was a "form of exile from heaven," and he wanted to live in courtyard garden and be in contact with nature. The return according to Shadi was to "your own house in the Old City where you buy land and sky but in an apartment you buy a cardboard box. You have neighbors all around you disturbing you. What could be 'arwa' (more wonderful) than living in a house whose markiz (center) is a garden-sun, light, oxygen, greenery, trees . . . for eight months we live in jinna (heaven)."

Shadi expressed the embodied difference between an apartment and a courtyard house where the power of aesthetics makes the latter superior. Moreover, if Damascus is paradise, then living in the city should feel like paradise. In all of these accounts, we see differentiation between the life-style in a bayt and in an apartment but also the contestation over ways of being modern. Farha Ghannam (2002) observed that in Cairo the popu-lation forcibly relocated from the center of the city to new apartments in the outskirts become modern by inhabiting a space, considered superior to their old homes. For the relocated population, this move to a differ-ent living space reflected an improvement in their social status. Similar attitudes can be found in Syria where many Syrians prefer to live in an apartment even when many of them are cramped and damp. The attitude of Shadi, Abu Sami, and Abu George toward the courtyard house is not a commonly held view.

Moreover, Abu Sami, Abu George, and Shadi were owners, not rent-ers. They lived in the whole of the house, and unlike in houses that were leased to several families, they did not share the courtyard with other ten-ants. Therefore, the paradise of the courtyard house was not only based on gender but also on social class. Being male and having ownership of

9. Courtyard garden, ca. 2004.

the house enhanced the experience of living in a bayt 'arabi. Later in this chapter, I will return to the gendered and class differences when I discuss the reasons the Shuwam abandoned the courtyard house.

Creating a Shami Sense of Aesthetics

The courtyard, with its garden and fountain, was designed to promote comfort and to replicate paradise. Based on local lore it is this experience that led to the Shami *dhawq* (taste) for beauty and finer things in life. After all, a persistent image of Damascus is as a paradise. Nizar Qabbani insists that the splendor of his Damascene home captivated him, it is the key to his poetry (1995, 35), and it is in the bayt 'arabi that he was trained to see and appreciate beauty; therefore, he had no choice but to become a poet of all things beautiful. Nadia Khost eloquently described how a bayt 'arabi instilled in the Shuwam a sense of aesthetics:

If you spend your childhood in such a house you develop dhawq (taste),
a feeling, a feeling for the decorations, the light, the shade. If you come
during the day, you can see how all these decorations are reflected on
the wall. You have a feeling for trees; you do not cut a tree because you
know you planted it. You have a feeling for the jasmine for the scents,
the perfumes that are made from them. Not like the imported European
scents of today. So that is why I say that the 'amara (architecture) is
very important for the education, taste, and morals of people. The new
city practically raised people who have no dhawq; they have no human
interaction with their neighbors; they have no feeling for 'asala (authenticity); they have no authenticity; they do not know that Arab zakhrafa
(decorations) are a namt haya (way of life).

In this passage, Khost describes the process of becoming Shami, where
being surrounded with beauty leads to refinement in lifestyle and in social
interactions. Hence, she believes the Shami culture was cultivated in the
courtyard house not unlike the trees and flowers found in the interior garden. In addition to meeting their need for shelter, the courtyard house
also nurtured the Shami desire for luxury, which is what Ibn Khaldun
observed in his explanation of cities and their inhabitants. Khost might
have been echoing Ibn Khaldun, but she does not see luxury as leading to
corruption and eventual decline as he forewarned was inevitable (Mahdi
1964, 207–9). Rather, the decline came from rural migrants and their
destruction of the beauty of the courtyard house.

The "material setting" of the courtyard with its fountain, trees, flowers, 'iwan, 'ajami, and 'ablaq is contrasted with modern apartments and
"dialectical interplay between these two modes" allows for the Shami
culture to "become" (Richardson 2003, 88). The difference in experience between inside and outside the courtyard becomes defined as Shami
dhawq, the cultural attribute that differentiates them from rural migrants.
Moreover, the harmony and beauty of the courtyard garden is replicated
in their social relations with one another.

In her eloquent defense of the courtyard house, Khost was speaking
against the cement building blocks that covered large areas of Damascus
outside the wall and had no aesthetic appeal since they were constructed

with the utilitarian function of housing people. The cement apartment complexes looked unappealing, at least from the outside, and were the result of the socialist modernist attempts of the 1960s and 1970s to build a city that was a "machine for living." Aesthetics not only wasted resources but also reflected bourgeois sensibilities. Therefore, the government built homes for people that reflected its own modernization agenda without considering social and cultural needs. This is another reason why some Shuwam believe the socialist Ba'th regime hated Damascus for being too refined and bourgeois. However, the modern buildings lacked any aesthetic appeal, and as a result, the inhabitants did not develop any dhawq; hence, Shami identity is the product of the Old City and cannot be replicated in the modern neighborhoods. The neighborhoods outside the wall were not organic but built by others, the result of architects, urban planners, and professional builders, some of whom were foreign and oblivious to local sensibilities.

Khost lived in an apartment, in an exclusive neighborhood constructed with stone; not all apartments are the same, but her concern is the government standard apartment building that rejected Shami aesthetics. As Damascus grew and land became scarce, apartments were more practical for housing the thousands of newcomers to the city. Based on the neighborhood where they were constructed they varied in quality.

Therefore, a sense of aesthetic for the courtyard house becomes "one dimension of a distant, self-assured relation to the world and to others which presupposes objective assurance and distance" (Bourdieu 1984, 57). Growing up in the garden courtyard sets the Shuwam apart from others and unites them in their appreciation of finer things. The finer things become associated with the interior of the bayt: the courtyard, with its black and white stone tiles, the fountain, the jasmine and citrus trees, and the red and black 'ajami and 'blaq decorations of the 'iwan. Hence, an appreciation for the interior of the bayt leads to dhawq and the "practical affirmation of inevitable difference" (Bourdieu 1984, 57). All things beautiful in the style of the interior of the courtyard and in social interactions differentiates the Shuwam from rural migrants.

Khost linked the aesthetics in the courtyard garden to how the Shuwam perfected social relations and interactions. An appreciation for beauty leads to refinement in all forms of social behavior and dhawq becomes the basis for the civility of the Shuwam. When someone is described as having no dhawq, it could indicate no manners, like not respecting elders or behaving with insolence. The lack of taste creates discord, such as not greeting people in the street or raising your voice in public during an argument. Once a neighbor in Harat Hananya said I was "*kulik* dhawq [all taste]." I had not seen him for several days, and when I asked my friend George about him, he told me he was sick, so as was customary, we went to pay him a visit and inquire about his health. He thought I was behaving in a very refined way, and I was naturally flattered with the compliment, coming from a Shami.

Many Shuwam are quick to explain that many rural migrants did not develop this dhawq. They were tenants living in crowded conditions that negated the impact of the house on its inhabitants. This brings us to another difference between the rural migrants and the Shuwam and once again to the issue of home ownership. It is assumed that when the Shuwam lived in the Old City they lived in houses they owned and were vested in their maintenance, preserving their aesthetic power. Rural migrants, however, were mostly renters living in one or more rooms and sharing the courtyard and amenities with other tenants. They were considered a transient population living temporarily in the Old City until they were able to move to better accommodations outside the wall. In many rented houses, the courtyard disappeared, as rooms were built, and the fountain removed to create living space. The courtyard gardens were not maintained, and the bayt 'arabi became a slum that inhabitants wanted to escape, as in Nora's case.

The living conditions of Nora and her family did not inspire an appreciation for the beauty of the bayt 'arabi that refined dhawq. Many of these houses were squalid, which depressed the soul and did not encourage tact in dealing with neighbors. Nora not only lived in slum conditions but also had to deal with several neighbors. It became challenging, especially with those with whom she shared the courtyard. To get to the bathroom or kitchen, Nora and her family had to cross the courtyard under the gaze of other families. During my fieldwork, neighbors constantly fought over whether the children could play in the courtyard. Nora tried to maintain

10. Courtyard in a tenement house, ca. 2004.

good relations with the neighbors, to make life bearable in such close quarters where every move was monitored and information about her daily habits could be used against her during a quarrel. She also complained she had no privacy in her house and was unable to do what she pleased in her own home. She complained that she could not do simple things like wear shorts on hot days in her house, because she always had to go through the courtyard and was under the constant watch of neighbors. Since many families lived in the same building, and they all used the courtyard for their movement, she had no control over who came into the building and had to be subjugated to the stares of strangers when she went to the kitchen or to the bathroom.

Resorting to the living conditions of long-term residents of rural origin as the reasons for their lack of dhawq ignores the socioeconomic factors that create tenement conditions in courtyard houses. Nora and others want their landlords to provide them with a decent standard of living.

Nora cannot afford to live elsewhere, and the landlord takes advantage of this. Moreover, the superiority of the Shuwam remains assured because even when rural migrants live in the Old City and in bayt 'arabi they are unable to become Shuwam. Therefore, their moral authority over the Old City remains strong even when others live there and they do not.

"Backward" Bayt

We saw in chapter 1 how the courtyard house has been described by modernizing agents as contributing to a "backward" mentality detrimental to national progress. It is in this tension between the "civilizing" aspects of the bayt 'arabi and "backwardness" that we see another important aspect of becoming Shami. Rapoport (2007, 58) described courtyard houses in general as "the inside-out city," a preindustrial form of dwelling that emphasizes culture-specific privacy, where most of the living happens away from the street. Inward-looking houses in Damascus supposedly emphasized the privacy of family life and effectively secluded women. The courtyard house heightens the difference between "inside" and "outside" and the level of social interaction in each space (Tuan 1977, 107). The lack of access to the interior of houses in Damascus inflamed the imagination of European travelers who were unused to mud dwellings and were curious about the inside, which they could not access (Abdul Nour 1982, 135). Because they could not see the inside, many travelers explained how the courtyard house was fundamental to Islam, ignoring the fact that the courtyard house was common in non-Muslim cultures and was the vernacular dwelling in the region long before the advent of Islam. Moreover, religious minorities in the Old City had the same type of dwelling. This observation by Orientalists contained a social critique leveled at Arabs and how the privacy of the homes implied a lack of social cohesion or community. Even Syrians, as we saw in chapter 1, attributed "backward" social traditions to the bayt 'arabi, especially those built during the Ottoman period. They also believed the enclosed interior reflected a closed mind when it came to women and their mobility outside the home.

According to some modernizing agents, the bayt ʿarabi had always been a gendered house designed to oppress women. In chapter 1, Hakki described how many Syrians consider old cities as resulting in gender segregation. The courtyard house with its internal open spaces allowed women access to the outside by remaining inside, therefore restricting their mobility outside the house. Moreover, in some larger homes, spaces were designated for men were formally known as the *salemlik*, and the spaces for women, as the *haremlik*. Men were free to move from the salemlik to the outside world; women were restricted to the haremlik.[7] Hence, because the house was inward looking, it created the insular mentality, especially regarding the role and status of women. However, in all of these gendered arguments against the courtyard house, there was the issue of class. Poor women did not have the luxury to remain at home like their rich counterparts and lived in houses they shared with other tenants.

In efforts to preserve the Old City, issues of social "backwardness" regarding the status of women were at the forefront of the debate on whether preserving the courtyard house was in the national interest. Hakki saw this as another hurdle in the attempt to save the Old City from demolition: "We want to liberate women but not through the destruction of place; we want to liberate women through social relations." The assumption was that modern neighborhoods, apartments, and wide streets supposedly allowed women more mobility, but that was not necessarily the case. Women could be willingly or unwillingly confined to an apartment without the benefit of the inside open space where they could be outside while remaining within the confines of their home. Moreover, social censorship of women who appeared in public and outside the house was strong in Syrian society and among women. The Old City and the bayt ʿarabi informed women's physical mobility and made it easy to delineate spaces where both men

7. These terms apply to sections of houses that belonged to the ruling classes, which became popular in the 1800s, perhaps in an attempt to emulate the sultan's palace Topkapi in Istanbul.

and women could or could not mingle. This mobility was largely based on the "idea of home," and it allowed women to negotiate new spaces by maintaining the proper demeanor associated with being in the home even in public (Newcomb 2009, 138).

Therefore, many women in the Old City limited their mobility and visibility outside the homes, not only to conform to local social norms but also to project their status. Siham, a Christian who lived in the Old City, did not know the price of a kilo of apples but was very well aware of the price of shoes. She did not shop for groceries because her husband was responsible for providing for the household, and she avoided the congested and chaotic produce market. However, she had no concerns about being seen in the fashionable shopping districts of Damascus looking for bargains on clothes and shoes. Many women shopped for groceries, sometimes out of necessity because they had no male provider. Since the early twentieth century, however, it has been considered indecent for upper-class women to be in the street; therefore, men have been in charge of the shopping (Thompson 2000, 180).

Although the haremlik and salemlik existed among the very rich and ruling classes that could afford to have a house big enough for more than one courtyard, the mentality of gender segregation was predominant even among those who lived in houses that did not contain more than one inner space. Modern buildings constructed postindependence continued to mimic the haremlik and salemlik bifurcation of old Arab homes. For instance, an apartment could have at least two and sometimes three entrances. One entrance led directly to the guest room or the apartment salemlik, separate from the rest of the house, where men could entertain their guests without having to take them inside the home. The second entrance opened onto the main living area of the house where the family spent most of its time, which in effect was the apartment haremlik. The third entrance led directly to the kitchen where supplies could be delivered without going through the family's private living spaces. Thus, building modern apartments did not necessarily eliminate gender segregation, and building "new" neighborhoods did not lead to a break with traditional social values. Nonetheless, the image remains strong that "backward" traditions existed in the Old City because the built environment encouraged them.[8]

The Social Construction of Privacy

While Khost and others argued the courtyard house allowed for refined Shami social interactions, others believed the courtyard house promoted isolation and distrust. It was assumed these houses were designed to safeguard the family's privacy. This was not only a religious injunction but protecting a family's privacy reflected suspicion and fear of neighbors. Therefore, distrust of neighbors undermined social solidarity in Damascus.

Abraham Marcus (1986, 166, 178) defined privacy as "the state of limited access to the person, attitudes, and experiences of an individual." He also observed that privacy could only happen in houses inhabited by members of the same family. This was not always the case, especially among the poor, wherein several families were exposed to one another; therefore, "access to privacy tended to be uneven." Nora's living conditions did not provide her with any form of individual privacy, where Abu Sami and Abu George controlled who could access their home. But the nature of individual privacy also varied in Damascus, where individuals did not necessarily have unrestricted access to their person, possessions, or personal information. As in Naples, another Mediterranean city, Walter Benjamin (1978, 171) described how "each private attitude or act is permeated by streams of communal life . . . the most private of affairs, is here, . . . a collective matter." His observation could apply to Damascus. In Western understanding, privacy as individuation differed from Damascus, where it could be best understood as *khususiyya* and is linked to the role and duty of the individual toward the community rather than the other way around. But it also a concept whose practice varies with the built form as Ghannam (2002, 92–93) noticed in the housing project outside of Cairo,

---

8. For more information on the incorporation of traditional methods for ensuring privacy in modern urban planning in Damascus, see Kheir al-Kodmany (1999).

where living in an apartment led to new ways of demonstrating privacy. The lack of shared spaces, such as rooftops and bathrooms, in the new complex meant that neighbors had fewer opportunities to interact. This lack of contact also curtailed sociability and led to a decline in reciprocity and exchange among neighbors. Hence, the apartment became a private space that limited interaction among neighbors, and the construction of the private self was in tandem with living in modern apartments. Furthermore, as Ghannam (2002, 99) explained, privacy in the modern apartment became a "relational concept that is context bound," where it is associated with sight, especially by what should not be seen by others.

In the bayt 'arabi, there is a specific form of privacy based on visibility among neighbors that allows fluidity in social interactions. It is the dialectics between the built environment and social relations that creates a khususiyya suited to the *al-nasij al-'umrani* (urban/cultural fabric). Ibn Khaldun used *'umran* for what was constructed and cultivated by humans, not only in the physical but also in the social sense. This was his concept for culture, or for the "living together, and being housed alongside each other in a city or a tribal community for the pleasure of companionship and the satisfaction of their needs because of their natural propensity for co-operation in acquiring their subsistence" (Mahdi 1964, 186). For 'umran to happen harmoniously, privacy at some level had to be maintained. Therefore, the blank exterior was not to exclude and separate but to moderate social interaction so that association with one another remained a pleasurable experience. The city in the premodern Middle Eastern example was about overcoming alienation and smoothing social differences so that residents fulfilled their desire for companionship. The bayt 'arabi and the neighborhoods were all part of the process of civility that allowed the Shuwam to attain a refined and civilized existence and to engage with neighbors who lived in proximity without fully forsaking their khususiyya.

The houses in the Old City were of such close proximity and life in these close-knit houses was porous that it was impossible not to be privy to what was happening next door. I was aware of the happenings in the house where I lived, and I could smell what neighbors were cooking and tell what and when they were eating. I knew when neighbors were at home or away, and I could hear conversations in the courtyards, especially at night. Neighbors could also see neighbors from the rooftop and second-story windows. They could see who visited and even guess the purpose of the visit, as when a young man is coming with his female relatives to the neighbor's house that has daughters of a marriageable age.

The rooftop becomes a very delicate part of the house since it allows access to the neighbors' courtyards. Most of the daily, mundane activities of women take place in the courtyard. Yet the rooftops, particularly on hot summer nights, offer a respite from the heat. Before the advent of electricity and air conditioning, many residents slept on the roof in the summer. Men who spend time on the roof were treated with suspicion, especially the *hammati* of the Old City or men who raised and trained the flock of pigeons seen in the Damascene sky, circling in perfect formation. These men were considered "odd" because they lived on the roof near their pigeons and were obsessed with the birds. According to local lore, their testimony was not accepted in court because they were considered morally deficient since they spent most of their time on rooftops where they could peer down into their neighbors' courtyards. Therefore, the privacy of a courtyard house depended on neighbors' acting in the appropriate way even when temptation presented itself. You could be on the roof but you did not look down into your neighbor's courtyard. This self-policing maintained the notion of privacy in the Old City.

To maintain civility, neighbors are expected to avert their gaze from front doors and rooftops. Hence, seeing becomes a tactic in maintaining social harmony; social actors choose what they see and hear. However, neighbors also policed what happened in the homes of other neighbors, a common practice since the Ottoman period to protect the well-being of the community rather than to support individual privacy (see Marcus 1986; Semerdjian 2008). Though both Marcus (1986)and Semerdjian (2008) wrote about Aleppo, their observations could apply to Damascus during the same late Ottoman period.

A common description of the urban fabric of the Old City, which I heard from the staff of the Committee for the Protection of the Old City, historians, Nadia Khost, and others, was the house of the poor was next to the rich, but you could not distinguish one from the other; they all had the same blank exterior. In this idealized Old City, a commingling of different economic backgrounds supposedly meant social harmony. Neighborhoods were defined by the characteristic of their residents rather than by class (see Khoury 1983). For instance, residents of Shaghur were known for their bravery and stalwartness in the face of adversity, whereas 'Amarah residents were devout. In present-day Damascus, modern neighborhoods outside the wall are increasingly defined by class and status (Salamandra 2004, 41). Ethnic and sectarian segregation in the Old City, where it existed especially during the Ottoman period because of the millet system, was based on ethnic and religious affiliation rather than on economic status. Again, poverty in the Old City was relative because the truly destitute did not live within the wall and the intramural neighborhoods were associated with better-off merchants and artisans. The new neighborhoods Qanawat and Suq Sarujeh were built to accommodate the wealthy who wanted to escape the congestion of the Old City. Nonetheless, there were various degrees of wealth in the Old City. The plain and blank exterior of dwellings was important for *satr*, literally defined as cover, conceal, or protect but socially implies protecting the sanctity of. Houses are described as *masturah* (guarding or protecting the sanctity of its residents).

Some people attribute the need for protection to fear of the evil eye of neighbors and authorities especially during the Ottoman periods of instability and insecurity, where the well-off feared for their well-being. Here the emphasis is on the need to protect rather than the need to protect the sanctity. Protecting the sanctity implies fear of the unknown or the vicissitudes of life and not necessarily because of the Ottomans. The Ottoman period is an unpopular period in Syria; many Syrians consider it a time of decline and decay (see Kurd Ali, n.d., 31–41; Hitti 1959). As one Syrian explained to me, "the Ottomans and the Mongols were the only two empires in the world that gave nothing to civilization. Five hundred years and nothing, not even a book." A friend cautioned that history books on the positive impact of Ottomans were misleading: "The Ottomans left us with everything backward and underdeveloped. They were horrible, creating problems between the different religions. They introduced the segregation of men and women with this whole thing of haremlik and salemlik." In this popular history of the Ottoman period, which has been debunked in academic circles, satr became a negative quality and is reinforced in the built environment, which was largely from the Ottoman period.

Hakki linked courtyard houses and social backwardness: "These buildings are from the Ottoman period and of satr especially of socioeconomic status. Whether rich or poor you try not show it, because there are greedy people out there. The *wali* (governor) becomes greedy if you are rich." He therefore connected satr to fear and the lack of legitimacy of the local authority among the people. However, his view reduces the relations between Damascenes and the Ottomans to dominant and subordinate and denies the collaboration and cooperation that took place during that time. Moreover, his belief that satr was "backward" because it oppressed women ignores gender relations during that period and assumes restriction on female mobility outside the sanctity of the home as negative. Hakki's interpretation of the built environment contradicts with his appeal for its preservation. He resolved this contradiction by stressing the aesthetic value, although it allowed "backwardness." He believed that the good could be distilled from the past. For instance, *takaful* (social solidarity) was something that he believed should be preserved, and he advocated a process that allowed for sifting through traditional cultural practices and discarding negative aspects such as female seclusion but keeping social cohesiveness. However, both social solidarity and female seclusion are intertwined and difficult to separate because they result from the same spatial practices and belief system during a specific historical moment.

Another aspect of satr is discretion, which allows for more social cohesion by not flaunting ostentatious wealth and abject poverty. Again, we return to the "misrecognition" necessary for maintaining the social hierarchy and power relations. In this instance, satr smoothed social relations between different classes because the exterior of their house did not betray their status. Therefore, class distinction was confined to the interior of the house where it is revealed to the inhabitants of the house and their selected guests. However, civility exhibited through masking wealth could also "be little more than the courteous style that oils distasteful inequalities" (Herzfeld 2009, 79). Furthermore, courtyard houses illustrate densely populated and highly stratified communities (Rapoport 1969, 81). Life in

Damascus was very porous, wealth was not a private or personal matter, and the rich were well known in the community. Because they were marked not by their houses but from their acts of altruism, they were able to maintain the cohesiveness of the community. Therefore, the satr and the harmony idealized in the current gentrification reflect an imagined past that "misrecognizes" social inequality. The appearance of equality becomes important in an environment that lacked state institutions to provide protection and security. The wealthy residents of the neighborhood had to provide their own security and safeguard their property, and they did so not by force but by kindness. It perhaps was less expensive than hiring security to protect their well-being.

As we saw in the previous chapter, wealthier merchants performed a religious duty when they supported the less fortunate members of their community by discretely leaving food supplies outside their homes. However, for this to happen, merchants had to know who was in dire financial straits; therefore, the houses did not conceal that kind of information from neighbors. In this setting, charity was valued when it was perceived as anonymous, and good deeds were more powerful when they were performed in private rather than in public. Not seeing the act of charity also rendered it a religious duty, done for God and not people. When the act is seen, it loses its authority and undermines social cohesiveness. Thus, the houses protected the status of the occupants and encouraged acts of kindness but allowed the social hierarchy to remain in place. Society in the Old City had very rigid social categories, as Schilcher (1985) has described in her seminal work on Damascene society during the late Ottoman period, and acts of charity by merchants ensured it remained in place. In the Old City, the social hierarchy was not translated spatially, with the rich living in specific neighborhoods isolated from the poor, and charity contributed to maintaining *tadamun* (solidarity) in a highly stratified society. This form of social solidarity was lost in the modern neighborhoods, where social stratification became etched in the landscape.

In this chapter, the Shami tajr is a product of the bayt 'arabi in the Old City, where he could demonstrate his superiority while undermining social friction or envy. By redistributing wealth to the poor, he allowed for reciprocity to be in-kind as tadamun. Through accumulating "symbolic capital" (Bourdieu 1977, 171), the tajr was able to undermine resistance to the power relations and rigid hierarchies that benefited him. Although many Shuwam might quibble with this interpretation of their social interactions, embedded in the Shami identity of today is a rigid social hierarchy that values wealth and men, if not Sunni, over other forms of affiliation. The danger is when tadamun becomes an ahistoricized practice considered to be civilized but masks social hierarchies. It also undermines other more inclusive forms of solidarity such as at times of national crisis and against foreign occupation.

Tadamun in its various forms remained important in defining Syrian society until the early 1990s when neoliberal economic policies encouraged new forms of consumption that led to the ostentatious display of wealth. Basma's family moved to Damascus from a village near Homs when she was a young girl. Her formative years were spent in the city during the 1970s and 1980s. She used to constantly criticize the new social transformations as a result of neoliberalism, which heightened the difference among the social classes in the city. According to Basma, a government minister lived in the same apartment building as a schoolteacher or a janitor. At school, the daughter of the minister, shopkeeper, and street vendor were in the same class. "We lived the same and ate the same, but today all this is changing," she lamented. Today's public display of conspicuous consumption has severely affected the tadamun of Syrian society. This could explain the resurgent nostalgia for the civility of the Old City and life in the courtyard house, as an attempt to understand the current social transformation resulting from neoliberalism. The shift from a command/socialist economy to a market economy has brought forth much uncertainty in people's lives. The liberalization of the Syrian economy is creating social fragmentation that even undermines 'asl, and the national unity project has been abandoned by the regime. The new entrepreneurs who have benefited from the new economic policies are not interested in tadamun with those who are not of the same class or share the same economic interests. Moreover, their interests are fleeting and capricious. The different meanings ascribed to the courtyard house and the Old City are part of the social processes to make sense of social change.

Kind Houses

The romanticized social interactions discussed above become part of the nostalgic memories associated with the bayt 'arabi. As I walked in the Old City with Ahmad, who, as I mentioned earlier, worked with one of the government agencies supervising the intramural neighborhoods, he pointed out how the fragile material of wood, mud, and straw and explained how they created *hanan 'umrani* (compassionate buildings). This compassion was etched in the cityscape in traditional courtyard houses leaning against one another. The leaning is the result of the material used in their construction and which does not include steel beams or cement to hold up the building. However, the leaning is not considered an architectural feature of traditional building material but as one building supporting another building. By extension, people who live in these houses built with mud, wood, and straw also support one another. By contrast, concrete is hard and cold, and people who live in apartment buildings are cold to one another. Malik attributed the "love" Shuwam had for one another to the built environment and specifically to the bayt 'arabi. When he showed me the changes he made in the bayt that he converted to the restaurant, he pointed to the wood left from the original structure and his additions during renovations. "Wood has soul; it gives warmth. Why does it give warmth? It is energy. Wood is energy. It keeps warmth among people." Therefore, in his restaurants, he was recreating the supposedly Shami environment that enhanced civility among people.

Hanan 'umrani became a common poetic motif, especially in the work of Nizar Qabbani. He said, "Each house . . . supports the weight of other houses" and "Damascene houses are houses in love" (1995, 68). But it seemed that this was not poetic license as much as local lore, and even Tergeman spoke of a narrow alley where the houses were so close to one another they "almost kissed and their walls from the intense love clung to another" (1969, 8). The anthropomorphic courtyard houses were compassionate, loving, and kind, important for the attempt to overcome difference, sometimes more than the people who lived in them. As social actors describe the houses, they are talking about themselves. Not unlike the Western Apache and how they "speak" about the landscape, when Damascenes speak about the bayt ʿarabi, they use the same values and morals in the construction of their selves and of their society (Basso 1988, 122).

The concept of hanan ʿumrani is a powerful image that directly links the built environment and Shami civility; it also justifies the preservation of the Shami city. Therefore, in many ways, Tergeman wrote to vindicate her past and to remind Syrians of the glory of Damascus. She condemned the demolition of the "mud and wood house" and its replacement with high-rises that encouraged "impertinent behavior" (1969, 33). The impertinence came about when apartment buildings were built next to courtyard houses. Courtyard houses were no more than two stories high, but the multistoried buildings allowed those living in the upper apartments to peer into their neighbors' courtyards. Therefore, the apartment building and courtyard house could not exist side by side. Again by extension people who live in apartments are unable to appreciate the civility of those who live in courtyard houses. Not only did the new buildings encourage incivility but they destroyed the civility of the Old City. Her plea was not so much to save the bayt ʿarabi as to save the civility it engendered in its inhabitants. The indictment was for a modernity that could be only attained by destroying the good in all that is traditional.

Nadia Khost (1989) also lamented the loss of sociability and civility in her book *Exodus from Paradise* with the move to apartment buildings. Nasr al-Din al-Bahra, another author of nostalgia memoirs of the ideal lifestyle that existed in the Old City, claimed that the new buildings created a psychological condition among the Shuwam that led to their renewed interest in the Old City (Salamandra 2004, 140). The lack of tadamun among residents in an apartment building was the result of modernization that created vertical linkages to undermine the social cohesiveness with neighbors who live either above or below you. Living in an apartment is "hanging," no longer being grounded. The relationship becomes highly stratified, and there is no hanan ʿumrani but iron beams, to hold up the building.

Therefore, the neighborhoods outside the wall are segregated by class because of the new form of dwelling. Apartments announce the status of the occupants, unlike the discrete courtyard house. A ground-floor apartment that opens onto a garden is considered more expensive than one higher up. In the United States, the penthouse is considered a luxury, but in Syria, it is where the disadvantaged live. Luxury in this instance is determined by the stairs you climb to reach the tabiq—the fewer, the better. Ground-floor apartments with direct access to their own gardens are considered exclusive but not damp and dark apartments in the basement. Of course, with elevators installed in many multistory buildings, attitudes toward rooftop apartments could change, at least until the next power outage. Nonetheless, the distinction between rich and poor is more readily apparent in an apartment building than in a bayt ʿarabi because of the neighborhood and the location of the apartment in the building.[9]

In highly emotive accounts that idealized life and the structure of the bayt ʿarabi, we see a condemnation of modern apartments where many of the authors who write in support of the Old City tend to live. Then it could be this contrast in lifestyle, between a bayt and an apartment, that allowed a deeper appreciation for the houses they left behind when they left the Old City. Salamandra (2000, 2004) attributed their nostalgia to finding themselves a minority in "their" city as well as their marginalization from power and within the Baʿth/Alawite-Shami/Sunni divide (2000, 187). She also allocated this nostalgia to a group of professionals and highly educated individuals underscoring its class dimension. However, other groups were also engaged in their own nostalgia for an idealized past. Basma, although not nostalgic for the Old City, wistfully remembered a simpler time when everyone lived the same. Although George was in his mid-thirties when I met him, he was nostalgic for the neighborhood of his youth when young men "protected" the alleys from "outsiders." Now he saw the young men self-absorbed and worried about their hairstyles and cell phones, not their community. The nostalgia of Basma and George is in part a search for an "abstract moral authority" that indicts the state for allowing these divisions to become more pronounced (Herzfeld 2005a, 154). Moreover, as Sudermann (2012, 40) has noted "nostalgia becomes

---

9. In a conversation with Rami Daher in December 2008, spatial distinction by class had spread to Damascus with the construction of gated communities on the outskirts of the city.

part of the national identity," and it has many uses and can be deployed by social actors for different purposes.

As we saw in chapter 2, the move from the historic city center was accompanied not only with local political transformation but also with turmoil in the country and across the region. The defeat of 1967, the rise of Islamic parties, the civil war in Lebanon, and the wars in Iraq, all had a deep effect on Syria and influenced domestic policy. Although Syria had long been a model of political stability and security, it came with a strong police state and regime repression that targeted many families and individuals. Moreover, it proved it was unsustainable, as security and stability quickly unraveled with the uprising in 2011. The problems facing modern Syria since independence are ongoing and have not been effectively resolved; therefore, the past in the bayt 'arabi becomes not a refuge but an attempt to explain contemporary sociopolitical conditions. The movement away from the bayt 'arabi occurred during a time of optimism when social actors were leaving the "backward" courtyard house for a more "civilized" lifestyle in an apartment. The improvement in lifestyle was never completed—some say never initiated—and today, it seems to be unraveling at an alarming pace.

This in turn brings us to the abandonment of the bayt 'arabi. In the previous chapter, I discussed some of the political and social changes in the Old City that led the Shuwam to leave the historic city center for modern neighborhoods in significant numbers since the French Mandate. The arrival of the Ba'th regime continued this trend. In this section, I add another layer to the cultural and political push factors and what Hikmat Shatta (1999) described as "fashionable" by emulating the French. The next section examines the social and pragmatic reasons for leaving the Old City.

Leaving Paradise

The nostalgia of writers such as Khost and Tergeman as well as other memoirists of the Old City never translated into an actual return to the bayt 'arabi for various political and economic reasons. In an interview with Nadia Khost, she explained that many people, including herself, were reluctant to invest in a bayt 'arabi since most of them were in districts that were always under the threat of demolition. Yet Hakki was perhaps the most honest of those activists working to save the Old City when he said that he preferred to live in a villa rather than in a bayt ʿarabi. Again, this did not preclude his desire to preserve the bayt ʿarabi. "I am one of those who fought for the Old City but decided not to live there. I built a villa outside of Damascus and many people ask me about this, and I say I fight for the continued existence of the old City, but I am not ready to live in a place where I cannot park my car or cannot do anything about the infrastructure, the sewage, and I don't know what. But there are people who were successful in the move."

Many of the activists who called for preserving the Old City but who did not live there have been criticized for wanting to preserve "squalor," while they live in modern, clean neighborhoods (Salamandra 2004, 78–79). I am not sure why living outside the Old City and advocating its preservation are incompatible; rather, it illustrates how spatial differences determine social distinction. The Old City is where "backward" people live and the modern neighborhoods are where "civilized" people live, and Khost, Tergeman, and others retain the belief that where you live defines you. Khost and Tergeman were well aware of the depressed living conditions in the Old City, but their support for it was based on its civilizational value. It was hoped that by preserving the heritage site it eventually would be developed, as in the recent gentrification, and attract the "civilized" people back. Perhaps Hakki was supporting the right to choose where to live for others as well as for himself, and if the Old City was demolished, there would be no choice to make, especially for long-term residents, who would like to remain in the intramural neighborhoods.

Hakki is choosing where to live because he has the means to do so, but this may not be an option for some of the people who live in the Old City. Ironically, the increase in property values is allowing those who own property to move. With this, we come to the lure of modern convenience and luxuries not available in the Old City that induced many to abandon the intramural for new neighborhoods. Besides the lack of space for a swimming pool and parking garage, the ring roads that surround the Old City are congested with traffic. The walkability of the Old City is challenged when cars compete for the same space as pedestrians. Shadi who made the move back conceded that living in the Old City required some sacrifice. "I was living in the center of the city—now I am stuck in traffic." He recalled his parents' considerations when they left the Old City in the 1950s:

> My family like the rest followed the fashion; it was like the domino effect and based on practical reasons. But I also think that there are social reasons. The move was done in the name of modernity and development. Old houses are backward. . . . Cars need wide roads not alleys of the Old City. Many people say they left for practical reasons. The bayt 'arabi is difficult to clean and maintain. Houses are not adaptive to modern life. In my opinion, all these reasons are not real. They have some truth in them but the real reason is how I want to present myself in this debate between modernity and tradition. So when my family left, like others they had these reasons.

Shadi distilled the desire to leave the Old City with the "debate between modernity and tradition." It also indicates how social actors defined themselves within this binary based on the space they inhabited. In addition to the political and economic changes that led many Shuwam to leave the Old City, we have the added social layer of "following the fashion." It became acceptable to leave the Old City to want to appear modern; those that remained for whatever reason did want to appear modern.

Shadi also mentioned the practical reasons that led the Shuwam to abandon the Old City that had to do with owning a car, keeping the house clean, and living as a nuclear family. Perhaps the most compelling argument made for leaving the bayt for an apartment was housekeeping. This is where gender becomes a factor in the reasons, leading to the abandonment of the bayt 'arabi, and provides insight into the patriarchal aspects of Shami life in the bayt beyond gender segregation and female seclusion discussed earlier.

Gender and the Bayt

Women were at the center of the debate of tradition and modernity, "backwardness" and "civilization," as well as abandonment of the Old City, largely because of how they controlled the domestic space. Although the house is owned by the husband or his family, women exercised considerable power over the management of the household, especially when keeping the interior of the house clean and well-maintained. A clean house not only reflected well on the wife and mother in caring for her family but also on the husband for choosing and having an industrious wife. Women through cleanliness exercised their moral authority over the family, asserted their right to the use of the domestic space, and staked their claim in the patriarchal home. Tidy and neat houses became a status symbol. Shadi mentioned that it was difficult to keep courtyard houses clean because the streets were filthy and the courtyard was open. I was amazed by the amount of time women spent cleaning, and usually, women or girls performed this household task. Cleaning was not only a gendered activity but men or boys mopping or cleaning a house when their female kin were available risked being ridiculed. Men could clean their stores for instance because it was a male domain, but the domestic sphere had to be cleaned by women. This gendered division of labor was not only in Syria or the Middle East but also in England where women who worked outside the home were still responsible for housework (Massey 1994, 207). Cleaning could also happen at different times of the day, especially if the woman of the house worked outside the home. Sometimes late at night, I heard or saw women mopping. In a city where social status comes from many factors, including cleanliness, keeping a spotless house reflects well on the woman's 'asl and upbringing. Hence, this emphasis on cleanliness differentiates the Shuwam from rural migrants. As we saw in the previous chapter, Pierre claimed villagers were filthy, but it was an unfair description because rural migrants were as fastidious about clean homes as were the Shuwam.

Moreover, housework became a negotiating point for staying or leaving the bayt 'arabi because of the amount of effort and time. Khadra and her family lived in a modest-sized bayt 'arabi. She had three rooms around the courtyard and three rooms on the second level. It was very suitable for her and her five adult children, but for a time, she was living in the house with her in-laws, two brothers-in-law, and their families. The house was crowded and difficult to keep clean. The women never agreed on whose turn it was to clean, and since they did not get along with one another, they did not cooperate. After her parents-in-law passed away and her brothers-in-law moved out, she had the entire house for her own use, though she did not own it entirely. One of her unmarried daughters spent most of her time keeping the courtyard and rooms clean. Unlike her sisters, she did not have a job, and keeping the courtyard clean became her contribution to the household. During the summer, the daughter told me she mopped the tiled courtyard three times a day. It was common practice by many local standards to clean whenever dirt was apparent, but the daughter's meticulous attention to fighting dust indicated her diligence in house-work, which would make her a more eligible bride. When the daughter marries and moves away, Khadra would most likely have a difficult time keeping the house clean to the standards set by her daughter, a situation that might lead her to decide whether she wants to stay in the house or move to a tabiq.

According to several interlocutors, the decline of the extended fam-ily was the result of women becoming too modern and wanting more independence. Doreen Massey (1994) illustrated the disruption in gender relations resulting from industrialization and capitalism in rural Eng-land. However, the disruption in Damascus was largely because of urban modernization in which many families wanted to adopt a modern iden-tity outside the Old City. Sometimes in jest, social actors would comment that women who became too modern led to the decline of the extended family. These women became modern not through seeking employment outside the home but by choosing new patterns of consumption, wanting a nuclear family, and living in an apartment. Women increasingly refused to live with their in-laws, and most important, they did not want to spend their time cooking and cleaning.

Although the decline of the extended family is the result of modern-ization, it is also a rejection of the patriarchal system that encouraged sev-eral generations to share the same living space. Within this system was another gendered hierarchy for men and women based on age and mari-tal status. A young wife married to the youngest son did not have much say in how the household was administered. Since women spent most of their time at home, this increased the friction among the higher-ranked females in the household, particularly between the mother and daughters-in-law. Nonetheless, to blame women for the rupture of the extended family ignores the fact modernization was transforming all aspects of life and that it was only a matter of time before it would affect gender relations. Modernization destroyed the delicate balance between daughters-in-law and mothers-in-law, the staple of numerous TV serials set in the Old City. Invariably, the good mother and the dutiful wife kept the family together and in the bayt ʿarabi since the decision to stay most likely hinged on the woman. The bayt ʿarabi was the province of women and in turn the "spiritual domain" of family, tradition, and national identity that marked the cultural difference with the West (Chatterjee 1993). As Partha Chatterjee argued in the Indian context, the spiritual domain became essential in defining the "new" woman who in the process of becoming new must maintain distinct "traditional" elements that maintained difference between her and the Western woman (1993, 9).

However, in Syria, a "crisis of paternity" brought about by World War I and the demise of the Ottoman Empire challenged patriarchal authority and introduced new gender roles before many Shuwam families contemplated moving outside the Old City (Thompson 2000, 6). Elizabeth Thompson described how the war demolished social norms. Men were expected to protect and provide for their families, a role made impossible when their families went hungry and women were in the streets begging for food (2000, 25). With the end of the war and the start of the French Mandate, the "crisis of paternity" informed new roles for women in public where their visibility rendered them the putative cause of social problems. The paternity crisis also shattered the illusion that a continuum existed in social practice from the late Ottoman period to the recent past.

Dreaming of a Tabiq

Several investors believed they did not displace long-term residents if those residents wanted to leave. Social mobility for many long-term residents continued to be attained through relocating to an apartment outside the Old City. Salim, an architect and investor, observed that not just women wanted to move to a tabiq: "Those people who used to live in an old house became disgusted. They have the right to be. They go to a flat with three rooms, a bath, and kitchen. The upkeep is easier. Here you have a house that needs more work. . . . So all people left for modern buildings. . . . Life has changed. Old life is not like new life. . . . Now you notice in your fieldwork everyone says they do not want to live in a bayt ʿarabi. They want to live in a tabiq."

I met several long-term residents that loved living in a courtyard house, which only highlights how the relationship between long-term residents and the bayt ʿarabi was a complex issue. It tends to be reduced once again to the difference between homeowners and renters. All the men introduced in this chapter lived in courtyard houses they owned, and they compared it to paradise, but tenants experienced the bayt ʿarabi differently. Many tenants lived in houses that lacked conveniences, such as bathrooms and kitchens, and had to make do with makeshift amenities. Landlords were less accommodating to the needs of their tenants and did not make necessary repairs or keep up with routine maintenance. In some instances, they did not mediate between tenants when conflicts arose, such as over the use of space or from high utility bills. Utilities were usually on one meter for the whole house, and landlords refused to pay the fees associated with having each housing unit on a separate one. Situations like these easily led many long-term residents who rented to become disgusted with the houses in which they lived. They complained about the mildew, the dirt from the mud walls, the annual maintenance, and the dust from the courtyard that easily dirtied the rooms. Many Syrians described these conditions as "backward," contributing to the decay and decline of the heritage in the Old City.

Nonetheless, the impact of being a tenant in a courtyard house effected women more than men. Bourdieu's (2003) work on the Berber house argued how the male and female use of the domestic space was an inversion of the social order that existed in the world beyond the threshold. In this instance, the bayt ʿarabi became a commentary on the social and gender inequalities that existed in the Old City and Damascus at large, which could no longer be ignored under new economic conditions. Living in a courtyard house was an ordeal for many women of the lower classes, not only because of cleaning but also because of their lack of control over their domestic sphere. If we return to Nora, her husband worked outside the home, returning for lunch and in the evening. This left her home alone most of the day with the neighbors. They were more of an issue for her than for her husband, since she was in constant contact with them. Her husband was able to maintain polite, formal relations with the neighbors, even when his wife was not on speaking terms with them. He would say, "This is women's business, to fight one day and make up the next." He was not going to follow his wife's lead and have social relations with the neighbors only when she did. But this was also a tactic used by men to maintain a channel of communication with the neighbors when the women were not speaking to one another. There might be a need to negotiate over rent, the electricity bill, or a new loud tenant and the men could still do this even if their wives were not on speaking terms. Therefore, Nora's husband probably disliked the neighbors more than she did, but in such closely intertwined lives, it was good strategy to maintain the channels of communication in case the need arose to negotiate over the use of common space. Hence, in the close quarters of a tenement courtyard house, a gendered division of communication is established; fighting with neighborhoods becomes the role of women while negotiating with these same neighbors, the role of men.

Nora was looking forward to the day when she would move to her tabiq, where she hoped she would control her domestic space: "It is much better in a tabiq. It is easier to keep clean, you can maintain your privacy, you do not have to associate with the neighbors, and you may never see your neighbors." She continued to say how she could not wait for the winter so she could close her door, gather her children around her, and have nothing to do with the neighbors in the courtyard. The closing of the door is easier to do in winter than in the summer and could be done without signaling ill feeling toward the neighbors. As Ghannam (2002, 95) observed, the door "regulates the inclusion and exclusion of others from the family's life" and "functions as a thermometer that indicates the fluctuation of the relation between neighbors."

The dream of a tabiq was more than escaping meddlesome neighbors. It was also a dream of social mobility for Nora and her family. Since they had been living in the Old City before it became fashionable to move there, they still maintained the notion that moving was an improvement on their current situation. This notion was reinforced by living in houses that did not provide tenants with a decent life, which rendered many long-term residents embarrassed by their bayt 'arabi, especially if it was run down and difficult to keep clean. It did not match their outward appearance in dress and behavior like a tabiq would. Some could be apologetic about visitors coming to dirty, cockroach-infested alleys and lanes to houses that smelled damp and were not properly maintained. Nora told me how she felt honored when her uncles, who lived in flats in the new neighborhoods, visited her. She considered her house beneath her wealthier relatives and was at pains to make them welcome when they came. The room in the bayt reflected her status that could not be concealed. Her situation and relation with the bayt contrasted sharply with Abu Sami, Abu George, and Shadi. They were men who also owned the bayt, hence the dissonance between ownership and renting. For Nora and other renters, it was not a piece of heaven, but more of a nightmare, especially during fights with the neighbors. It did not awaken any feelings of beauty, but rather a desire for luxury in a tabiq. I did not hear of many tenants in the Old City who wanted to buy a bayt 'arabi, and these days it has become beyond their reach, as prices have increased astronomically.

Cultural Affinity

However, many investors were able to use the desire of many long-term residents for a tabiq against them and as proof for their lack of attachment to the Old City. Salim owned several houses in the Old City he was refurbishing as hotels. He was pleased with the new rent law that would enable him to evict tiresome tenants who held up his project by refusing his earlier offers to move. Before the rent law came into effect in 2004, he had made each family an offer of one and half-million Syrian pounds (approximately $30,000) or an apartment in Jaramana, a congested suburb of Damascus, to relocate. Now he did not have to be as generous and could evict his tenants legally. I asked him about the future of long-term residents in the Old City as result of the law and gentrification. He answered,

I don't consider those people as residents. They only live here because they have no choice. Is this one maintaining a house, look [here he points to a house bordering his property]. They are renters. . . . They did not move here because they wanted to live in the Old City. These houses were the cheapest available in Old Damascus. Now this house has eight families, each room has a family and each family is seven or eight members so what do they feel about the Old City. . . . I consider they are bad for Old Damascus. Old Damascus means nothing to them, and we can go and see houses that are rented, they are a treasure but who has destroyed this treasure? The renters. They painted the stone; they removed marble and put in ceramic tiles. They are all like that. They do not live here to preserve Old Damascus. I do not consider them at all. I consider they are harmful to Old Damascus. And it means nothing to them.

Salim dismissed long-term renters as transient residents who did not belong in the Old City because they were unable to "feel" the beauty of the courtyard house and were impervious to its aesthetics. Social distinction between rural migrants and Shuwam based on lack of taste made it easier for investors such as Salim to evict them even though he was not a Shami. Yet this eviction was not displacement according to Salim since the long-term residents did not belong in the Old City, which continues to be associated with the Shuwam. He was saving houses from long-term residents who were polluting the historic alleys of the Old City and damaging its heritage.

Brett Williams (1988) described the difference in perception between renters and homeowners in one neighborhood in Washington, DC, undergoing gentrification. Renters were considered "socially incomplete" since homeownership indicated responsibility and maturity. Moreover, homeowners were considered to be permanent members of the community and therefore vested in the future of their neighborhood unlike renters who were considered transitory (74). Although Williams illustrated the commitment of long-term residents to their community, they were more vulnerable to gentrification because they were easier to displace. Salim expressed similar attitudes toward the tenants who he sees as irresponsible and uncaring to the well-being of the property they inhabit. Compounding their shortcomings as responsible residents is that they live in a heritage site and remain impervious to its value. The heritage of the Old City remains the patrimony of the Shuwam and deprives long-term residents to any claim to the space and denies their contribution to place making. Similar attitudes toward long-term residents and users emerged in the preservation of Times Square (Reichl 1999), Harlem (Jackson 2002), and East Harlem (Davila 2004), where they were criminalized and accused of contributing to the economic decline of the city. John Hartigan, Jr. (1999), reported that the racialization of poor whites from the South in Detroit marginalized their claim to space. Incidentally, historic preservation like gentrification has been associated with marginalizing long-term residents as well. Michael Holleran's (1998) work on the history of historic preservation in Boston described how Italian and Irish immigrants were blamed for the decline of Brahmin Boston and spurred the efforts to preserve historic neighborhoods in the city.

In Damascus, rural migrants were considered the cause of decay and decline because they also engaged in criminal acts, selling the wood panels of rooms or ornaments they hacked from courtyard houses. The Department of Antiquities regularly sends teams to houses under its authority to be sure residents have not defaced or removed ornaments and decorations. This was the case in a courtyard house under state control occupied by several families. In one room, a curtain covered an intricately carved small marble alcove. When I asked the wife what it meant, she rolled her eyes and said she did not know, but government employees from the Department of Antiquities came to inspect it periodically. I thought it ironic the Department of Antiquities was monitoring a simple decorative stonework of no artistic or historic value while the rest of the house was deteriorating. This procedure implied the government's concern that the residents, in this case Palestinian refugees, would sell the alcove because they lacked an appreciation for its value. The lucrative heritage industry and the black market for stolen artifacts encouraged some individuals to traffic in relics or objects from courtyard houses. But it was also a reminder that the Palestinian refugee family did not belong in the heritage site.

Salim, without being a Shami or needing to claim to be a Shami, designated himself the steward and protector of this heritage in the bayt 'arabi from the very people who live in it. Possessing this affinity had become a necessary qualification for anyone who wanted to invest in the Old City under new economic conditions. Therefore, as a heritage site, the Old City should belong only to those who know, and in turn appreciate, its historical and aesthetic value. Furthermore, cultural affinity does not necessarily come from having lived in the Old City; rather, it is a feeling one develops for aesthetics and heritage.

In this chapter, we saw how the bayt 'arabi could be used to articulate a unique Shami identity when it approximated the garden/paradise of an idealized past. The guests in the beginning of the chapter were satisfied with their expectations of a courtyard garden in the art gallery because it affirmed their notion of a Shami home. The courtyard remains important in creating cultural differentiation between the Shuwam and rural migrants that underscores political transformations in the country as well as class and gender differences in embodying the bayt 'arabi. It is also important for navigating social change and transformation, where in addition to contributing to the civilizing process of life in the city, it could be the cause of backwardness.

The aesthetics of the courtyard house and their role in developing a Shami cultural identity are significant in the gentrification of the Old City since it allows for another aspect of differentiation between the investors and long-term residents. Moreover, an appreciation for the Old City was measured by the desire to remain in a bayt 'arabi. Since most of the long-term residents in the Old City are tenants, their desire to remain in the Old City is determined by other factors contingent on gendered issues, such as privacy, cleanliness, and sharing a bayt 'arabi with several other families. Moreover, social mobility among many long-term residents is attained by dwelling in an apartment not unlike an earlier generation of Shuwam who exchanged the courtyard house for an enclosed flat.

Nonetheless, the purported difference between the rural migrants and Shuwam propels the current gentrification where many investors see their role as ensuring that the Old City remains a distinct Shami space though much of their material heritage is being commodified in new forms of cultural consumption. Rather what remains important in the gentrification of the Old City is the creation of the garden courtyard and the narratives it inspires on Shami sociability and civility. The next chapter will continue the examination of the bayt 'arabi but through an analysis of how the preservation of architectural elements in the house is leading to new forms of being and belonging in the Old City.

4

"People Living in Houses Ruin Them"

During the course of my fieldwork in 2004, I was introduced to a Syrian couple who had purchased a house in the Old City. The Turkis were part of a growing number of people buying courtyard houses in the Old City to restore to their "original" condition. This group was not restricted to Syrians but with economic liberalization included non-Syrians as well who were motivated by opportunities in the heritage industry of the Old City. They had spent two years searching for *the* perfect investment property and were eager to show me their house as it was being renovated. I met them early one Friday morning on Straight Street, and we walked to the bayt 'arabi they had purchased in a residential neighborhood not far from the main road in the Old City. We stopped before a nondescript iron door that opened onto a courtyard and 'iwan, where reconstruction was under way. The walls were stripped of paint and plaster to a layer of mud bricks and wooden lath, with a few red tiles embedded between the bricks. Anything beyond this layer would mean demolishing the walls, which was, at least hypothetically, not allowed according to the preservation guidelines of the Committee for the Protection of the Old City (CPOC). Parts of the courtyard were dug out, and the roof had collapsed, rendering the entire upper level a ruin.

The Turkis were noticeably excited about their work and spoke of how restoring the house would occupy them for months, if not years, as they painstakingly researched and renovated its architectural elements. Throughout the tour, the couple emphasized the history and heritage of the house. The house was located where it is believed the Roman city had once existed. Mr. Turki pointed to the thin terra cotta tiles in the wall and read, "Roman tiles," visibly proud that his house contained proof of a genealogy that went back to ancient times. In the gutted courtyard, he pointed to terra cotta pipes that he labeled "Roman aqueducts"; an example of a "civilizational air conditioner": water in the pipes alleviated the summer heat. I was not sure whether the tiles and the pipes had been authenticated as Roman; nonetheless, he planned to install glass bricks when he repaved the courtyard so that the "Roman" pipes could be displayed.

Mr. Turki's family originally came from Midan, but the couple lived in one of the modern and upscale neighborhoods of Damascus. Mr. Turki remembered an ancestral courtyard house but did not mention he lived in it, and he probably only went there to visit relatives on special occasions. He could claim the nostalgia for childhood memories in a courtyard house propelled him to buy the bayt 'arabi. Yet this well-educated and highly professional man, who traveled abroad almost every year, typified the new group of cosmopolitan Syrians who sought to own a piece of the heritage in the Old City, now that it had become fashionable to have a second address in the intramural neighborhoods.

I take my understanding of cosmopolitanism from Ulf Hannerz (1996, 102–3), who used it to describe "a perspective, a state of mind" of a group of people who were willing to engage with diverse cultural experiences that they saw as alien or incompatible with their own culture. Cosmopolitans are at ease anywhere in the world and are not restricted to one particular locale. Therefore, for someone like Mr. Turki, being Syrian was inconsequential to his interest in the courtyard house; rather, he approached the bayt 'arabi as another instance of a global cultural experience distinct and distant from his own experiences even though he lived in the same city. It was common among the upper class and the Western-educated Shuwam to see novel and exotic experiences in the Old City of their ancestors (Salamandra 2004, 142–43).

The new economic policies of the 1990s led to a boom in the heritage industry of the Old City, which attracted investors to buy the vernacular dwelling, once decried as an obstacle to national progress. As Suhail, a Shami and long-term resident still living in the same courtyard house his father and grandfather were born and raised in said, "Until recently

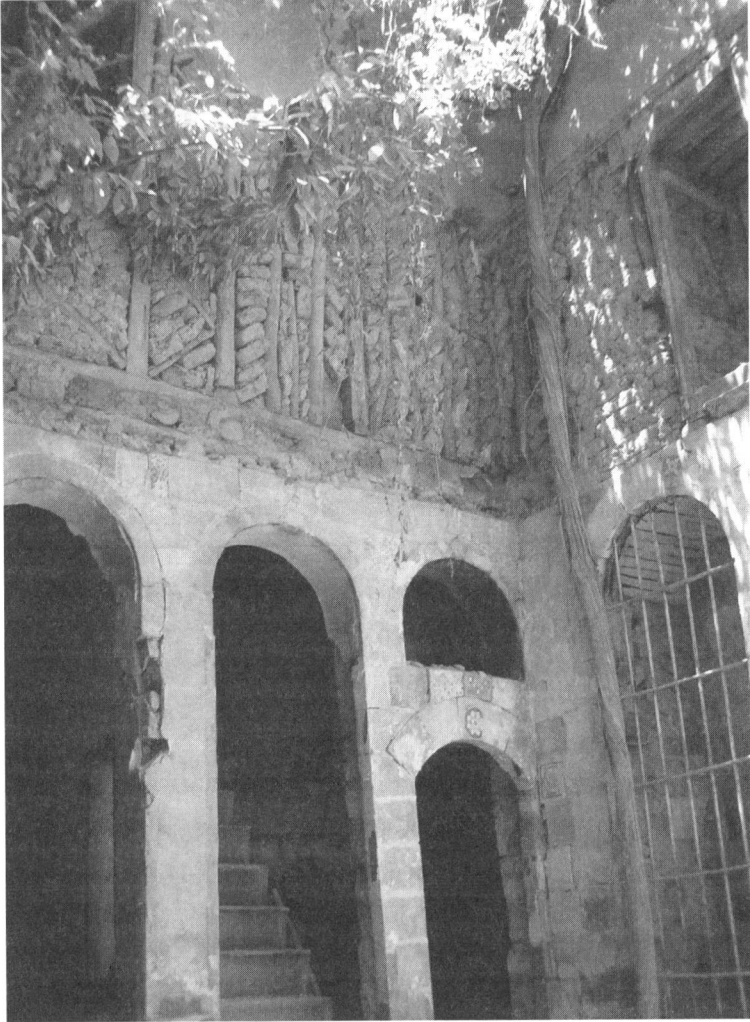

11. A stripped wall in a courtyard, ca. 2004.

people would tell you go sell your bayt 'arabi and buy a tabiq. Now they say you are lucky to live in one." Yet the luck was not in actually living in the house but in possessing a cultural artifact of history, a link to the "authentic past." Whereas for long-term residents the bayt was home, for investors such as the Turkis, it became an "ethnographic object" (Kirshen-blatt-Gimblett 1998), detached not only from its immediate surroundings but also from its immediate history. The house was valuable for its Roman elements and not because it was embedded in the local community. The architectural elements that could be preserved were more important to a house's value than the role it had in the social interaction in the neighborhood. Furthermore, the bayt was fragmented into its architectural elements rather than taken as a whole, and when these parts supposedly possessed historical value they were displayed. The act of displaying objects "mediate[d] and thereby transform[ed] what [was] shown into heritage" (Kirshenblatt-Gimblett 1998, 7–8). The bayt became less important for forging connections with other long-term residents and building social solidarity within the neighborhood but significant for connections with cosmopolitans of other nationalities who possessed the same affinity for heritage anywhere in the world. We have seen an example of Europeans purchasing the riad in Morocco and with economic liberalization in Syria foreign investors have found opportunities to own Old City heritage. Through their work in preservation cosmopolitans regardless of origin can claim ownership of the history in the Old City. Yet what remains specific to the historic preservation in Damascus is that the heritage saved continues to revolve around the Shami cultural identity. We will see how the preservation continued to uphold idealized aspects of the Shami home.

A major difference between cosmopolitans and long-term residents was the return ('awda) because it was mediated by a specific form of cultural knowledge and appreciation for the heritage of the Old City, which long-term residents supposedly lacked. For the Turkis, and other cosmopolitans, there was an attraction in the aesthetic of the courtyard house, which allowed them an intellectual engagement with previous civilizations. Even though Khost argued against the past as a foreign country, for many Damascenes who did not venture into the intramural neighborhoods prior to the "rediscovery," the past was an exciting new frontier. Some investors, not unlike the Turks, spent years searching for a bayt that appealed to their idea of a Shami house or one with the potential to be restored as such, but the search was part of the process of "discovering" the Old City. In addition, the time and effort invested in the transformations of a dilapidated house into an ideal Shami dwelling enhanced the restorers' credentials as true connoisseurs of the past.

In this and in the next chapter, I will focus on two types of cosmopolitans in the Old City who were involved in this process of displaying the heritage of the bayt ʿarabi buried under the layers of "backwardness" of the long-term residents. In this chapter, I introduce the group I call the "returnees," and in chapter 5, I discuss the mustathmirin (plural for *mustathmir* investor). Although both are investors in the Old City and their aim is to preserve the courtyard house, they have different uses for the restored homes. The "returnees" maintain the residential function of the bayt, whereas the mustathmirin, convert courtyard houses into hotels or restaurants. Although both are involved in the gentrification of the Old City, their intervention in the intramural neighborhoods introduced different and new spatial practices. The mustathmirin were commodifying a distinct Shami identity for local and global consumption of an "authentic" cultural experience, thereby encouraging more cosmopolitans from outside the wall to come to the Old City. The returnees challenged the sociability and social interactions in the residential neighborhoods because many were not permanent residents in the Old City and their houses beautifully restored stood vacant most of the year.

The returnees and mustathmirin were both involved in the process of *trajiʿ ila al-ʾasl* (return to the original) again bringing to the forefront the theme of ʿawda that has dominated the discussion on the gentrification of the Old City. By restoring the house to its origins and revealing its heritage and "authenticity" as a Shami dwelling built and inhabited during a period described as "civilized," cosmopolitan investors were returning to the idealized Shami city and in the process designating themselves as stewards of the Old City. This process further marginalized long-term residents and reduced the Shami identity to easily commodified cultural practices and aesthetics. Although Sharon Zukin (2010, xiii) described authenticity as a "cultural form of power over space" that allows for class differentiation among social users of the space, in the Old City the cultural form remains exclusively Shami and any group that wants to lay claim to the Old City must deploy the Shami cultural attributes that we have discussed in the previous two chapters. The attributes of the Shami identity were mediated through the bayt ʿarabi; hence, the courtyard house becomes shorthand for being Shami. However, by the same token, investors who took liberties with the Shami identity in their restoration of the courtyard house were accused of damaging the heritage of the Old City. Therefore, as this chapter will also demonstrate, not all returnees were contributing to "saving" the Old City rather distinction among them was based on how well they attained Shami sensibilities. Some were accused of doing more damage than long-term residents.

Gentrification and historic preservation are two different processes of urban change, but in this instance, they could be easily conflated because they are the same process in the Old City. Moreover, historic preservation is the only recourse for transforming the built environment, because the Old City is a protected heritage site, and, theoretically, no modification should take place that alters the physical layout. Historic preservation is also loosely applied because, technically, it requires the least modification in the structure of the building (Fitch 1990, 84). However, social actors in the Old City speak of preservation by returning to the original historic form of the building, and I decided to privilege their approach in what they are doing. Therefore, this book is not about the techniques of historic preservation but rather its social implication. There are similarities between the gentrifiers in Damascus and Southern California who also were "experiencing a sense of history rather than reliving actual chronological events" (Lawrence-Zúñiga 2010, 224). Their concern for the distant past in the Old City stemmed from nostalgia brought about by civilizational anxiety. Although nostalgia is mediated by a sense of loss (S. Stewart 1999, 145), in this instance, loss is not real but imagined, resulting from the decades of discourses surrounding the decay and decline of the Old City. None of the returnees I interviewed were returning to a childhood home, but the image of the decayed bayt became a powerful "poetics of space" (Bachelard 1964) that evoked bittersweet sentiments.

As Esra Ozyurek (2009, 9) illustrated, neoliberalism in Turkey created a nostalgia that "becomes a convenient desire that can transform public concepts such as the national past or identity into personalized commodities." It could also transform the cultural present into an object that could be acted upon (K. Stewart 1988, 228). Nostalgia for the bayt leads to the restoration and renovation projects in which the Shami past becomes a commentary on the social conditions of the present.

Class or Social Acts?

Although historic preservation and gentrification are class-based activities meant to establish a distinct social identity (Zukin 1995, 2010; Jager 1986; Redfern 2003), in this instance, it is difficult to determine the contours of any one class or any one identity in the transformation of the Old City. In his work on the gentrification of Melbourne, Australia, Michael Jager (1986) described how middle-class anxiety over their identity as distinct and distant from the lower classes was expressed in the restoration of houses from the Victorian period. The Melbourne middle class were appropriating the sensibilities as well as the patrimony of the Victorian bourgeoisie.

According to Redfern (2003, 2362; emphasis in the original), the "importance of class in gentrification issues is not therefore the supposed difference between the (so-called) middle class and the (so-called) working class, but the *experience* of class." He explains that gentrification is significant because of how it is deployed by the class with means to create a "place in society" by making a place in the city. The lower classes are also vested in making a place in society, but they are overpowered by the upper classes. Redfern (2003, 2364) concludes that there is no evidence that gentrifiers are a class or gentrification an "evolution in class structure" but that urban renewal is the process to resolve social anxiety and fear of marginalization.

To reduce the gentrification of the Old City to social class anxiety and differentiations ignores how local discourses on being and belonging in the Old City have long stressed another form of anxiety over the loss of the Shami city. Although there is an element of class bias in the evolution of the Shami–rural divide, the current long-term residents are of disparate social backgrounds. Whereas renters tend to be of the lower classes, many property owners tend to be wealthy according to local standards. Hence, to assume that gentrification of the Old City is the relocation of the lower classes by the middle class is inaccurate. Moreover, it neglects how gentrification has provided long-term residents who want to move with the opportunity to do so. At the center of the gentrification of Damascus is a group of investors who, although looking to make a profit, expressed their investment as a cultural affinity for heritage that supposedly long-term residents lacked. Moreover, investors came from diverse backgrounds and what they have in common with one another is their return to the Old City. Here, one must distinguish between short- and long-term investment; some houses are "flipped" at an incredibly fast rate even before restorations are completed. Therefore, rather than approaching the gentrification of the Old City as the middle class appropriating the historic urban core, I put forth that urban changes are the rearticulation of the Shami–rural divide but where an affinity for heritage supersedes origin-based anxieties over the meaning of space.

In this chapter, I define gentrifiers in the Old City by what they do rather than by who they are, which, in this specific instance, is to return to the Old City to restore houses to their imagined origin. As a group, they lack any common political, economic, or social interests beyond this act. This allows me to discuss individuals from diverse backgrounds—middle class, upper middle class, elites, bourgeoisie, Syrian, Damascene, European, Christian, Muslim, and Arab—that compose the returnees to the Old City. It also includes architects in the discussion of the gentrification of the Old City since they work on projects funded by returnees and share an affinity for the heritage of the Old City, which they express in their renovations. These architects become important in the process of gentrification since they are actually the ones restoring the courtyard houses, and their input is important to returnees. Unlike other parts of the world, where a strong cadre of preservationists exists, in Damascus there are few experts in historic preservation who are trained in the appropriate techniques and methods. Many architects develop experience in preservation by working on returnees' projects. The individuation of preservation and heritage protection due to the lack of experts and technicians leads to further social fragmentation and new forms of contestation over the history and heritage of the intramural quarters.

An important aspect of returnees is how they differentiate themselves from long-term residents. Gentrification in the Old City is not concentrated in one area but is dispersed throughout the Old City. Some returnees tend to look for houses in the Christian quarter because of its perceived openness and receptiveness to outsiders. Other returnees buy houses in traditionally Muslim and theoretically sequestered quarters, since these houses supposedly have more 'asl, not only in decorations but also in architectural elements from before the late Ottoman period. Historically Damascene elite Sunni merchants tended to be richer than other Shuwam, such as Christians or Jews, and their houses were more elaborately decorated, especially before the Ottoman Tanzimat, when elite Sunnis controlled the economic, religious, and political positions in the city. Therefore, the bayt 'arabi, the target of much of the preservation efforts today, belonged mainly to the merchant class that came to prominence in the late Ottoman period. The elaborately decorated and spacious dwellings with multiple courtyards or the "treasure houses" (see Keenan 2000) became the coveted houses for investors in the current gentrification process. Although Christians had a long history in Damascus, the riots of 1860 destroyed large parts of the Christian quarter, including the homes of the rich that were pillaged and looted. Many wealthy Christian families left Damascus in the aftermath of the civil unrest, and though the quarter was later rebuilt and populated, it was not by the same Christian families. Therefore, there occurred a break in the continuity of the Christian presence in the Old City that affected the social composition and status of the neighborhood. Hence, returnees were more interested in the courtyard house than in the neighborhood and community. Although some returnees lived in their refurbished houses, their participation and presence in the neighborhoods was limited. On the other hand, long-term residents lived in ethnic or religious communities they belonged to and were integrated into the daily life of the neighborhood.

'Asl among the Ruins

I asked Mrs. Turki why it took them more than two years to find a house, and she replied that were looking for a house that was least altered by its inhabitants, preferably empty because, "people living in houses ruin them." The house the Turkis showed me had a collapsed roof, which rendered the upper level uninhabitable. The previous owners only used part of the first floor. According to the Turkis, the residents wanted to sell because they could not afford to fix the roof. However, that may be due to their inability to comply with the government guidelines to restore their home rather than lacking the financial resources. Although the owners were eager to sell, they hesitated when the time came to finalize the sale because they had nowhere to go. It took a few months of negotiations before the sale was finalized to allow them to find new accommodations. Therefore, in some ways, the heritage industry in the Old City provided long-term residents with opportunities to improve their living conditions and not be overburdened by historic preservation laws. It is interesting to note that a house with a collapsed roof would have been difficult to sell prior to the rise of the heritage industry.

The collapsed roof had "saved" the house from modification and lent the bayt 'arabi an aura of distress, appealing to investors who could play the role of the savior and restore the bayt to its 'asl. When Mrs. Turki gave me a tour of the second floor, stepping over fallen wooden beams from the ceiling, dirt, and debris, she pointed to the round ceramic light switches on the walls and explained how they dated to the 1940s when electricity first became widespread in Damascus. The outlets, switches, and wiring harkened to the time when Damascus was inhabited by the Shuwam. This not only lent "authenticity" ('asala) to the house, but gave the Turkis the details they will use in constructing the narrative for their house and through which they could construct ties to the heritage of the Old City.

This incident brings us to the concept of 'asala and how it is manipulated in the current gentrification. In the Syrian context, Jonathan Shannon (2006, 57) posits 'asala as the "converse of hadatha [modernity]" when speaking about the aesthetics of music in Syria, but that still retains the "connotation of rootedness and pure descent." Although Salamandra (2004, 19) also sees authenticity as a response to modernity, in Damascus it is not necessarily in response to westernization, but rather "the stuff of social distinction in contemporary Syria, and lies at the heart of arguments over who is perceived to rule, who once ruled, and who no longer rules." 'Asala (authenticity) in the genealogy of the bayt is significant in the gentrification process because it was hidden under layers of "backwardness." The 'asala has always been there; it is the essence of the dwelling, much like the Shami essence of those said to be from the historic areas of Damascus but live elsewhere.

Authenticity as a concept was constructed to promote individualiza-tion (Handler 1986, 2) and has remained quite resilient over time, even when it proved to be manufactured (Gable and Handler 1996, 568–569). Returnees remain attached to authenticity in the courtyard house because it enabled them to achieve self-realization. The "contact with authentic pieces of culture," in this case the architecture and building material of the bayt, allowed returnees "to appropriate their authenticity, incorpo-rating that magical proof of existence into personal experience" (Han-dler 1986, 4). In the process of appropriating the authenticity of the bayt returnees differentiate themselves from long-term residents and promote themselves as the successors of the Shuwam. In an overt political move, they affirm the superiority of the depoliticized Shami culture, and they maintain the social hierarchy in Damascus, where they assume its upper layers. In the gentrification of the Old City, the new class that emerged with economic liberalization has ascended the social scale. Therefore, "the notion of authenticity is not so much a determinate concept as it is a node of associations and interpellations, a trope by means of which the his-torical world is reduced to a particular order, and a token which marks off social and political groups and forges and reconstitutes historical identi-ties" (Al-Azmeh 1993, 41). This flexibility allows social actors to engage in the restoration of the Old City, determining what is authentic and what is not, regardless of their own 'asl.

Authenticity requires an original (Benjamin 1968a, 220) and whether this original is fabricated or not remains irrelevant. The interplay between origin and authenticity is clearer in the Arabic terms 'asl and 'asala, where the latter, "lexically, . . . indicates salutary moral qualities like loyalty, nobility, and a sense of commitment to a specific social group or set of values. It also indicates a sense of *sui generis* originality; and in association with the sense previously mentioned, 'asala specifically refers to genealogi-cal standing: noble or at least respectable descent for humans" (Al-Azmeh 1993, 41).

The genealogy of the house needs to be carefully documented, hence the peeling of layers in any restoration project to find the 'asl and proof of 'asala. Yet the proof could be anything linked to the past. The Turkis found what they believed to be Roman tiles and aqueducts that gave their house its 'asala. Their house is also located where the Roman city is believed to have been. What is consistent about authenticity is that it becomes the "authority of the object" (Benjamin 1968a, 221). Amir Mufti (2000, 87–88), taking his cue from Walter Benjamin, talked about how some cultural practices possessed a "kind of aura, as the practices themselves came to be seen as resources for overcoming the forms of alienation that were the result, and the subjective dimension, of the colonial encounter." In this instance, the bayt 'arabi becomes a distillation of Shami civilization, not only because its layers could include Roman tiles but also because it is located in the Old City of layered civilizations. Under all these additions, the "true" city wants to break free. The bayt 'arabi of other neighborhoods in Damascus was not imbued with this kind of 'asala because it was not inside the wall. It becomes important to find these artifacts and layers in the house, because they lend the bayt 'arabi a "respectable descent" much like the Shuwam. When they are not found, anxiety ensues, and many returnees add these elements, not necessarily to fabricate an 'asl, but because they believe they were somehow lost over time.

Adding these missing elements enable returnees to establish the authenticity of a house, hence "claiming authenticity can be a means of gaining ownership" (Zukin 2010, xiii). By documenting a genealogy for the house, they give one to themselves, since it is they who could sense its 'asala underneath all these modifications. They are therefore in possession of Shami dhawq and distinction. Hence, historic preservation is not only about the consumption of heritage but also about the "construction of a self" (Lawrence-Zúñiga 2010, 212).

Returnees are not the only social group involved in the construction of self, and in some cases, they are not even the ones doing the constructing but under new economic conditions outsource the process to local architects. Nadeem, an architect who worked with the government, also supervised restoration projects for many returnees on the side. He explained how he acquired the feeling for the origin of a bayt 'arabi by peeling layers to get to what he believed was the true house: "In many houses they put new layers on top of old so the level raises and the feel of the courtyard is not correct and doors are squeezed." He knew when to stop removing layers when "I feel that I am going deeper than I should. . . .

I feel a certain part is the real part of the architecture." He explained how it was practical for long-term residents to add layers upon layers rather than to strip the work done before. This leads us to another distinction between long-term residents and returnees, the adding compared to the removing of layers. Did the long-term residents add layers to obfuscate the 'asl of the house and remove traces of the Shuwam in their attempt to make the houses their own? After all, many of them were of rural background and were snubbed by the Shuwam when they first came to the city. They had no need to be constantly reminded of the previous inhabitants of the house or their own social inferiority in the city. Or did the long-term residents, who were confident of their own 'asl, have no desire to seek a genealogy in a house built by others? Rather they made the houses their own much to the chagrin of the Shuwam.

Whatever the reasons, layers of paint and plaster added by long-term residents in many ways preserved the Shami essence of the house and made it easier, if not cheaper, to restore houses to their origins in the current gentrification. Long-term residents had their own notions of preservation even if inadvertently. Yet sensing this essence was subjective as Nadeem explained: "The more you work with old houses the more you appreciate [architectural] details and you must respect this. You can feel the importance of every small detail and this is not taught in universities." For a non-Shami, Nadeem acknowledged that developing an affinity for the Old City and for the bayt 'arabi was not based on 'asl in a genealogical sense, but it developed with the right kind of spatial embodiment. Nadeem believed he acquired this knowledge from a combination of being and seeing: "You have to experience old houses . . . respect old architecture." Hence, this sense for space comes from receptiveness to the stimuli in the built environment. His seeing and embodying are sharper and in focus because he came from outside the wall, and he implied the years of living in the Old City dulled the senses. We therefore return to the concept introduced earlier, that the Old City could only be understood by those who returned there because they wanted to, rather than the long-term residents who were supposedly living there out of necessity

In this section, I demonstrated the importance of the architect in the preservation process; they tend to be missing in most of the work on gentrification and historic preservation. Nadeem was able to provide returnees with a valuable service: the needed understanding of the bayt, especially for those investors who bought property sight unseen. Nadeem was following his own instincts and not the orders of the returnees who hired him for the job, in fact, he may have been hired for having this very quality. I have heard of other architects that are selective in the projects they undertake and avoid working with returnees who do not heed their advice in the preservation process.

In the new market economy, Nadeem and other architects become the brokers of authenticity for individuals who possess the means to buy but not necessarily the sense of aesthetics for what is authentic in the Old City. He spoke of possessing the code for understanding the Old City as a lifestyle based on the aesthetics of the bayt ʿarabi. He is paid for being able to understand and decipher this code for others. In the process, he was also reclaiming the space from long-term residents for the returnees. By removing the layers made by the long-term residents of the house, he was also able to remove their trace and in turn their claim to the new urban space. He becomes the agent of the new classes, their tool to use authenticity as "a cultural form of power over space that puts pressure on . . . who can longer afford to live there" (Zukin 2010, xiii). Even for long-term residents who wanted to remain in the Old City, their ownership of houses is undermined by the lack of authenticity in their homes because of their modifications, which obscures the historic architectural elements of the bayt under modern modifications. The work of middlemen like Nadeem complicates the class dynamics in the gentrification of the Old City, where the class with means uses a class with lesser means to relocate the class with the least means.

Saving Whose City?

According to one of the directors of the CPOC I interviewed, "preservation is *tarjiʿ al-bayt ila al-ʾasl* (reverting the house to its origin). If we include innovations, the old and unique urban fabric of the city disappears. Its [the Old City] importance stems from being old." It is difficult to determine the origin of any city, and with Damascus a palimpsest of numerous civilizations, it is certainly illusionary. Nonetheless, it was understood fully by social actors involved in the protection and preservation of the Old City that the 'asl was the Shami city of the immediate past. In Decree 826, that also included guidelines for preservation and which was based on an earlier French law, established a building's origin between 1926 and 1927 until 1948.[1] This law temporalized 'asl for houses, which was institutionalized in the cadastral maps drawn by the French.

In 1925, the French subdued resistance to their occupation of Syria that began in 1920 and started the process of state building. This included mapping the urban areas for purposes of taxation and organization. Maps were common tools used by modernizing agents to impose order and control and to simplify the reality of urban activity (J. Scott 1998, 3). In the mid-1920s, a French team of surveyors, with little experience in the local conditions or familiarity with the city, produced the cadastral maps to assist in the colonial administration of Damascus, but they became a document of authenticity for the courtyard houses in the current gentrification. Cadastral maps provide a manageable and controlled register of local property for taxation purposes, a shortcut for the state to exploit local resources (J. Scott 1998, 36). The cadastral for the Old City included a detailed description of the property, such as the thickness of the walls, ownership of the walls, the courtyards, fountains, staircases, and awnings. This information allowed Syrian urban planners to monitor the changes in the built environment over the past several decades (Gaudin 1992, 194). To obtain a permit to restore or renovate a building, a copy of the cadastral map for the property must be attached to the application. The restoration or renovation must result in a building that approximates the cadastral map, although this is rarely the case especially for houses converted into restaurants and hotels. When I asked an architect at CPOC about using colonial documents created for taxation in the restoration projects, she

1. The copy I have of Decree 826 that deals with the built environment in the Old City was last updated in 1996 and was based on French Mandate period laws. According to the CPOC it was still used, though in 2008, I heard there were going to be some revisions.

shrugged and said their use was not an issue because they were accurate and factual. I felt some admiration for the work of the French urban planner in her comment. Therefore, according to this staff member, the maps assume a historical authority and become the document of authenticity for any property within the wall. The maps fixed the built environment in time and undermined any alterations to houses that were lived in. Buildings change to accommodate the needs of social users who inhabit them, but any additions to the building not included in the French plan were considered a slight to integrity to the courtyard house and by extension the Old City. Hence, the removal of modifications not included in the maps is a required to preserve the integrity of the building and the city, thereby privileging the heritage of the built environment over the needs of long-term residents.

Many long-term residents challenged the authority of the maps because they were impractical and restricted their daily use of the building. Suhail, for instance, was enraged that CPOC would not allow him to build a staircase to the roof because one did not exist in the cadastral plan. He complained bitterly about the rigidity of the preservation law that made no sense and did not consider the evolving needs of residents. "If my grandfather did not go up to the roof, does this mean I cannot go up to the roof?" he ranted. As we will see in chapter 6, rigid preservation guidelines frustrated investors even though there was more government support for nonresidential use of the courtyard houses.

The cut-off year 1948 is significant for several reasons and indicates how the bayt 'arabi became associated with an idealized Shami presence in the Old City. In 1946, when Syria gained its independence, many Shuwam opted to leave the Old City for modern neighborhoods outside the wall, evacuated by the French inhabitants. Two years later, Palestinian refugees found their way to Syria, and many were housed in the Old City, thereby contributing to the crowded conditions in the city. Therefore, 1948 signals the beginning of the end of Shami dominance in the Old City and, supposedly, the decline of the intramural neighborhoods. The modifications to the bayt by the Shuwam was accepted as part of the 'asl of the house since it was assumed they were implemented by the rightful owners, highly attuned to the aesthetics of the courtyard house. The electric outlets that Mrs. Turki found in her bayt added an elegant touch to the house undergoing modernization in the 1940s to meet the contemporary needs of its "original" inhabitants. Ironically, some of these Shuwam became slum landlords when they rented their property to rural migrants and failed to maintain them.

Saving Ruins

Returnees such as the Turkis were attracted to distressed houses because they could play the role of savior, salvaging the house not only from decay inflicted by long-term residents but also from government bureaucracy that could stifle attempts to maintain houses. I will address the issue of government bureaucracy in chapter 6. Munir, another returnee who actually lived in the house he restored, described the house he purchased as "*kharab*" (ruin) and expressed surprise that it was actually inhabited when he bought it. He always wanted to live in a courtyard house because his apartment made him feel *makbut* (stifled). "My goal was to live in a bayt, and in five minutes I bought the house." Munir was saving a house from ruin while saving himself from cramped living conditions. He sounded like Abu Sami and Abu George who found freedom in the courtyard houses. However, perhaps Munir was driven by the challenge to convert the ruin into his image of a bayt that reflected his wealth and status. I will return to Munir and how he created his dream house later in the chapter.

The search for the ideal bayt 'arabi became a spiritual quest for a house that needed "saving." The Turkis mentioned "the spirit of old houses" and how the house "spoke" to them before they bought it. They knew it was the right house once they walked in. The bayt like houses in Southern California were endowed with agency and selected their future owners (Lawrence-Zúñiga 2010). This created a bond between the buyers and the house, strengthened during the restoration process when they got to know the house intimately. As Christoph Brumann (2009, 288) found among Japanese restoring and renovating the traditional dwelling in Kyoto, the *machiya*, they also spoke about the house "being alive." He attributed the animism associated with the traditional house as a "countermovement" to the modern material culture overwhelming social actors (289).

The bond with the bayt was not restricted to Syrians. Julian, a French expatriate who worked with international organizations, welcomed the new law that allowed foreigners to own property in Syria and was wavering between purchasing a bayt ʿarabi either in Aleppo or in Damascus. After visiting twenty houses in Damascus, he found what he was looking for: "I came back from Aleppo saw the house on Tuesday and bought it on Thursday. No regrets. The quality of walls, decorations, and architecture drew me. There was no discussion."

Many of the long-term residents did not speak in spiritual and mystical language when it came to the bayt ʿarabi. Nora hated living in the courtyard house and could not wait to move. She would have scoffed at me if I spoke of the spirit of the bayt ʿarabi and the feeling it evoked in people. She would have pointed to the crumbling musty walls and said, "This is the spirit of the bayt ʿarabi." Though Abu Sami also might ridicule this spirit talk, he did have a bond with the house he was born and raised in. But it is a bond strengthened not by restoring the ʾasl of the house, but by making it more compatible to his notions of convenience and comfort. For many of the long-term residents, the bayt ʿarabi was not a happy space. It could be a crowded home shared by several other families or a house crumbling with no means to repair it.

Thus, the bayt ʿarabi can communicate different things to social actors and does not necessarily speak only to Shuwam or even to Syrians, but to anyone who is able to appreciate and understand its ʾasl, therefore reinforcing the universality of its heritage. Moreover, aesthetic values, which varied from one returnee to another, made the house come alive. For the Turkis, a house almost in ruins spoke of a dwelling minimally altered, but for Julian, he could feel the quality of the decorations under the layers of paint and varnish. Munir found a kharab he could rebuild into his dream house. Yahya, another returnee, described what a bayt ʿarabi inspired in people. "Unless you live in it you cannot find a word for it. Houses in the Old City have a language, the courtyard light coming from inside. There is a fixed language about the house. It has a unique feeling. One house leaning, one standing by itself, another squeezed. Houses have a soul; it might talk to you or to someone else. You can say the same thing about apartments but only after you live in it. In the Old City, it is a different case when you walk into a courtyard house. Even if it is an abandoned house you get a feeling, the feeling of any courtyard house."[2]

Yahya directly referenced the aspects of the bayt that have contributed to the formulation of a distinct Shami identity discussed earlier. It demonstrated his full understanding of the appeal of the Old City and how this understanding informed his decision making in the restoration. But he was also a returnee of another sort. His family once lived in the Old City before moving to an apartment outside the wall. However, he does not live in the Old City. Nonetheless, he demonstrated his generation's yearning for the bayt their parents abandoned, and perhaps, for some like Yahya, these poetic images influenced their return. For Yahya's generation, the courtyard house becomes the "space that has been seized upon by the imagination [and] cannot remain indifferent space subject to the measures and estimates of the surveyor. It has been lived in, not in its positivity, but with all the partiality of the imagination" (Bachelard 1964, xxxvi). They did not have to experience the bayt as their parents did but could retain romantic notions of life in one. Gaston Bachelard (1964, xxxv; emphasis in the original) referred to "*felicitous space*," and perhaps this was why returnees developed strong bonds with the bayt 'arabi. Because they had not lived in one, they could ignore or gloss over the challenges of a home built for a premodern lifestyle and lacking modern conveniences.

Kind Houses, Kind People

When I asked what was so special about a bayt 'arabi in the Old City, many returnees described the aesthetics of the courtyard, the fountain, and decorated rooms. Some mentioned the sense of community or that residents of in the intramural neighborhoods were real and cared for one another, unlike the endemic selfishness of today. Moreover, many of these imagined lives, mediated by the numerous Syrian TV drama series, idealized and glorified communal life in the historic neighborhoods and in

---

2. The interview with Yahya was conducted in English.

beautiful courtyard houses during the Ottoman and mandate period and before neoliberalism.[3]

In addition to being attracted by the aesthetic qualities of the house, Julian felt that in the Old City "life is real, it exists" unlike in Aleppo where "it was all business and trade." Although he avoided the Old City on his earlier trips to Damascus, he discovered how wonderful it was when he rented a room in Bab Tuma in 2003 to study Arabic. He "felt good, felt comfortable liked the atmosphere, the way of life and kindness of people. It was a historical city but not a museum. It was alive. Children playing in the streets, there were schools." He pretended to be looking for a house to rent or buy in order "to gain access to the bayt 'arabi" though he did not intend to do either "but wanted an excuse to visit houses." Living in a bayt allowed Julian access to community life and to experience a vibrant historical city. He wanted the sociability of life in the Old City for the few weeks in the year he lived there. As a European, Julian saw community where many long-term residents were convinced it was gone. It is perhaps an aspect of cosmopolitans who lack deep roots anywhere in the world and are constantly going from one place to another to appreciate the permanence of others.

Yahya also spoke of the community in the neighborhood where he was restoring a house, and it was this sense of solidarity that encouraged him to invest in the neighborhood. He told me about the shopkeeper who knew everyone in the neighborhood. The shopkeeper would leave his store unattended to carry the bags of groceries home for an old lady. If a child from the neighborhood is sent on an errand by his mother and did not have enough money, the shopkeeper would tell the child not to worry, he will get the rest from the father on his way home from work. According

---

3. Salamandra (1998, 2004) discusses the ambiguous feelings of many Damascenes (her term for Shuwam) over the dramatized series about life in the historic quarter. Although there seems to be consensus that interest in Shami history is welcomed, there were concerns over the depiction of some aspects of neighborhood life, relations between the sexes, and the accent. There was also come criticism over non-Shami actors chosen to play Shami character since some believed they could not channel nor convey the essence of Shaminess (Salamandra 2004, 111–15).

to Yahya, shopkeepers guarded the street, and this is true, especially in residentially and commercially mixed neighborhoods. Although, this form of supposedly benign neighborhood watch appealed to some as a sense of community, others saw it as another form of control and surveillance by the nosy neighbors and the government. In my neighborhood, the *mukhabarat* (intelligence police) were known to stop at grocery stores when they were looking for information on residents. Shopkeepers were accused of being state agents, but these images of mukhabarat in the neighborhood mar the poetics of life in the Old City and are not always mentioned.

Yahya evaded answering whether he planned to live in the house he was restoring. He was not committed to living there and ironically is contributing, albeit indirectly, to the eroding the community he idealized. The Turkis saw their house as a potential summer retreat. Julian told me he had two other homes in Europe. Perhaps it was easier to extol the virtues of community when one did not deal with its members on a daily basis, but it also indicated the change in the social relations in the neighborhood. Although both Yahya and Julian emphasized how their house was part of the greater community and both men had strong romantic notions about the neighborhood, they were speaking nostalgically and abstractly. Julian lived in Damascus a few weeks a year, and Yahya rented his house to foreigners who wanted to experience life in the Old City. They were not contributing to the survival of the community and were encouraging the commodification of social relations in the Old City.

Moreover, many returnees enjoyed living in the bayt 'arabi but not the neighborhood. One returnee talked about wanting to keep her door closed because she did not want the neighbors "in her business." She implied they lacked the appropriate status. Also the new notion of privacy—the Western understanding of individuation in which private matters remain within the house and are not shared with the neighborhood—needs to be considered. Returnees want to eliminate the porousness of the bayt. Therefore, the houses of Qabbani no longer supported one another because a rupture had been erected between the house and its social milieu. The rupture was caused by profit-seeking returnees as well as by their personal privacy concerns.

Yahya was one of the few individuals who admitted that some of the returnees were involved in speculation. Mr. Turki mentioned how profit became 300 percent once the house was restored. Returnees did not want to appear as though they were purely motivated by profit, which would place them in the same category as long-term residents who sold their homes. Yahya would have liked his project to be an example for others to buy houses to restore rather than to turn them into a café or a restaurant. He acknowledged that he was participating in gentrification, with all of the negative Western connotations. He preempted my questions on the matter and said that in the United States gentrification is considered a bad thing. But he saw his work as different and important because of his attention to detail in the restoration process. He was attuned to the spirit of the house and was working to bring out the 'asl, which surely placed his intervention in the Old City at a different scale. Therefore, gentrification of the Old City means maintaining the Shami feel in the neighborhoods. What this entails has become a contentious issue.

Authenticity in Mud and Straw

Yahya was fastidious in his preservation of the bayt 'arabi, insisting on the use of only traditional material and building techniques. By choosing traditional materials and construction methods from other times, he was finding new ways to create "gratuitous products [in this case a bayt 'arabi] whose sole purpose is to signify his own capabilities through his *work*" (de Certeau 1984, 25; emphasis in the original). The specialized knowledge that comes with the use of traditional building material created a connection between Yahya and the Shuwam of earlier times as well as distinction between him and other returnees and architects who did not adhere to traditional techniques in their restoration projects. Therefore, Yahya saw his work as preserving the true essence of the Old City. According to Yahya, "This architecture is an accumulation of long tradition and experience of what fits in the environment and I don't think I could use a whole different technology." His respect for the architecture underlined his belief that this is the spirit of the house that needs to be saved from misguided or ignorant efforts to use modern material. Although many returnees preferred to work with cement, since it was more durable than mud and according to some workmen easier to work with, cement was the not the essence of the bayt and could eventually be harmful to the structure and the environment.

The debate on modern versus traditional material in the reconstruction and restoration of the bayt indexed the lack of expertise on preservation or a guiding philosophy on how to preserve in Syria. In the gentrification of the Old City, preservation was open to interpretation, and each architect and returnee had their own understanding. Yahya was not entirely wedded to the idea of traditional architecture and explained that, whereas there were no bathrooms or kitchens on the upper levels of the house, he added them because "you need them for the modern life." He seemed defensive when he went on to explain, "I think my respect for the accumulation of expertise and tradition should not confine me. If they had this facility they would have been used, but I am against building a house entirely of cement [in the Old City]."

Yahya did not deny he was an investor, though he maintained that he followed certain principles and that he was conscientious, perhaps more than other returnees, about the impact of his actions on the neighborhood in particular and on the Old City in general. He told me how he would not purchase house parts such as doors, ceilings, or decorations from poor people to put in his house. He also would not add 'blaq and 'ajami because the house he purchased was simple and did not have them. He was convinced that his house served as the servants' quarters for the larger homes around it, and this will be the narrative he will construct for his bayt 'arabi.

There was a level of awareness in his actions that transcended the immediate investment opportunity. He was channeling the Shami concern for neighbors and their sociability in a new direction aimed at improving the Old City. Yahya was portraying his economic investment as more of a cultural and social investment, as he emphasized his civilizational anxiety over other returnees with financial gains in mind and what they were doing to the bayt 'arabi in the name of preservation. Therefore, his approach advocated that gentrification should be viewed positively when it was initiated by someone as conscientious as himself. It was not about displacement of long-term residents (as a matter of fact he does not mention the residents at all) but rather the improvement of the neighborhood and maintenance of the heritage of the Old City.

Nadeem had similar feelings toward gentrification and was also distancing himself from other architects who worked on restoration projects with his attention to detail and vast knowledge of the Shami home. He was adamant he was unlike other architects who had no respect for the integrity of the house in the Old City, who allowed cement and aluminum in their work. But not all were fastidious as Yahya and Nadeem. Munir believed his house was "probably two or three hundred years old," but there was "nothing old in it so I tried to bring back the old." When I asked him what he meant by this he said, "The spirit of the old means that it is three hundred years old and there is nothing three hundred years old in this house only the stone walls. The 'ajami ceiling in the living room was not there, but it is well known that it existed in these houses. I tried to bring back the old as much as I could, though it cost me a lot." Therefore, Munir did not consider his actions as fabrication or faking the essence of his bayt but rather as restoring what *should* have been there. He insisted that his intentions were honorable when he referred to the amount of money he spent on restoring his house to a new origin. He bought what he could not find under layers of paint and varnish. As we will see, Munir and his intentions were not always well received by neighbors and other returnees. This also highlights the problem with different interpretations of the preservation guidelines. Regardless of whether it is an "invented tradition" (Hobsbawm and Ranger 1983) or an imagined past, these houses were built and inhabited by the Shuwam. Hence, in trying to restore the houses to their 'asl, and regardless of their own genealogical origins, returnees are seeking to connect with this Shami identity that they believe can be found in the bayt 'arabi. Authenticity becomes a privatized and individualized process when the heritage making and preservation process is no longer controlled and monitored by the state or officials for nationalistic purposes (Handler 1988; Herzfeld 1991) or to promote specific narratives as to the founding of the nation (Handler and Gable 1997).

The demand for 'ajami and 'blaq created a black-market trade, locally and abroad. The wood panels plaster, and frescos were stripped from abandoned houses or by residents and sold. One returnee showed me a fresco that depicted flowers his workers brought from another house they were working on, and he was debating where he should incorporate it in his restoration project. He asked me not to photograph the fresco because he knew it was an illegal acquisition.

Nonetheless, the restoration of the bayt ʻarabi by returnees not only demonstrated their taste and architectural knowledge but also how they positioned themselves in the debate between "civilization" and "backwardness." They used the restoration projects to illustrate their belief system and how they resolved ethical dilemmas. The commodification of architectural elements of the bayt ʻarabi was destroying houses that existed outside the wall to save houses inside the wall. Some returnees justified purchase of stolen parts to install in their own when houses outside the wall were slated for demolition. The traditional dwellings in historical districts outside the Old City were not all located in protected areas and were still being demolished to build multistory buildings. This gives heritage as "cultural salvage" a somewhat different meaning. Yet the cannibalization of some courtyard houses to save those located in the Old City suggested that the locus of ʼasl and heritage is more valued in the intramural neighborhoods, thereby reducing the historical significance and value of the historic neighborhoods outside the wall. Areas such as Midan, Suq Sarujeh, Qanawat, and even parts of Muhajirin may not have the longevity of the intramural neighborhoods, but they still possess significant religious and vernacular buildings. Furthermore, as we have seen in chapter 2, the Old City did not exist until the middle of the twentieth century and was continuous with the neighborhoods beyond the wall. An official attempt to concentrate heritage preservation within the intramural neighborhood could contribute to the demolition of historic buildings and neighborhoods beyond the wall.

The bayt ʻarabi occupies precious land in a tight real estate market. The Old City might become an island of heritage in a sea of modern and new buildings, which could quickly lead to its "museumification." However, activists have been working on obtaining protection for neighborhoods outside the wall. The emphasis is on the continuity of the Old City with the rest of Damascus to ensure that it remains a viable neighborhood.

The privatization of historic preservation is casting some doubt on the role of the government in protecting the heritage of the Old City. Some Damascenes and many Shuwam have complained that the fragmentation and individualization to preserve the Old City is a deliberate attempt by the regime to destroy Damascus. Returnees who come from various backgrounds, and a few can claim to be Shuwam, are guilty in their restoration efforts of distorting the "true" bayt ʿarabi. These accusations are in keeping with local discourses of the animosity between the predominantly Alawite regime and Shuwam who see any intervention in the Old City as a deliberate attempt to undermine the Shuwam and to corrupt their culture. Although the Syrian regime is brutal and violently suppresses any form of opposition, for many Syrians discourses on attempts to dismantle and disabuse Shami culture speaks more about their own social relations and politics, which are also circumstantial.[4]

The "Criminal"

I focus now on the house that Munir restored and how he created dissension among his neighbors. While he insisted he was improving the neighborhood, long-term residents accused him of destroying the essence of the Shami bayt and neighborhood. He serves as a good example of how returnees were creating social and cultural rupture in the Old City, which

4. At a conference, I met Syrians who were upset with a European who, when speaking about the changes in Damascus, referred to the dichotomy of Alawite regime and Damascenes. They insisted that outsiders simplify relations between the two and ignore that authoritarian power is not absolute. The binary maintains a simplistic approach to complex local politics. What is also interesting is a group of Syrians, albeit very critical of their regime and government, who do not want to dwell on its authoritarian feature since it is not in keeping with the image they seek to construct of themselves as modern subjects. For them, dictatorship connotes "backwardness," and the well-educated, well-traveled cosmopolitans reject such a representation of their country. What tends to be forgotten is that living in an authoritarian country becomes the norm, and its normalcy is worth defending. But, then, this was before 2011.

led many Syrians to observe that some of investors were doing more harm to the Old City than were long-term residents.

When I first passed Munir's house, I thought it was a restaurant, since the façade was painted in a pastel color rather than in the drab gray or whitewash common in the Old City. I looked for a sign advertising the latest eatery in the neighborhood; not seeing one, I assumed that it had not opened. Since it was located in Naji's neighborhood, I asked him about it. Naji, a Shami, lived in his ancestral home and was one of the few individuals I met that could speak as a long-term resident and investor; he not only was living in a bayt 'arabi but also was interested in the new economic opportunities in the Old City. We would meet regularly to discuss changes in the Old City and the work of the CPOC with whom he had a conflicting relationship. He was friends with some CPOC employees and supported their work; however, he was more wary of the administration, which he did not trust to safeguard the Old City. In trying to entice me to interview Munir, Naji clarified that Munir was restoring a house, not a restaurant, and he would be interested to hear what Munir had to say. Naji was being uncharacteristically cryptic, and I soon found out why.

It was easy to find Munir because the front door to his house was open. I simply announced myself, but to be on the safe side, I mentioned that I was a friend of Naji. From the onset, it was obvious that Munir was proud of his bayt 'arabi, as he took me on the tour of his recently restored dwelling. "Many people swore that this was not a house but a hotel or restaurant and that we were living here for a short period of time because this amount of renovation and money paid did not make sense if it was not an investment. The neighbors came three days ago and said this is *tamwih* (cover up) you want to make this into a hotel. I did not think of the income that I could get from this house. I had offers up to four thousand dollars a month to rent it out but I refused."

I could see why Naji was upset, Munir had blurred several boundaries between private and public space, long-term residents and returnees, and residential or nonresidential use of the courtyard house. He also conflated his role as returnee and mustathmir with resident. Munir was one of the few returnees I met who was living permanently in the house he restored.

This was not a second or even third home. Yet this aspect was not apparent from the way he restored the house, which was proving problematic for some of his more fastidious neighbors. Many refused to believe that the amount of money he was spending on restoring a bayt ʿarabi could be just for a home; that kind of investment in the Old City was expected for restaurants and hotels that would return the investment. I asked Nora if, assuming she had sufficient funds, she would buy a bayt ʿarabi or an apartment. With no hesitation, she opted for an apartment outside the Old City. Like many long-term residents, she did not believe it was a wise decision to buy a bayt ʿarabi that required constant maintenance because of the traditional material used in its construction. Munir was not renting out the property to recoup some of his investment nor converting it into a hotel or restaurant; therefore, his neighbors thought he was being deliberately obtuse or misleading. Either situation did not endear him to the long-term residents in the neighborhood. Then there were his own modifications.

He added a retractable roof over the courtyard and made the windows double glazed to keep out the noise of the restaurant across the road. He justified the roof over the courtyard by saying that his children could play inside all year long, regardless of the weather. The exterior of the house and the colored façade were an issue with some people in the neighborhood. Munir was proud that he mixed six different shades of paint to get this particular tone. "The façade is a color I mixed together. I wanted it to be different from the beige color and gray. These are old colors. I had to paint the façade seven times before I got to this color. Of course, I was criticized and was told this was bad, but I insisted."

The façade of the bayt ʿarabi, as we saw in the previous chapter, did not reveal anything about the interior of the house or the status of the owner. The façade of the houses should be mute and somber to encourage social cohesiveness in the neighborhood. Class distinction was maintained in the interior of the house. Speaking of Morocco, where the government mandated the color beige for building exteriors, Clifford Geertz (1989, 302) observed, "to change the face of the city (or the façade of the house) is to change the way those who live in it understand it and to put under pressure the cultural frames by which they have been used to understanding it and the terms of which they have been used to living in it." Munir was making his own changes to the neighborhoods without consideration for the neighbors, and this was where his innovations became controversial. Moreover, he was flaunting his wealth, which we saw in the previous chapter went against the main aspects of the Shami civility and sociability in the Old City. Long-term residents did not like to be reminded of his wealth and status. Although he was a returnee, he became out of place and a polluting element (Douglas 1966) in the Old City, violating the code that distinguished returnees from long-term residents. Therefore, he was neither accepted by other returnees nor by long-term residents.

There was a growing distrust of wealth in Syria, especially among those who benefited from new economic opportunities but still lacked an appropriate 'asl and dhawq as well as an affinity for national or local identity. The fear and distrust of the nouveau riche is common in the region, and the accumulation of wealth in what is considered a short time typically underlies illegal activities or collusion with the ruling regime. Nadia Khost called this group that emerged in the new economic reality *tabaqa tayarah* (fleeting class), meaning that they lacked roots and were only attached to their economic interests. Several others have also mentioned that members of this class are corrupt and corrupting.[5]

Therefore, Munir's wealth was contributing to the falsity of the Old City by turning it into a "theme park" (Sorkin 1992), much like restaurants, which is the topic of the next chapter. As Michael Sorkin (1992, xi, xiv) has shown in his discussion of the theme park city, it became completely "ageographic," privileging a city of simulations and "urbane disguises." Naji was quite upset with Munir for this reason though he did not let on

---

5. The widespread interest in the bayt 'arabi coincides with the liberalization of the Syrian economy. Many Syrian expatriates and non-Syrian investors were encouraged by the new laws governing foreign currency and private property to repatriate their wealth (see Keenan 2000). Moreover, according to an architect who works with CPOC, numerous Gulf and Saudi firms and individual investors sought business opportunities in Syria and other countries in the region after 9/11, when many feared the impact of the war on terror by the West could lead to confiscation or freezing of accounts. See also Daher (2007, 22) on how the tourism boom in the region is linked to 9/11.

12. A colorful exterior stands out in the alley of otherwise plain walls, ca. 2006.

before I had a chance to see Naji's house. "His wall from outside has nothing to do with Old Sham. The restaurants are also wrong. These façades
can be from anywhere from Rio, from Italy. He wants a place *muzarkash*
(embellished) with brocade embroidery decorated, brocaded." Munir was
undermining the same Shami culture he supposedly was restoring by rendering it tacky. Though he was wealthy, he lacked dhawq, but he was part
of the new class that was blamed for the new wave of social ills in the
country associated with market liberalization.

When Naji insisted that the Old City was not Rio or Italy, he was rail-
ing against the tawdry replication of the Shami bayt 'arabi by investors.
Not only did these houses insult the senses but they mixed in elements
they eclectically borrowed from other regions of the world. Many houses

were not accessible to the public, and most of the fake decorations and foreign designs and styles were installed in restaurants, which resembled a Shami-themed park. Naji considered himself a true son of Damascus, born and raised in the Old City and living in his bayt. He believed the city needs to be inhabited by those who appreciated its history and showed neighbors respect. Furthermore, he insisted on aesthetic standards set by the Shuwam to prevent innovations in restoration projects by social actors who did not comprehend Shami aesthetics. Introducing foreign elements was an added insult to the already offended Shuwam. Unlike the incident in Rethemnos, where the state imposed aesthetic standards that undermined popular aesthetics (Herzfeld 1991, 257), in this instance, the Shuwam who live in the Old City demand aesthetic standards. The government includes preservation guidelines, and supposedly, government officials and the architect monitored Munir's work. That the government allowed these forms of innovation on Shami aesthetics was troubling on several levels. For the Shuwam, who remain distrustful of the government and the regime, this confirmed that the CPOC and other agencies were destroying the Shami city through preservation. The less suspicious see this as another example of inept and bumbling bureaucrats who cannot impose their own government guidelines or hire architects lacking expertise on the Shami city.

Naji wanted to emphasize the foreignness Munir's work in the Old City, which already claimed unique architecture: Munir was corrupting what should not have been corrupted, the 'asl. The Shuwam of yore perfected living and life in the Old City, and someone like Munir had no right to tamper with it. Retaining the exterior was also about maintaining the solidarity and sociability in the neighborhood, as Naji explained: "The façade is owned by everyone. People cannot change it, so he must do the same as his neighbors. Even if I am walking in the street, and I saw something that is not right, not coordinated, you cannot say, 'this is my bayt and I want to do what I want.' I have to think of the neighborhood, not myself."

I suspected that Naji wanted me to interview him to confirm that Munir did not belong in the Old City. Furthermore, Munir was treating his house as though it were a restaurant, and he even said that "people enter the house and think it is a restaurant. Tourists come in if the door is open. I leave my door open," which was how I was able to interview him. Munir had different notions of privacy, and he was proud of his home, but houses in the Old City were not meant to be inviting and open. He encouraged, even welcomed, the "gaze" of others and blurred the boundaries between home and restaurant. I had to wait for months for an invitation from Abu Sami to visit his house, and both the Turkis and Yasser kept their front door closed. Moreover, many of the restaurants in the Old City were exclusive, as explored in the next chapter. All these issues added to Naji's civilizational anxiety regarding the Old City's fate. In principle, he thought it was a good thing that the Old City was now receiving the attention it deserved; however, he worried that some of this attention harmed the urban fabric and would dilute, if not eradicate, the essence of the historic site.

Nonetheless, I thought that Naji would at least concede that it was better someone had bought a house to live in, rather than convert it for nonresidential use, further reducing the number of inhabitants in the Old City. After all, Naji had told me the new joke on the street: "Someone bought a restaurant and turned it into a bayt 'arabi." He was referring to the alarming number of restaurants that kept opening in the Old City. The number of returnees did not come close to the mustathmirin converting courtyard houses into boutique hotels and restaurants throughout the Old City. Moreover, a restaurant was across the street from Munir, and its owners were notorious for their rudeness to the neighbors. When they first came to the neighborhood, they coerced the neighbors to approve their project. They were not concerned with the neighborhood and did nothing to curb the impact of cooking fumes or clients' noises. This proved Naji's point. Everyone could see that the restaurants were an innovation on the bayt 'arabi, but Munir's restoration assaulted the senses because it lacked taste.

Hence, gentrification of the Old City continues to raise concerns over who should live in the Old City. Long-term residents were accused of polluting and destroying the Old City, but then returnees were also met with misgivings. The different parties—the government, the Shuwam, the returnees, the preservationists—seemingly cannot agree who should live in the Old City and how. Issues of 'asl and cultural affinity continue to inform who belongs in the historic district.

Naji was not against new forms for the bayt as long as sociability among the people in the Old City was preserved. During another conversation, when I asked him about a hotel planned near his house, he expressed admiration for the owner and his delicate Shami taste. He said, "I would prefer someone who comes and does justice to the Old City than some *badawi* (literally a Bedouin) who will ruin it." I was surprised that he used the term badawi, but he was singling out those who did not belong there. Nonetheless, Naji was angry over the new class that have benefited from neoliberalism and who considers usurping the Shami identity because they lack one. This feeling is clear in his usage of the term badawi.

Ibn Khaldun (n.d., 148) described *bedu* as groups with tribal solidarity, who work together to provide for their survival either through cultivation or animal husbandry, and do not provide more than their basic need. The opposite of this group was found in the *hadr* who were able to exceed their basic needs, work in industry or in commerce, and live in luxury (149). According to Ibn Khaldun, the hadr were accustomed to refined living and luxury therefore could only live in cities where they formed group solidarity beyond kinship. For the bedu to become hadr, they moved to the city and acquired city ways. But Naji and many others rejected bedu in their midst because they believed the bedu were immune to the civilizing process of the city. Whereas someone like Naji would provide the newcomers with tutelage into the ways of the city, under new economic conditions, this tutelage is rejected. Many newcomers to the city refuse to be Shamified and someone like Munir is accused of having no respect for Shami culture. His purchase of the courtyard house was to follow latest fashion in ostentatious consumption.

Under new economic conditions, Naji did not consider the bedu an earlier or primitive lifestyle but as an alternative state to the "civilization" of the historic city. He believed the bedu were imperious to the sociability and civility of the Shuwam and therefore do not belong in the Old City. Naji had no problem with the bedu as long as they lived away from the historic city, enjoying their different lifestyle. Naji's anxiety stemmed from the fear that the Shuwam were losing their established differentiation in the very site that made them a unique social category.

In this case, we see how "civilization" and "civilized" were not necessarily about economic status and wealth but the cultural values and sociability that money could not buy. Hence, even with his money and consumption habits, Munir was a badawi, thereby dividing the different groups in the Old City, not only between long-term residents and returnees but also among the returnees themselves. There was more fissure among those who wanted to protect the Old City than initially thought. When I next saw Munir, I mentioned that some activists on behalf of the Old City had singled out the façade of his house as having no relationship with the Old City. But he was unfazed and said, "I have been called a criminal because I am killing the spirit of old Damascus." He almost made it sound like it was a badge of honor to go against the grain in Damascus.

Furthermore, Munir countered that he was working for the betterment of the neighborhood and was trying to do what he thought was best for the Old City. "I tried to bring change to the neighborhood and fix the alley. I was willing to pay eighty percent of the cost to pave the street with stone but the others do not want to." He also distinguished between himself and the restaurant owners, who he called mustathmirin (investors). He saw himself as vested in living and staying in the neighborhood, whereas they would sell and leave. He had a point, but staying in the neighborhood still did not make him belong to the Old City, especially in Naji's eyes. Munir was boastful about his status and wanted everyone to see his wealth. He was not concerned about smoothing over social differences but inflamed them instead. Although the Shuwam have a moral claim to the historic neighborhoods, their physical presence has been dwindling. However, not all newcomers are considered good for the Old City, which further foments issues about whose city it should be.

I began this chapter with the 'awda of the returnees to the Old City for those who were seeking a new cultural experience through the restoration of the bayt 'arabi to resemble the ideal Shami home. I concluded with an example of a return that was not only unwelcomed but also considered harmful and corrupting to the essence of the Shami city. Although gentrification of the Old City was premised on restoring its Shami identity and heritage, it revealed how contested pasts are about contested presents. The returnees were negotiating the Old City's history as well as its Shami legacy in their projects, attempting to demonstrate not only their ability to undertake heritage preservation but also their moral right to the Old City. Their presence underscored long-term residents' experience with the historic center. Issues of cultural differentiation arose between the investors and long-term residents mimicked the Shami–rural divide. As we will see in the next chapter, the mustathmirin maintained this distinction and argued that the houses were no longer practical for living. The only way they could be preserved was through their conversion into restaurants, hotels, or art galleries.

In this chapter, we saw a new form of civilizational anxiety, resulting from the peculiarity of the interpretations of Shami heritage and its preservation. These differences were causing division among returnees on whether their projects could benefit the Old City. The different approach to restoring the house, as we saw with the Turkis, Yahya, Julian, and Munir, illustrates the idiosyncrasy associated with preserving the Old City. Hence, the civilization of the Old City was currently under threat when returnees veered from the local understanding of Shami civility and the sense of aesthetic that made the Old City. These returnees could be more damaging to the historic city center than the rural migrants. I will return to the theme of civilizational anxiety in chapter 6 and illustrate more of its multilayered dimensions.

The 'awda (return) to the Old City was initiated by the early entrepreneurs who converted the bayt 'arabi into restaurants and cafés that encouraged many Syrians to venture back to the Old City, when in the past, it was shunned as poor, backward, and filthy. Restaurants became in many instances the introduction for Syrians living outside the wall to the heritage of the bayt. The success of these early restaurants also inspired many investors to buy a bayt 'arabi for other purposes, such as hotels and art galleries. Restaurants in the Old City also encouraged the creation of new venues for visible consumption. As one of my neighbors in Sha'lan once told me, "we now dress to go to the Old City like we were going on an outing." The Old City was considered an exotic destination, and for many Syrians living outside the wall, the "other" was found in long-term residents. To visit the Old City was to see how others live. Hence, we next turn to these nonresidential uses of the bayt ʿarabi where mustathmirin also tackled issues of authenticity, which led to new forms of civilizational anxiety, further questioning the role of investors in preserving the Old City. We will also examine the effect of restaurants on new visitors in their quest to connect with the history and heritage of the Old City.

5

"Khay! Now We Pay to Enter a Bayt 'Arabi"

"**D**id you hear the latest joke?" Majid asked as we sat in his shop on Straight Street in the Old City. "In the Old Sham between a restaurant and a restaurant is a restaurant." But Majid was not laughing. He was thinking of yet another restaurant opening near his bayt 'arabi. The impact of the restaurants on the Old City was our usual topic of conversation. "Now we search for the bayt among the restaurants," he added with an attempt at levity, as he sipped his coffee and I stared at my tea, contemplating how many restaurants the Old City could support. This conversation took place in 2006 when restaurants in converted courtyard houses were becoming a worn-out cliché signifying change in the Old City and were met with dampened enthusiasm by long-term residents and visitors. In the beginning of the 1990s, restaurants were a novelty, exciting places for Syrians to rediscover the "exotic" Old City. Among the young and trendy, they became the "hipster" spots, the places to see and be seen. Inhabitants welcomed them in their neighborhood when their numbers were few because they brought services, interest to the Old City, and increased the demand for courtyard houses, which led to higher prices, benefiting many owners. Problems with restaurants in residential areas became apparent when their numbers increased dramatically, and there was no policy to regulate them.

In 2002, I was able to map the various restaurants and detect a pattern in their location and name. Most were found in the main tourist area next to the "central rectangle." Many had folksy or whimsical names, such as Bayt Jabri (Jabri's House), Piano Bar, Casablanca, Elissar (after an ancient Aramaean goddess), Marmar (from a folk song), and Oxygen.

13. Signs pointing to several restaurants in Bab Tuma, ca. 2006.

In 2004, it became difficult to track restaurants in the Old City, and in 2006, I gave up trying. The Committee for the Protection of the Old City (CPOC) had planned to restrict the tourist areas in the Old City to the main axes, surrounding the Umayyad Mosque, along Qimarriyyah Street that connected the mosque with Bab Tuma, and on Straight Street. But many investors, especially those with direct connections to the regime, circumvented the CPOC and its planning. The CPOC lacked the authority to prevent powerful investors from undoing their plans to separate tourist areas from residential neighborhoods (Sudermann 2012, 47). There were also the usual whispers of corruption among some Damascenes that certain CPOC directors accepted bribes and undermined their own urban planning.

Restaurants and cafés opened in the Old City in Christian or in Muslim neighborhoods, near mosques and churches, in cul-de-sacs, almost anywhere and in anything that used to be a bayt 'arabi, a shop, a bakery, a woodshop, or a stable. Staff at the CPOC brushed aside my question on the number of restaurants the Old City could feasibly support. I wondered whether a "restaurant bubble" was possible. Restaurants were supposedly contributing to the economic well-being of the historic center and in the process were introducing new social practices and consumption habits that challenged the residential aspects of intramural neighborhoods.

Moreover, the restaurants were increasingly indistinguishable by their setting, food, or service. Owners changed faster than it took to be served in some places. What may have begun as a favorite destination for the upwardly mobile degenerated over time and became the place respectable Syrians avoided. Other restaurants were reinvented as nightclubs or menus were changed to serve global ethnic cuisine (at one point, an Armenian restaurant became a Chinese food place, which emphasized authentic cuisine by employing Chinese workers). Some restaurants received new names and décor with each new owner.

In this chapter, I revisit Nora's deft comment; "Khay! Now we pay to enter a bayt 'arabi" to explore the social and cultural ramifications of restaurants in the Old City. I examine how restaurants combined economic and cultural factors to facilitate the 'awda to the Old City. Restaurants were lucrative investments in marketing the Shami identity, and their interior was made to resemble an elite Shami home. The menu consisted of traditional Shami food and owners demonstrated the extent of their "Shamification" in how they integrated into the neighborhood. Moreover, some of the new tourist venues catered exclusively to Damascenes' sense of nostalgia and created an ambience that triggered longing and desire for an idealized past.

I will also illustrate how restaurants were framed as saving the Old City from long-term residents by preserving the form of the bayt 'arabi for future generations. As we saw in the last chapter, investors insist the courtyard house is incompatible with a modern lifestyle; the only way the traditional courtyard house could be saved is through nonresidential use. Although I have interviewed owners of art galleries and hotels during my fieldwork, I will focus on restaurants and their impact on the sociocultural aspects of the Old City. The prevalence of restaurants highlighted the shortcomings of the government's preservation guidelines and the challenges of the heritage industry in lived areas. Restaurants demonstrated the ineffectiveness of existing government policies that failed to comprehensively address new businesses, their activities, and residents' needs in the Old City.

Moreover, restaurants were the first form of investment to appear in the Old City in the early 1990s, and the past two decades provide a good assessment of their social impact. They reflect new consumption practices in Syria because of economic liberalization and globalization. They also largely cater to the local consumers and not exclusively to tourists or the expatriate community as do hotels and art galleries. Hotels in the Old City were designed as five- and four-star tourist accommodations to discourage backpackers and budget travelers.[1] Art galleries were very selective and beyond the means and perhaps interest of most Syrians. Therefore, restaurants initiated the renewed interest in the Old City as a heritage site that encouraged Syrians to "return" to the Old City. This 'awda was mediated by restaurant owners and their heritagization of the vernacular built environment rather than an appreciation for a national monumental past.

I begin this chapter by introducing the concept of mustathmirin and compare them to long-term residents to delineate the new spatial practice they have brought to the neighborhoods. They are "place entrepreneurs" (Molotch as quoted in Zukin 1995, 7), who see economic opportunities in the removal of "backwardness" from the Old City by adding their notion of "civilization." As place entrepreneurs, mustathmirin were engaged with the "symbolic economy" or the "symbiosis of image and product, the scope and scale of selling images on a national and even global level" (Zukin 1995, 8). I will include a discussion of some restaurants and how they marketed the Shami identity by making it appeal to a Syrian nostalgia for an idealized past. I also emphasize how the "symbolic economy" in

1. Many of the hotels in the Old City that were being built target tourists who are willing and able to pay US$100 and more per night. Syrians seem to consider wealthier travelers to be better for the economy and have less of a disruptive social impact. Some believe that vices associated with tourism, such as drugs and prostitution, would be less problematic with wealthy tourists, although I am not sure how this perception came about. But overt classism permeates local discourses on morality and associates it with the upper rather than the lower classes regardless of nationality.

the Old City superseded other forms of entrepreneurship by inhabitants, which further undermined their claim to the Old City.

I will conclude this chapter with the effect of restaurants on the Old City. Some of the demographic transformations in certain neighborhoods are irreversible, which raises the question of whether the Old City is actually "saved" by restaurants. The number of returnees lags far behind the mustathmirin, and no sustainable measures have been adopted to keep residents in the Old City as either tenants or property owners. Moreover, restaurants also may be causing another form of destruction to the fragile built environment that could rival if not supersede that of the perceived neglect by inhabitants. There have been complaints about fumes from restaurants affecting the air quality and noise pollution in residential neighborhoods. The increase in vehicular traffic not only results in vibrations harmful to the fragile built environment but also adds to the noise and air pollution. Moreover, Tourism in Syria has been a volatile endeavor. Not only are travelers fickle and are always looking for the next trendy attraction but tourism is harmed sometimes irredeemably from political instability and civil wars. This discussion will lead into chapter 6 on the national ramifications of gentrification and heritage preservation and the conclusion that addresses the ongoing civil war.

Place Entrepreneurs

While such concepts as gentrification and gentrifier do not have a direct equivalent in Arabic, *'istthmar* and mustathmir come close. Numerous signs on stores and shops in the Old City have signs for sale or investment. As we recall, Yahya in the previous chapter was defending his gentrification of the Old City, but he was correct in that the negative connotations associated with gentrifier and gentrification in the United States do not come across with the local terms mustathmir and *'istthmar* in Syria. These terms reflect the new reality in Syria and denote the ability of some individuals to take advantage of innovative economic opportunities. Many inhabitants of Harat Hananya, as well as officials in CPOC, referred to owners of restaurants as mustathmirin, though the term was not restricted to the Old City. It was part of the wider investment movement in other economic sectors and throughout the country. It included the ability to transfer capital into the country and to tackle the bureaucracy of conducting business in Syria, which implied the investor had connections with government officials to overcome investment hurdles.

The term had several implications in the Old City that underscored the transformations in social relations. New forms of investment were associated with the shift in attitude among investors from dependency on the state to private entrepreneurial activity. Kjetil Selvik (2009) interviewed several entrepreneurs who saw the public sector workforce that resisted change as the obstacle to free enterprise, not the state. Hence, business and state interests were aligned against the "backward" mentality of intransigent government workers who were more concerned about their personal interests than the national good. Raymond Hinnebusch (2009, 20), however, highlighted a gap within the political elite and between generations in which the younger cohort was more willing to accept change than their parents. Nonetheless, entrepreneurs supported the policies of the regime and forged different types of partnerships and alliances that could be seen in the gentrification of the Old City. The urban changes in the intramural neighborhoods, as Yannick Sudermann (2012, 34) argued, was the result of the regime permitting "urban spaces for a transnational capitalist lifestyle." However, the scope and scale of this cosmopolitan lifestyle was based on local discourses on the Old City and its Shami identity.

The mustathmirin, similar to the returnees, were transient and distinguished themselves from long-term residents by their cultural affinity for Shami heritage. Many mustathmirin also did not live in the neighborhood where they invested and some sold their projects even before the restoration work was completed, but their impact was more visible on the community since a restaurant is more disruptive to the local community than a restored home of a returnee. Therefore, mustathmirin introduced new spatial practice in the intramural neighborhoods though they did not live there. Those who actually lived and in many instances worked in the neighborhood had a strong sense of belonging, of rootedness to the harah unlike investors.

Before the boom in the heritage industry, some long-term residents struggled with the decision to relocate or to sell their bayt. Majid spoke admiringly of his father who in the 1960s was having financial problems and though he had mortgaged the house and had renters he was about to declare bankruptcy. The father seriously contemplated selling the house. He found a buyer, but when the time came to finalize the sale, he could not go through with the transaction. A few years later, the father wanted to sell the bayt but again could not. Majid interpreted these two incidents as proof that the house was part of his father and an unbreakable bond linked his family to the Old City. However, the new demand for houses by investors was making it difficult for homeowners to resist the need to sell.

The mustathmirin were outsiders and difficult to assess because their 'asl was obscure. It was not that they were foreign to the neighborhood but they were not maintaining social distinction based on origins. Rather, many members of this new class of entrepreneurs tried to embellish or obscure their background (Perthes 1991, 35). Moreover, it was not clear who truly owned the restaurants. Many mustathmirin claimed sole responsibility for their work: "I insisted that the fountain be removed" or "I personally selected the paintings." The claim I heard most was, "I had to deal with the bureaucracy of the CPOC." Yet there were, in most cases, partnerships, with either other family members, government officials, or silent partners from abroad; therefore, the supposed owner was actually the front person for a family, company, or group of investors. Globalization made it harder to track the flow of capital into the country, and some Syrians worried about the intentions of investors. In Syria, the culture of paranoia is pervasive and encouraged by the regime to maintain control and dominance. In addition, it was unclear how well or highly connected some of these mustathmirin actually were. Approval for a restaurant or hotel permit was supposedly contingent on neighbors' consent, but it was not always transparent how consent was obtained. In a few instances, investors threatened long-term residents if they did not support a new restaurant, and there was no recourse for the threats.

Nonetheless, many investors tried to show their goodwill to their neighbors and offered home improvements to smooth relations. For instance, if a neighbor's wall overlooking the courtyard of the restaurant was damaged, the investor would fix and paint it. The exterior walls of houses next to the restaurant were painted free of charge, sometimes annually to maintain a respectable appearance for the surroundings of the venue. Many property owners were able to extract other services from investors in exchange for their consent, and the mustathmirin tried to maintain the smooth relations while they owned the establishment so that visitors to the restaurant will always feel welcome in the neighborhood.

The presence of the mustathmirin in the Old City disrupted the "rhythm" of the quotidian life for long-term residents (Lefebvre 1996). The demographic changes that accompanied the increase in the number of restaurants and hotels altered the sociability of intramural neighborhoods. Before I discuss how inhabitants navigated new spatial practices and interacted with mustathmirin, I will examine how investors encouraged new users to come to the neighborhoods and exploited the popularity of courtyard houses as restaurants.

Saving Civilization

Salim, the architect and investor I introduced earlier, believed the courtyard house was an anachronism, and it was a matter of time before it was abandoned for a tabiq. But Salim and other investors insisted they were also improving the neighborhood. As Ali who had a restaurant in the Old City explained, "The neighbors are happy because now people come to the neighborhood. When I first came, I found garbage all around, and I worked out an agreement with the garbageman to keep the alley clean. I also called the electric company to fix the light in the alley. We get visitors who are diplomats, oil company executives, and tourists, and we must present a view of the real Sham before it was distorted."

By promoting his role in improving the neighborhood, Ali underscored local discourse of decay and neglect in the Old City. Streetlights and sanitation services tended to be haphazard in the poorer neighborhoods because residents lacked the political clout to demand these services from the government. Ali had the influence needed to bring municipal services to the neighborhood. But he also "privatized" state service by offering additional incentives to the garbageman who was already getting a salary to clean the alleys. This is an example of the new "mentality." Ali did not wait for the government to clean the streets. He was proactive in improving the neighborhood, buying services where the government fell short. In the process, he became the self-anointed advocate for the neighborhood, taking on the role of the traditional strongman. Other investors were candid about how the improvements they introduced to the neighborhood increased the price of the courtyard houses. It was a dominant theme in many of my conversations with investors: The demand for courtyard houses allowed several owners to benefit from the new economic climate and improve their living conditions. Moreover, Ali believed he was doing his patriotic duty by revealing the "true face" of the Old City, hidden under the years of neglect and decay. Ali was involved in more than reshaping the Old City; he was making it a place "of creation and transformation" (Zukin 1995, 8).

Malik, the restaurant owner we met in chapter 3, interpreted his contributions to the neighborhood as a patriotic duty when he created a sanitized environment for tourists. He assumed responsibility for improving the experience of tourists in the Old City, and based on his account, he allowed tourists who were not customers to use the toilet in his restaurant because he knew there were no other amenities available to them when they visited the neighborhood. He invested in social relations and as a mustathmir; Malik obscured the lines between the local and global, public and private, and national and regional by downplaying the business aspect of his presence in the Old City. He was a good citizen and neighbor, contributing to the improvement of the neighborhood. He was also a "good Shami" putting the interests of the neighborhood first and engaging in neighborly civility, though as discussed before, he was not Shami by descent. Malik's deployment of the "good" Shami demonstrates the "particular strength" associated with the Shami identity and the uses of "Shamification" in the gentrification of the Old City. He deployed local conceptions of the urban–rural binary, and his use of stereotypes is "interesting for what they tell us about the relationship between daily social life and the intellectual imagination" (Herzfeld 2009, 80).

Malik insisted his actions and practices demonstrated his "*intima' lil balad*" (attachment to the country) and that he "*bahib al-balad*" (loves the country). He wanted "a good reputation for Syria" because of this love, which is a part of him as a "Shami" and propels him to doing what is best for the community. However, there were different ways to interpret the bursts of patriotism I encountered in some people I interviewed in Syria. At times, I dismissed it as their way of making sure their words cannot be construed as disloyal and antiregime. Malik could have used the interview to demonstrate his "compliance" to the regime and its domination (Wedeen 1999). But it also demonstrated the alliance between private investors and the state on economic reform and liberalization that exceeded compliance. The Ba'th, especially under the Bashar al-Asad, the elite business communities, the merchant, and investors aligned their interests because economic reform benefited all of them (Perthes 2004, 109–10). But there are local social discourses that even the regime cannot control and that have long been established in terms of the urban–rural binary and its current manifestation as "civilized" and "backward." It is this dichotomy that continues to inform local social action. Although many have described alliances between the government and investors as co-option, in the case of the Old City there was the agreement that "backwardness" resulted from rural migrants and long-term residents. The investors were not challenging this categorization because it worked in their favor, and the regime saw that it was to its benefit to encourage entrepreneurship in the Old City. The regime and the investors believed it was necessary to remove the "backwardness" for the full potential of the heritage industry could be realized and the removal is by investors and not the government. Therefore, investors are sanctioned to discriminate against occupants in the gentrification of the Old City for the benefit of the nation. Ironically, as in the case of Malik, he is a rural migrant, but he is able to distance himself from this particular stereotype for one that carried more social capital under new economic conditions. Market liberalization has allowed local social actors to bypass the restrictions of 'asl and to construct a fluid identity that is not constricted to a place of origin but is adaptable to the new social and economic reality.

The rhetoric of patriotism and national duty offered an appropriate framework for the preservation project undertaken by Malik and other mustathmirin. The intramural neighborhoods were changing physically and demographically, yet by invoking the good of the nation, Malik emphasized the positive in this change. Investors were also enforcing the new mentality that did not encourage dependence on the government. He had not displaced residents, as much as improved the neighborhood, not only for those who continued to live there but also for visitors, local and foreign. Gentrification is an attempt to reclaim the glorious past of urban spaces (Smith 1996, xiv). Malik and other investors were the "new urban pioneers" who, through urban renewal were "remaking the geography of the city [and] simultaneously rewrit[ing] its social history as a preemptive justification for a new urban future" (Smith 1996, 27). Investors were supported and celebrated by officials because they possessed the creative mentality of entrepreneurs by finding new economic opportunities and renegotiating local discourses on the decline and decay of the Old City. They also were assuming private responsibility for public services. They were defining the forms of "urban entrepreneurialism" (Harvey 1989), not because the local government was reducing services but because it was not meeting the demand. The government is never completely absent in the Old City. After all, we are talking about an authoritarian regime, and it is present officially through police and bureaucrats as well as unofficially through its intelligence network (according to some sources the garbagemen work in surveillance). However, the gentrification of the Old City is redefining how the regime is embedded in the daily lives of people through its new proxies, entrepreneurs. Therefore, it is no coincidence when investors doing the government's work are accorded certain rights and opportunities denied groups not working within the government's agenda (Sudermann 2012).

I am not suggesting that the investors I have mentioned actually work closely with the regime or have been designated as its official representatives. I did not ask any investors on their relationship with the regime, because I considered such questioning improper and off limits, but it was easy to discern how the regime was heavily involved in all aspects of society. Moreover, asking these questions would have placed me in a vulnerable position because my ability to conduct fieldwork was premised on its apolitical nature. Nonetheless, I was more intrigued by how authoritarianism becomes normalized in daily life and how social actors lead productive and meaningful lives under such a regime. The differences between the regime and investors were apparent during interviews. The investors began with unprompted praise for the regime and economic liberalization, but then gave a litany of complaints on government inefficiency and crippling bureaucracy, and ended with the declaration that the regime does not do enough to create a business-friendly environment.

Moreover, authoritarianism discouraged autonomy in social action, and several of the Syrians I interviewed were not concerned in overcoming these constraints because they provided them with a structure for activism. Ironically, since their choices in social action were limited, they were not overwhelmed with the "freedom of choice" and were able to do effective work within the constraints. Other Syrians spoke honestly of how they preferred political stability over political freedom, citing Iraq and Lebanon as two countries that have relatively more freedom and are considered more democratic but lack stability and security. Until the beginning of the civil war, stability and security in exchange for compliance were part of the social contract between the regime and citizens. Many Syrians I met insisted on a flexibility in their relationship with the regime, one that included collaboration, coordination, co-option, resistance, and opposition. The flexibility allowed social actors a measure of freedom to determine the best course of action to achieve their ever-changing interests.

Bringing "Civilization" Back?

I asked Abu George what he thought about the restaurants in Harat Hananya, and he replied without hesitating, "It is a good thing. The restaurants have improved the neighborhood. Now you see people in the streets at night. I used to come home around eleven p.m. from the coffeehouse outside the Old City and walking through deserted alleyways I would be terrified. I would not see a living soul. Now there are people, there is light, and there is life. You feel the neighborhood is alive." My landlady also confirmed that restaurants were good for the neighborhood. "They light up the alleys. There are people, and you do not feel like the alleys are deserted." Abu Ahmad who lived on a another neighborhood added, "Restaurants introduced the world to Old Damascus and Old Damascus is not ashamed when people get to know it because Old Damascus makes one proud."

However, not only long-term residents saw the positive impact of restaurants but businesses did as well. According to Kamel, a shopkeeper in Qimarriyyah, "five years ago [the interview was in 2004], there was no one in the streets after nine. There was fear in the streets, and they were not thriving with people like now." Qimarriyyah was becoming a main artery for the Old City, connecting Suq al-Hamidiyya with Bab Tuma, where many restaurants have opened (Sudermann 2012). People walk through Qimarriyyah to get to the restaurants, and it is alive well into the night.

All of these comments have one theme, people in the street equals normalcy. Yet many residents were indirectly recalling the troubled decades of the 1970s and 1980s, implying that the emergency laws limited the assembly of people outside and at night. Stores were required by law to close at eight, or nine in the summer, and people were discouraged to be out at night. The restaurants not only reflected the political and economic changes in the country but also created nightly entertainment for people if only to see where these new venues are located. A main source of entertainment for many people was strolling the streets at night, especially in well-lit areas with stores and restaurants. Hence, restaurants, people in the streets, and stores opening later were creating an atmosphere of normalcy among Syrians. Even though the draconian emergency laws were still in effect, they were not enforced. The appearance of normalcy was important to attract more investors and visitors to bolster the local economy and to present a new and "civilized" face to the world. Ironically, the emergency law in Syria was lifted in April 2011 in the early phases of civil unrest.

Visitors to the Old City also came to see the "other." In an anecdote that Nadeem told me about a conference on the future of the Old City, one attendee said that dwellers in the Old City should wear *tarbush* (fez); because they were in the historic district, they should dress the part for tourists. However, the Old City was too vibrant and alive to be converted into the Williamsburg model (see Handler and Gable 1997). No one seemed to support this idea at the conference, but it indicated that as the Old City becomes historic, its residents, if not accused of destroying the heritage, were in danger of becoming living exhibitions (Kirshenblatt-Gimblett 1998, 96–105).

Many inhabitants reversed the gaze and watched the new visitors to the Old City. Many sat outside their houses or stood on rooftops or balconies to watch the alleys. At least that was my experience in Harat Hananya where the visitors became part of the summer evening's entertainment for some, who would turn from their TV sets and "gaze" at the newcomers to the harah. Neighbors were aware that someone important was coming to Casablanca when the staff rolled out the red carpet and the alley was scrubbed cleaner than usual by the restaurant staff. Neighbors sat outside their doors or by windows, and the next day they could tell stories of how they greeted the president of Syria, who was an occasional guest at the restaurant, and gave his wife flowers.

However, not everyone I met was sanguine about the restaurants in the Old City, especially when their numbers increased dramatically and they were haphazardly opened in cul-de-sacs and in residential neighborhoods far from the street. In the early days when their numbers were small and they were a novelty, many long-term residents welcomed them and appreciated the services and the efforts of investors to promote the Old City as a site of "civilization" rather than of "backwardness." However, as the negative aspects of restaurants in residential neighborhoods became apparent, many did not want to live near one. Hikmat Shatta (2005) was a returnee and wrote an editorial in the newspaper *al-Hayat* that restaurants were a catastrophe and accused restaurateurs of systematically destroying the Old City. He worried about the effect of the large number of restaurants on the Old City and claimed modern Damascus was "raping" Old Damascus. Although he was not against restaurants and nonresidential uses of courtyard houses, he saw their proliferation as ripping apart the urban fabric. The privacy of the bayt 'arabi was desecrated when rooftops became dining areas. His editorial complained about the lack of urban planning. He thought preservation was done incorrectly, and there were no accommodations for occupants who wanted to remain in the Old City but not live next to restaurants and their inconveniences.

Other Damascenes feared the regime was deliberately attempting to destroy Damascus by transforming it into a tawdry version of its illustrious past. Others worried that the shoddy preservation of the courtyard house was actually hastening the deterioration of buildings. Although the CPOC had received numerous complaints about restaurants, it lacked a comprehensive strategy on how to deal with this new phenomenon in the heritage site. Mustathmirin, returnees, and long-term residents complained about the ineptitude of CPOC and its staff, but most important in the attempt to move forward in the gentrification of the Old City, questions were asked that had no clear answer: What was being preserved and for whom? I will address the issue of corruption and bureaucracy in the next chapter, but it does intertwine with the concern many inhabitants felt about the chaos caused by restaurants in their neighborhoods.

Forgotten Histories

Local conditions legitimized certain actions, and produced knowledge that was codified in new social realities (Asad 1987, 607). Current gentrification of the Old City, as led by the mustathmirin with support of the government, met with the approval of many long-term residents though it "silenced" their ongoing efforts to improve their neighborhoods and living conditions. Such I discovered in the case of Abu Ahmad who was long involved in promoting his neighborhood long before it was popular with investors. Abu Ahmad was one of the few Shuwam living in the Old City who allowed government-sponsored activities in his courtyard. I asked him about opening his house for the public, and he replied this was part of his effort to show what the Old City was about. "If we were in the West and we had a city like this they [meaning the government] would have worked much more and provided more services. They are not concerned with the city. Now it has become somewhat cleaner. At least you see sweepers in the streets. I had spoken to the governor when he was here for an event about opening more roads in the Old City. He promised to do something but did nothing."

This added another layer to the matter of services mustathmirin purportedly brought to the neighborhood. Services Salim and Malik provided were missing because of government neglect, and neighborhood occupants lacked the necessary connections to bring them, especially since they were not considered powerful or important. They have been discriminated against for living in the Old City, as we have seen in previous chapters. But they were also denied the role of improving their situation because such a role did not adhere to the narratives of decline and neglect they supposedly caused in the Old City. The saviors of the Old City can only be the returnees and the mustathmirin because they were part of the new movement who discovered the heritage of the Old City. Moreover, while the services investors brought to the neighborhood benefited residents, they were mainly for the visitors to the Old City. Thus, the global became more important than the local, and it very likely they were not be permanent but are linked to consumer interest in the Old City. Perhaps Abu Ahmad was accurate in his assessment of the situation when he stated that if the Old City were in the West it would have been better maintained because the current improvements were implemented with the comfort of global tourists and not local users. We turn next to how investors were involved in the gentrification of the Old City and in heritage preservation of the Shami home.

Heritage in Any Form

The popularity of restaurants in the Old City created an interest in any building that could be converted into a tourist attraction: workshops, stores, and bakeries, though the goal should resemble the ideal Shami home. The building that eventually became al-Makan was not even a typical courtyard house but was a nondescript house assembled from three different ones.[2] The investors were more interested in the location near the main street than in the actual bayt, and their restaurant became an interesting case study in heritage preservation when there was no actual heritage to preserve but only the idea of one. Three mustathmirin purchased the building at the beginning of the restaurant craze and when the Old City was attracting more investment than other places in Damascus because of the heritage industry. They also sought to capitalize on the interest in the Old City because of the popularity of TV dramas that promoted the interest in the bayt 'arabi and historic neighborhoods. Yet the investors insisted

---

2. This is not the actual name of the restaurant.

that their main aim in buying the house was preservation, as one of them explained: "If we don't keep Old Damascus, then there will be nothing left of Old Damascus."

Nidal, the architect hired by the three mustathmirin to convert the bayt 'arabi into a restaurant, explained that his task was to convince his employers that they should not recreate the historic elements of the ideal bayt 'arabi but aim for something new.[3] "The house was a very a simple building," Nidal rationalized, "nothing in common so I think that each façade came from another house or was rebuilt from another ruin, you can always invent theories so you can see that the house has been altered, [because] doors and windows are all different." Therefore, he was already dealing with a house that did not even exhibit the main architectural elements of a courtyard house. But it was within the heritage site that lent it an aura of distressed authenticity, and his restoration was aimed at redefining the concept of the bayt 'arabi. He worked with the idea of a courtyard house rather than the actual architecture of the house and tried to create a variation on the ideal Shami home. He was interested in the design, not the structure. "You can't really change the structure, courtyard, 'iwan, and rooms. So the creative part is design—the architectural use of space or in Arabic *tasmim*."

Nidal was familiar with the bayt 'arabi since he worked on the architectural documentation of different historic neighborhoods in Damascus when he was an architecture student at the university.[4] This knowledge was useful when he designed a restaurant differently from the ones in the Old City. He lamented, "If you have seen one restaurant you have seen them all," and in my experience, I understood what he meant. Most had tables in the courtyard and the surrounding rooms, and many reconstructed the 'ajami and 'blaq that did not exist in the original structure to lend their restaurants a genealogy.

3. Interview with Nidal was conducted in English.

4. Courses in architecture and fine arts at Damascus University include field visits to the Old City. I remember one day coming out of my room in the Old City and finding a group of students bunched up in the tight alley leading to my front door sketching. I asked one of my neighbors about them and he said "It is their season."

14. Typical restaurant setting in the Old City, ca. 2004.

The different interpretations of how to display and promote heritage in the Old City had been based on what various mustathmirin believed would attract the right customers to their establishments. Since any structure in the Old City was heritage, their role was how best to display that heritage through restoration. In the reinterpretation of the Shami heritage, the personality of each restaurant reflects its owner. In al-Makan, Nidal retained the layout of the building but experimented with colors and design. He believed "the colors of the walls in Arabic House (his term for bayt ʿarabi) were white, black, red, green from the trees, brown and blue. Decorations were mainly the primary colors, such as red and yellow. Walls were usually whitewashed because of the material used in their construction. Bedrooms were usually pastel colors." In the restaurant, he had three main colors: red floor, dark blue walls, and yellow lights the colors of the bayt but with his variation. The courtyard floor was damaged and instead of recreating a traditional courtyard floor with white flagstones and black trim, he decided on something radical, polished red marble for the floor and fountain.

Many Damascenes were outraged by what Nidal, a Shami, did in al-Makan and thought he tampered with heritage and tradition. He had been accused of taking too many liberties with the bayt, but he was aware of this criticism and responded, "The Arabic house is a form, a terminology, a cause, and an ideology. However, the house itself did not lend itself to restoration. It was a simple family dwelling made of several connected homes. It had different style windows and doors indicating it never stood as a whole." Therefore, he was able to argue that he respected the integrity of this particular house rather than the generic idea of a bayt ʿarabi. He was interested in "restoration only when it was worth it like the two facades [the black stone wall of the original structure]." Nidal was trying to show the value of the old house with a new function and give new meaning to the bayt in a contemporary setting.

One of the partners admitted that he was not convinced of the liberties Nidal had taken with the restoration, but he was persuaded in the end. He did not elaborate on why he hesitated, and I assumed he was worried that clients would not be reminded of the Old City in his restaurant and may not want to return. Nonetheless, he appreciated the distinction between al-Makan and other restaurants: "People do not come for the food, they come for the experience . . . it is a totally different house, only the black stone walls are left of the original." Hence, this owner wanted to promote the "quality of the experience" that shifted the authenticity of the bayt from the architectural elements and motifs to the concept of Shaminess that could transcend the Old City.

Heritage preservation remains fraught with controversy and contradictions. The many interpretations for what constitutes heritage and how

best to preserve it in the Old City also reflect the sociopolitical contestation as well. Historic preservation is a very political issue that is inevitably
exclusionary of certain social groups or histories. What is preserved, how,
and for what purpose reveals the social dynamics in politically sensitive
settings where different groups vie to promote their interests over those
of other groups (Handler 1988; Herzfeld 1991, 2009; Handler and Gable
1997). It is also easy to conclude that the heritage preservation of the Old
City is another manifestation of the Shami–Baʻth binary where the former
accuse the latter of undermining the "authenticity" of their Shami past.
But since some investors, architects, and supporters of the gentrification
of the Old City of Damascus tend to be Shami, and much of the criticism comes from non-Shuwam, this conclusion is problematic. How social
actors support or oppose heritage preservation is commentary on their
role in the shifting marketplace of consumption. They accumulate social
capital in the gentrification of the Old City either by participating in the
production or consumption of the urban heritage.

Perhaps the multivocality in heritage preservation in the Old City
is rooted in the causes for the sudden interest in the courtyard house.
Whereas in other parts of the world where historic preservation is spearheaded by governments to protect a national patrimony or by individuals seeking to escape the materialism of the modern period, in Damascus
it is about seeking economic opportunities. Nonetheless, it is important
to understand what social actors engaged in historic preservation say
about their work. Following the work of Arjun Appadurai on the "social
life of things," Brumann (2009) argued that common assumptions about
heritage preservation had negative connotations and did not include the
"emic" point of view. Therefore, in many studies it resulted in understanding preservation through one of four explanations "falsification, petrifica-
tion, desubstantiation, and enclosure" (277). However, in his work on the
preservation of the traditional dwelling in Kyoto (*kyo-machiya*) he found
that urban heritage preservation did not adhere to any of the explanations
listed above. Kyoto residents were interested in the spiritual aspects of the
kyo-machiya as an antidote to the materialism of modernity. Moreover,
their restoration of the traditional dwelling did not include innovations.
Rather he argued that the urban setting was better documented and had

a higher concentration of "intellectual and creative resources" than the countryside, which made it difficult to innovate in preservation projects (291–92). Access to documentation, historical records, and the fact that the preservation was performed by local actors allowed for less innovation in the local traditions (292). Brumann described Kyoto local actors as tending to be less inventive in the preservation of the traditional dwelling, because the origin of the house is not obscured but available. It is difficult to define what Nidal did in al-Makan as anything but innovation although the restaurant is in an urban setting and there are documents to determine the origin of the house. He is also Shami and is knowledgeable of the traditional courtyard house. Unlike in Kyoto, in Damascus innovation comes from overexposure to the ideal Shami home as in the numerous restaurants found in the Old City. Nonetheless, and as Brumann stressed any study of heritage preservation must include what the preservationists say about their work (295). Therefore, although investors claim to be preserving heritage they are also marketing ethnicity and as the market for Shami culture becomes saturated and ways of expression limited, many of the investors seek to create a dining experience that stands out and encourages customers to return to their restaurant. Investors in Damascus insist they are protecting the courtyard home from disappearing by making it relevant to the younger generation of Damascenes. This relevance must be powerful to lure visitors and therefore should include some creativity.

Coming Home

Although several investors believed that the bayt 'arabi was no longer practical as a residence they were commodifying nostalgia for home and encouraging a form of homecoming. This nostalgia was not necessarily for the courtyard house, since many visitors were not raised in one, but for the idea of home, by creating images of the *"felicitous space"* that inspired the imagination and created intimacy with the new form of the courtyard house (Bachelard 1964).

Ayman, a young university student working at the French research center where I spent much time in their library, noticed I was asking mainly for books on Damascus, and he became intrigued by my research topic. I explained my interest in the Old City and the bayt 'arabi, and he began speaking almost lyrically about how he would love to live in an old Shami house because it would be "more relaxing and comforting than his apartment." The sound of water and the trees in the courtyard were all "spiritual," he said. When he told me he was from a village outside of the coastal city of Latakia, I became intrigued with how a coastal boy was so enamored with a Shami bayt 'arabi. He described the house his family owned in the village surrounded by trees and how he would love to live there but could not because of the lack of job opportunities. His next best option, he thought, was to live in the Old City, which he had gotten to know by going to restaurants and cafés. He felt at ease and content when he went to refurbished restaurants and cafés. I pointed out some of the realities of living in the Old City based on my own experience. He agreed saying, "If I lived there, it would be anything but romantic." But he still wanted me to see how he experienced the new cafés and restaurants in the Old City and offered to take me to one of his favorite spots because it was a "felicitous space."

A few days later I went with him and his girlfriend to al-Bal, one of the trendy restaurants in the early 2000s that catered to a decidedly intellectual and artistic young crowd. Ayman and his girlfriend were on a mission to convince me of the aesthetic qualities of the bayt 'arabi. They both explained how much they loved al-Bal pointing to the fountain in the courtyard, the stone walls, the fact we were in the Old City, one of the oldest cities in the world and the seat of Arab and Islamic empires. It was obvious why the Lebanese English-language newspaper the *Daily Star* called them "Hipster Houses." One patron even said, "Old Damascus represents a lifestyle. It is our identity, our collective memory and a place to meet people."[5] The journalist should have added "like-minded people" since Ayman and his girlfriend were part of the generation who were developing new national sentiment and an appreciation for the past from these restaurants and

---

5. Agence France Presse, "Hipster Houses: Trendy youth reviving the spirit of Old Damascus." *Daily Star*, February 14, 2006, www.dailystar.com.lb/printable.asp?art_ID=22169&cat_ID=4.

cafés. These establishments established the *lieux du memoire* that recreated bonds between people and the past (Nora 1989). Ayman had been able to develop a new appreciation for his family home by going to al-Bal but also from the Old City, which he could also claim as his own though he comes from the coast. The type of architecture that existed in the intramural neighborhoods allowed for nostalgia and "when formalized as heritage, nostalgia goes a step further: it produces legitimacy through aestheticization" (Roy 2004, 65). In this instance, al-Bal nostalgia was not defeatist or an attempt to escape the present but was empowering young people, like Ayman, to think of a future that included a comfortable and happy home. Moreover, restaurants were fueling nationalist pride as the Shami heritage was appropriated by Syrians from other parts of the country.

However, nostalgia "cannot be sustained without loss" (Stewart 1999, 145). In al-Bal, Ayman felt content remembering happy feelings associated with his family home in the village but it was also a feeling of bittersweet loss because he cannot live there. If anything, the mustathmirin invested in the nostalgia industry, which we saw earlier was part of the national identity (Sudermann 2012, 40). Bittersweet makes the feeling more authentic, but not painful and it is this sentiment that contributes to what it "mean[s] to be modern in Syria today" (Shannon 2006, 55). As Jonathan Shannon demonstrated, Syrians constitute their modern subjectivity through how they embody "affect and sentiment" and though he was speaking about music, it can also apply to the nostalgia of the courtyard house.

In *Cultures of Cities*, Zukin (1995, 53) described how the Disney urban model made the "symbolic economy" seem viable because "it abstracts both the technical and the architectural elements of a place and the motions that places evoke." Disney idealized urban space to create a safe and sanitized environment for the "public culture of civility and security that recalls a world long left behind" (52). A similar process was taking place in the Old City where mustathmirin, evoked memories of a childhood home, in how they restored and redesigned a Shami bayt ʿarabi. As the Turkish wooden house became "a socialization mechanism aimed at a new generation who posited problems of compliance" (Bertram 2008, 144), the bayt as restaurant served a similar function in the Old City. Not only did it allow for a continuum with the past for the younger generation,

it also served to remind visitors of a simpler time. One of the social ramifications of the new economic realities is the widespread yearning for an
idealized past. Whereas we saw in the last chapter that many of the Shuwam who wrote memoirs about the Old City expressed their nostalgia for
the bayt of their youth and life in the neighborhood, now we were seeing
that nostalgia became generalized for a bittersweet loss of innocence and
bliss. Since society was already indulging in nostalgia, the restaurants created a safe and sanitized environment that allowed this feeling to overflow.

Moreover, going to restaurants sanitized the realities of living in the
Old City, and social actors could experience the Old City without having
to live there. Perhaps this was why the restaurants in the Old City were
more popular with Syrians than with tourists. Though this nostalgia was
not an escape to the past, it became the process through which local social
actors negotiated the rapid pace of social and economic transformations,
which were not only engulfing the Old City, but also other aspects of their
daily lives. The "urban nostalgia, as a process, as a reaction, as a kind of
mapping of time onto place, for example, can be used constructively to
help residents, urban experts, and scholars understand how normative
(and sometimes negative) meanings of the 'new' and 'historic' city are
created to pursue socially exclusionary nationalist agendas in the present
based on utopian visions for the future" (Till 2005, 57).

Ironically, al-Bal was a renovated woodshop but that again became
irrelevant because it was redesigned to create the ambiance of the bayt
'arabi, mainly through the fountain in the courtyard. Moreover, visitors
expected they were going to a converted bayt when they went to the Old
City and not a carpenter's shop. Al-Bal served no alcohol, only tea, coffee,
and juice. It also offered light refreshments. It played the music of Fairuz,
the famous Lebanese singer, continuously. One of the owners told me that
he was aiming for three themes in his café: art, leisure, and Fairuz. Why
Fairuz, I asked? He replied: "Fairuz is a symbol not only an artist. She is
'asala (authenticity) in lyrics and music." But he was also talking about a collective memory shared by many Damascenes who woke up in the morning
to the sound of Fairuz. It was something I experienced living in Damascus.
In the morning, one heard Fairuz on the radio at home, on the bus or in
the taxi, or wafting from open shops. It was still too early for the cacophony

of the Arab techno-pop music that was played at earsplitting volume, and Fairuz was just right in tone and style to ease one into the chaos of the day. The owner like many of his generation listened to Fairuz on the way to school and was able to capitalize on this nostalgia for childhood and perhaps for simpler times by playing her music continuously in his café. In creating a site for personal memory to flourish, he was also encouraging an environment for the "collective memory" and where remembered past events need to be localized in a social environment (Halbwachs 1992).

According to Maurice Halbwachs, "in order to remember, one must be capable of reason and comparing and of feeling in contact with a human society that can guarantee the integrity of our memory" (41). One reason restaurants and cafés are popular with Syrians and Damascenes living outside the wall is that even with all of the modifications and innovations on the Shami bayt they maintain an amount of integrity that allows for the social act of remembering. The environment in a restaurant or café is replete with memory triggers from a common past, such as Fairuz. There is an authenticity in the songs of Fairuz that upend the café experience as a mere act of cultural consumption of the past. Rather, the past evoked by Fairuz becomes personal and individualized. Astute entrepreneurs realize the local demand for nostalgia, perhaps because they have experienced it and are able to supply triggers and cues in their cafés and restaurants to aid their customers to remembering happy times.

However, Fairuz is not only soothing for Ayman, his girlfriend, and other "hipsters" who come to al-Bal. An earlier generation also sought solace and comfort from the anxieties of time in the voice of Fairuz (Tergeman 1969, 328). Fairuz is one element of the continuity with the past and across generations. Although she is a Lebanese singer, her concerts were as popular in Syria as they were in Lebanon, and she was just as beloved. Tergeman's memoir of historic Damascus includes an entry on Fairuz. Through her songs about Syria and Damascus, Tergeman relives the love of Syria, and she is proud to have lived in the "age of Fairuz" (333). Hence, Fairuz represents continuity between generations and their relationship with the Old City.

Fairuz was well-suited for the courtyard house since many of her song were whimsical and nostalgic. The café al-Bal, was named after one of her songs, meaning "on my mind." Her songs also dealt, as the owner reminded me, with the *day'ah*, or the village, and how life used to be before moving to the city. It was incongruous that Fairuz was appropriate for the Old City, because her songs were about the tranquility and simplicity of the village, but the feelings of longing that they evoked were not specific to the city or country. The owner of al-Bal came from a village but was raised in the Old City. Like Ayman, the stones and courtyards of the Old City reminded him of the village. In many ways, he too was remembering a faraway place in distance as well as in time, which happens to be what Fairuz usually sang about wistfully—loss.

The contrast between the city and the countryside is necessary for understanding social and cultural change during periods of economic transformation (Williams 1973; Harms 2011). Al-Bal and other restaurants are able to undermine the difference between the city and the countryside with a generic sense of loss that allows social actors to feel nostalgia either for the city or the country. This is perhaps the reason for the popularity of such venues such as al-Bal. They do not overwhelm the sense of sight with artifacts from a Shami past rather by focusing on the sense of hearing and inundating it with the songs of Fairuz patrons can decide their own sense of loss and for what. Sitting in al-Bal Ayman remembers his village, but someone else may remember a childhood home in the Old City. It is never clear what triggers memory in these settings, but the less clutter of objects allows for a more personalized trip to the past. Hence, it is not really about finding the village in the city but the search for meaning in the chaos of the present.

The choice of Fairuz was in some ways a critique of the techno-pop Arabic music dominating the airwaves in the Arab world, which is associated with neoliberalism. Singers are difficult to tell apart, the music is jarring, the lyrics are forgettable, and bordering on the vulgar. A top song today is barely remembered next week and forgotten a year later. Some of the local social critics considered techno-pop a cultural invasion that had no roots or relation to authentic Arab music. It was empty of meaning and value, disrupting the "experience of the origins" since it did not evoke the Old City or the home like Fairuz. In many ways, new songs reflected the current reality in many of the modern neighborhoods, where they too were indistinguishable; the buildings looked identical and lacked any spirit. The authenticity of the Old City required another authenticity, that of Fairuz. The owner encouraged young high-minded college students such as Ayman and his girlfriend, who disliked techno-pop and were seeking an alternative authenticity, to find it in the Old City. They found social distinction from their cohorts who listened to techno-pop through their desire for tranquility in the bustling city. Some restaurants and cafés became nightclubs on weekends. They played the loud jarring techno-pop but then catered to those who were attracted to the Old City for the night-life thriving in neighborhoods around Bab Tuma and Qimarriyyah.

The Problem with Restaurants

Perhaps the biggest change that mustathmirin introduced to the Old City was redefining public/private space in the Old City. Majid like many long-term residents did not like to see strangers in the alley outside his house because it was an extension of his home; the alley was both semiprivate and semipublic. Neighbors understood and adhered to a code of behavior that governed these spaces. Outsiders who went to the neighborhood restaurants did not. Before the 1990s only residents and their guests accessed these neighborhoods. Now restaurants attracted all kinds of visitors, and occupants of the neighborhood could not prevent them from invading their living space. The influx of people to formerly secluded neighborhoods disrupted the daily rhythm of life for many inhabitants. A German woman who lived in a bayt 'arabi explained:

> Living in the Old City the streets are semi-public. People go out in pajamas in the morning to buy something. In the Christian quarter, women wearing nightgowns go out to throw the garbage. In a way, you know who is in the harah but with foreigners coming you don't. It destroys the privacy people have in their little streets not to mention the noise pollution. I think there are enough restaurants. It would be a pity if houses in the Old City become like those in the historic city centers of Europe, restaurants and discos. The idea of three restaurants around me is making me consider moving somewhere else within the Old City.

Long-term residents not only complained of the influx of strangers to their otherwise secluded residential neighborhoods but also complained of noise and fumes, drunkenness, and loud or inconsiderate behavior. Some restaurant owners had their door attendants quietly instruct departing patrons to keep quiet in the alleys so that "a sick neighbor" would not be disturbed.

In 2002, Fathi, who worked with the CPOC, said that restaurants were allowed in neighborhoods as long as they preserved *"adabiyat al-mintaqah"* (morals of the area); now chaos prevailed, as Hikmat Shatta wrote about in his editorial. According to Fathi, religious prohibitions for each neighborhood should be observed, but he reduced these injunctions to the consumption of alcohol which forced some and restaurants that served alcohol in Muslim quarters to be closed. By 2004, there were several restaurants in the traditionally Muslim quarters that openly served alcohol, and many complaints were lodged against restaurants regardless of what they served and where they were located for reasons not limited to their beverage menu. Such was the case with Opalin, mentioned in the Introduction, located deep in the Shaghur neighborhood, but it was owned by the sons of the then vice-president Khaddam and therefore immune from prosecution. When Khaddam resigned from his post and left Syria for exile in France the state expropriated his and his sons' property. There were rumors that another government official had taken over the management of Opalin. Other restaurants in Qimarriyyah, a predominantly Muslim neighborhood, also served alcohol, but then as management and ownership changed so did alcohol policies. Many Muslims in Syria drink alcohol. Restaurants that serve alcohol tend serve drinks to whomever orders.

Restaurants also perpetuated generalizations of neighborhoods based on sectarian differences where alcohol has become a new marker of Muslim and Christian difference. Drinking alcohol is forbidden in Islam but just because it is condoned in Christianity does not mean Christians consume it freely. Moreover, restaurants reduced sectarian characteristics to certain stereotypical practices and were also fixing boundaries among the neighborhoods in the Old City where in the past they were fluid. Nonetheless, focusing on where alcohol could be served as the cause of friction between restaurant owners and residents ignored other equally important objections. Neighborhood occupants regardless of religious affiliation did not like to see outsiders roaming in semiprivate neighborhoods nor did they appreciate the increase in the air and noise pollution.

The ethnic and sectarian composition of neighborhoods in the Old City survived from the late Ottoman period, even with the movement of people in and out of the intramural neighborhoods. As Fathi once said, each neighborhood attracted people of the same religion and social class. Newcomers were expected to integrate in the neighborhood and not change the neighborhood to suit their values. The *mustathmir*, who focused more on the quality of the house and its access to the main streets instead of the neighborhood's social composition and values, wanted the neighborhood to change to accommodate his presence. The neighborhoods differed in their thresholds for tolerating disturbances created by the restaurants. Fathi like many in Syria maintained that the protection of morals in the neighborhoods was more widespread inside than outside the wall. One of the biggest challenges for the CPOC was the attempt to introduce legislation to preserve the tranquility of the residential neighborhoods. I was walking in Bab Tuma on a Friday night, amid throngs of pedestrians and revelers, including young men traveling in packs. A woman standing at the entrance of the cul-de-sac that led to her house yelled at a group of young men who wanted to enter, saying, "there is nothing, there are no restaurants or cafés only houses why do you want to go in there." The anger in her voice frightened me and the men probably sensed it too and continued on their way. The anger was probably the frustration experienced by those who lacked control over the transformations to their neighborhood.

The number of grievances logged with the CPOC against restaurants increased exponentially throughout the Old City. Long-term residents complained about the noise of loud patrons and music. The air quality was another issue since many of these restaurants served water pipes and the smell of tobacco was overpowering in the alleys. These complaints created tensions between investors and inhabitants, which in some cases led to lawsuits. In recent surveys and polls by the CPOC, residents preferred hotels to restaurants. Hotels were perceived as less disruptive, quieter, and

better for the neighborhood.[6] Therefore, they were not against the investment opportunities in the Old City but wanted to participate in decision-making process and ensure that their concerns and grievances are
addressed.

Majid summed up the contradictions of restaurants in the Old City by
placing them within the wider discourses of heritage and social hierarchies
discussed in previous chapters. As a Shami living in the Old City, he continued to blame the deterioration of the historic center on rural migrants.
The CPOC and government encouraged investments in the Old City but
did not plan for the disruption they would cause. Restaurants were changing the spatial practices in the Old City if only by attracting visitors from
outside the Old City to the residential neighborhoods. Although some
inhabitants could not afford to go to these new venues, restaurants also
restricted the type of consumer they aimed to attract, thereby creating
new forms of inclusion and exclusion in the Old City.

No Status, No "Shami" Identity, No Service

The owners of al-Makan did not advertise their new restaurant, and during the interview, they did not tell me its name. I found it out when I
saw the sign for the restaurant. The owners were circumspect about the
date of the opening and the clientele they aimed to attract. One partner admitted that it was through their connections they hoped to build
a solid clientele. They knew the people they wanted as regulars, and in
the words of the owner, from "mouth to ear, people I know will bring
others." The restaurant was geared toward clients who were of a certain
social class. Much like the high-end coffee shops in Cairo, restaurants
become "controlled" and "socially closed" spaces that allow owners to
"secure an unambiguously classy clientele" (de Koning 2009, 534, 541).

---

6. One issue with hotels, especially in the time of political upheaval in Syria, is they
rely on tourism. There have been reports that hotels have taken in displaced people so this
could be a new use for them in times of crisis. Restaurants, however, can operate because
they cater to a local consumer base.

Customers need to feel comfortable being seen in the restaurant and to maintain their social distinction in an open public place by avoiding contact with lower classes. Restaurant owners in Damascus were upholding the boundaries that already existed among the different social groups outside the restaurant. The social hierarchy was no longer confined to the Shami-rural binary but encapsulated taste for aesthetic and an appreciation for heritage. At Opalin, a golf cart ferried passengers from Straight Street, where they parked their cars, through narrow alleys that led to the restaurants so that customers did not have to walk in the Old City and risk contamination.

Although restaurants also catered to tourists, they were more selective when it came to local customers. Foreign tourists offered another challenge for many restaurants in the Old City. Owners willingly accommodate tourists, because they were sometimes charged more than locals. As transient customers, tourists were not subjected to local social scrutiny because they were not part of the social politics in Syria. Nonetheless, it was a delicate issue to deal with tourists. Many restaurants did not want to be perceived as tourist establishments that deterred locals.

Prices at many restaurants (typically entrées ran from five to seven hundred Syrian pounds in 2008) were well beyond the reach of the majority of Syrians, where the per capita income in 2008 was US$4,800.[7] Some establishments subtly dissuaded undesired clients. Staff would tell local customers that there were no reservations. The staff was also well aware of 'asl and how it was manifested in accent, in clothes, and in behavior. One restaurant owner was blunt: "Each restaurant has its customers." Hence, restaurants maintained the local practice of discriminating among people, based not only on their 'asl (as we saw in chapter 2) but also on the type of consumers they wished to attract under new economic conditions. Restaurants retained the spatial distinction for consumers who lived outside the wall in segregated neighborhoods based on class. These spaces of consumption were not for residents, but for visitors from outside the Old City, so they could be introduced to the heritage of the Old City. Since

7. Exchange rate during this period hovered at 50 sp = US$1.

the middle and upper classes avoided the Old City because it was a site of "backwardness," restaurants had to create a safe and sanitized environment that protected them from the "polluting" effect of the intramural neighborhoods by allowing them to intermingle with others of their ilk even in the Old City.

No restaurateur I interviewed openly admitted to their exclusionary practices or the type of clientele they wanted to attract. However, each restaurant developed a reputation and was favored by a specific group. Yet one group that seemed to be always discriminated against were young men, who were turned away by establishments that wanted to appear family friendly or safe for women. Young men were perceived as a potential problem because of the probability they might misbehave and cause discomfort for young women or families. Anouk De Koning (2009) examined the politics of gender and class in upscale Cairo where coffee shops and restaurants used "social closure" to appeal to upper-class men and women, excluding members of the lower classes. Sawalha (2012) described how some Beirut coffeehouses catered to the middle class and intellectuals before the war. Although coffeehouses were largely a male domain, some women felt comfortable transgressing the gender divide in upscale Beirut coffeehouses (92). Expensive restaurants and coffeehouses proliferated after the end of the civil war in Beirut. However, they excluded the typical preconflict clientele, which reduced the available venues for middle-class women to socialize outside the home.

In a fascinating reversal of gender roles, I had seen nightclubs prevent groups of young men entry unless they had a female chaperone. Certain coffee shops and restaurants in conservative areas or that catered to a more traditional crowd had two sections, one for families and another for young men. Although these establishments were not quite recreating the haremlik and salemlik of the courtyard house, the concept was similar, in that segregation was based on status and gender. The gaze of young men was threatening to the social order inside the restaurant. However, men with families were allowed to sit among other women they were not related to since a young man within a family will not misbehave. Hence, restaurants that appealed to Syrians from outside the Old City made semiprivate alleys more public but created semipublic private spaces for their clientele. Some establishments created comfortable environments for intellectuals, trendy hipsters, or high-ranking government officials. In some ways, the bayt 'arabi retained aspects of its restrictive access even as a restaurant.

Return or Exodus?

Nidal, the architect who worked on the conversion of al-Makan into a restaurant, was not sure whether opening restaurants preserved the Old City. "What are we going to preserve?" he asked. "Buildings, social networks, there are lots of deserted houses in ruins. *Shuwam* don't live in these houses. Do people who come from rural areas to live here for cheap rent, do they have the same responsibility?" He added: "Things are moving in a direction, and I am not sure if it is positive or negative. I don't necessarily think it's a negative thing. It could be constructive in a place where nothing was happening socially and economically, so this is good."

The impact of social change on the historic neighborhoods remains largely unaddressed and the fast pace of gentrification renders any solution temporary. As we have seen in this chapter, mustathmirin created an idealized bayt 'arabi through weaving emotions, nostalgia, local discourses on social hierarchies and distinction. However, creating a Shami "theme park" to evoke nostalgic memories of a home, merged preservation with urban development in the Old City, and brought to the forefront the challenges of using market strategies to decide unresolved relations between collective memory, local history, and development (Page and Mason 2004, 16).

Many long-term residents appreciated the services and the positive publicity restaurants brought to the intramural neighborhoods after decades of neglect and negative hype. They were able to show pride in their residential neighborhoods that now attracted elite visitors, from outside the wall. Yet to return to Majid's attempt (discussed at the beginning of the chapter) to joke about the situation, the high number of restaurants concentrated in a relatively small area created new problems and challenged the notion of community and privacy in the Old City. Moreover, there were concerns about what was actually being preserved in these establishments whose main purpose was to generate profit. This concern is fueling the civilizational anxiety over the future of the Old City and compounding local fear that the preservation of the historic quarter could lead to its destruction. The next chapter brings together the challenges of gentrification and heritage preservation in the Old City that have been mentioned throughout the text, examining the meanings and causes of civilizational anxiety and what this means for the future of the Old City and Syria.

6
"Who Has No Old Has No New"

We met Salim, the architect and investor, several times in the preceding pages. On this occasion, I was walking through a dilapidated bayt ʿarabi, which, according to Salim, once served as the Austrian Embassy in Damascus during the early twentieth century. He was describing how he would restore it, given the chance. He shared his thoughts with me on preserving the built heritage of the Old City and why it was important: "The new has its space; why should I destroy the old? I go outside [the Old City] to build. If you see any house built out of concrete in old Damascus no matter how beautiful it is, it is deviant (*shadh*). *No matter how beautiful it is, it will still be shadh* [his emphasis]. If I want to build something new, I go outside the Old City."

Salim, like many Damascenes I have met, supported the "dual city," where the contrast between the modern and traditional in Damascus is a physical manifestation of social and discursive binaries modernity–tradition, urban–rural, Shami–rural migrants, "civilized"–"backward." The interplay between these contrasting modes of being also allowed social actors to construct their understanding of cultural and social change. Under new economic conditions, actors continued to negotiate the spatial distinction between the new and Old City, to make sense of their rapidly changing world as well as their place in it.

I felt like playing the devil's advocate and waited for him to pause in his praise of old houses and old cities and why they should be preserved before I asked, "But why bother? Who really cares?" He was taken aback, and I felt bad. He had graciously taken me on tours to several of the properties he had purchased in the Old City, which were in various stages of conversion into restaurants and hotels. He assisted me in my research by introducing me to other investors. On numerous occasions, he had asked me to try to convey the "true" meaning and significance of the Old City in my work because he believed I shared his passion for the preservation of the Old City and understood the value of its heritage. After a long pause, he finally said, "*hik inti kharabti al-dinya*" [with this you have ruined the world]. I laughed but insisted, "Seriously, why preserve?" It was then that he rationalized his position with: "There is a saying *'ili ma lu qadim ma 'ilu jadid*" [who has no old has no new]. How they used to think, they used to think in a correct way, and we today cannot think in their way. The way they used to build was one hundred percent correct."

By appealing to a common saying, Salim legitimized the authority of the past in addressing present concerns and issues. As shown in chapter 2, issues of the past in the present and the role of heritage were the basis of the debate on modernity and tradition in Syrian society. In the current gentrification, these issues become the center of the debate on the historic preservation of the Old City. Salim is expanding on the meaning of turath (heritage) to include the vernacular past and is according it the same authority as the written classical heritage to guide and instruct the present. Embedded in the bayt 'arabi is the knowledge needed to make sense of the present, which is revealed to social actors as they restore the house. Architects, returnees, and investors who are committed citizens and are attached to the nation are able to unravel the code of the past and use it to guide their actions in the present to build a better future. In fact, the gentrification of the Old City allowed ordinary individuals to navigate the issue of the past in the present in daily urban experiences.

Salim did not consider the past alien or foreign; rather, it was pure "one hundred percent" correct and therefore the authentic guide for living in the present. His respect for the past, though idealized and fabricated, reveals how he defines his role in the current gentrification of the Old City. He creates a continuous genealogy of builders beginning with the anonymous individuals who perfected the courtyard house to the recent architects who restore them. In his work, he aims to emulate these early builders in technique and commitment. The superiority of the older generations of builders was largely the result of their way of seeing; their attention to detail, their craftsmanship, and their skill in working with locally available materials to construct houses that have survived to the present in one form or other using simple technology. Perhaps this is why Salim used shadh (deviant) to describe the introduction of anything from the modern period onto the tradition of the bayt 'arabi. Although we have seen in chapters 3, 4, and 5 how the courtyard house continued to evolve to accommodate new tastes in fashions and innovations in building methods, gentrification of the Old City required freezing the courtyard house in time and place (Brumann 2009, 277). Salim was harsh in his condemnation of any form of innovation in the house as shadh, thereby revealing his lack of faith in modernity to resolve contemporary social problems. His use of the term also underlined not only the "aura" of a supposedly "pure" past but also how caution is needed in the restoration process to avoid the introduction of elements that might dilute the authority of the past. Moreover, Salim did not name "them" as Shuwam, preferring a more anonymous social group that could encompass anyone who was part of this legacy, regardless of their 'asl.

The valorization of the past and its producers led to new concerns as how best to preserve their legacy, especially by those with no Shami 'asl, as demonstrated in chapter 4. By acknowledging the past, Salim also justified his own modifications in the reconstruction and preservation process, where he did not hesitate to use modern material and building techniques. He admitted to the use of shortcuts in his own construction projects because of financial or time constraints, but his admission emphasized the different historical moment under which he labored. Although his work in technique and product will not approximate that of the builders of yore, the fact that he is aware and in awe of their superior craftsmanship preempts any criticism of his work.

In this concluding chapter, I bring together the different strands that I have introduced in the preceding pages on the meanings and uses of "civilization" and "backwardness" in the gentrification of the Old City My question still stands, why preserve the past? I seek to examine an answer to this inquiry that expounds on the role of the past in navigating present concerns. One of the major social and political challenges in the current gentrification of the Old City is civilizational anxiety. The civilizational anxiety we encountered in the previous chapters, especially with how investors expounded on the meaning of the vernacular past in their projects, is creating a new fear that heritage preservation is actually heritage loss.

I begin this chapter with local discourse on civilizational anxiety, expressed in the cityscape. I explore how this anxiety is rooted in the fear of al-ghazu thaqafi (cultural invasion) that attacks the essence of being Shami from within and has severe consequences for Syrian national identity and unity (Salamandra 2004, 19). Local social actors are the villains especially individuals who are ignorant of the past; hence, they are more destructive than an actual enemy invasion. I also examine how this ignorance illustrates the contemporary national malaise. The rise in anxiety over al-ghazu thaqafi correlates with the instability in the region, especially with the increase in the influx of global investment capital into vulnerable local economies. As some concerned Damascenes complained, it was difficult to track global capital, and they wondered whether investment came from groups hostile to Syria, an insidious form of Trojan horse investing that will destroy the essence of the Syrian national identity from within. Moreover, the increase in foreign direct investment coincided with the aftermath of 9/11 when many rich, oil-producing Gulf countries were wary of investing in the West and sought regional opportunities. The influx of capital in Syria from these Gulf states was invested in real estate and the heritage industry. Government agencies that supervised the preservation of the Old City were under scrutiny, for fear they are participating in destroying what they claimed to protect as they conceded to powerful Gulf interests. Although some Syrians interpret foreign investment as another plot by the Ba'th regime to profit from the destruction of the country, neoliberalism undermines national solidarity and pivots state interests toward creating a business-friendly environment rather than protecting social welfare (Harvey 2005). I conclude this chapter and the book with a summary on the impact of gentrification on the Old City. This chapter will be followed by an epilogue to address the ongoing civil war in Syria and to extrapolate about the future of gentrification of the Old City during the crisis.

Civilizational Anxiety

One evening I went to the movies with Tariq and George, two young men I had gotten to know while living in Harat Hananya. We decided to walk from the Old City to the movie theater in Sha'lan. Halfway, we passed a park built where once stood a local market that sold fruits, vegetables, meat, fish, live goldfish, pigeons, chicken, turkeys, small household animals, spices, household items, and clothes. Vendors had stalls inside a makeshift barrack with cement walls, dirt floor, and a tin roof. Almost overnight, the vendors were gone, the barracks razed to the ground, and grass planted over the vacated space. The suq became a little green space in a bustling part of the city. Although it was evening, some vendors, perhaps the former stall owners, were selling sundry items on the sidewalk. I said, "*Haram*-[what a pity] they did away with the market." But my companions were not sympathetic. Tariq mocked me, replying, "*Shu haram? kan hatha manthar hadari*?!" [What do you mean a pity? Was that a civilized sight?]" I was taken aback by the emotion in Tariq's voice and decided not to argue over the use of urban space.

This incident is significant because it led me to think about the changes in the Old City in terms of "hadarah" and "takhalluf." It also offered insight on another important aspect of urban renewal: how social actors wanted to live in a physical environment that reflected them. As an American expressing sympathy for what local users considered to be a filthy and noisy nuisance in the center of a modern city, I was perpetuating the image of Damascus, and by implication Tariq and George, as "backward" though that was not my intention. The vendors' point of view was inconsequential in our debate because they transgressed on urban space and created a village market. George and Tariq believed the vendors were in the wrong for the pollution they caused not only to the city but to its "civilization"; therefore, as polluters, they had no right to the city. Pollution in this instance is not merely the selling of smelly livestock in an urban setting but performing acts that are out of place in the city. Moreover, with a contested urban identity where the Shuwam are pitted against rural migrants, pollution becomes important in creating social distinction (Douglas 1966, 161). Hence, the Old City and by extension Damascus represent the Shuwam, and they had to be protected from the pollution of rural migrants and their rustic ways.

The urban landscape, as a representation of the people, has long been an issue in Damascus. As Kevin Martin (2010) observed, the International Exhibition in Damascus in 1956 served as an opportunity to alleviate civilizational anxiety over "urban disorder," such as begging and street vagrancy that marred the image of the nation-state. By enforcing order in the city, the state modernizing agents and public intellectuals wanted to control the image of the nation and how it was viewed by international visitors to the exhibition. The exposition assumed the twofold purpose of representing Syria to the world and the citizen at home as "modern," "progressive," while possessing an "authentic" culture. The search for an authentic culture, as Martin explained, was threatened by the filth and chaos of Damascus streets that led to the exposition. Urban planners and government officials undertook the "proper ordering of Damascus's physical environment through the banishment of all forms of 'filth' [that] was absolutely fundamental to the overarching goal of the Damascus International Exposition, the ethnographic construction, and presentation of Syria's "true" identity to the outside world" (398). Although Martin did not explicate on what was the "true" identity, it was certainly not the armies of beggars, flies, and insects swarming the markets and pack animals in the streets of Damascus. Hence, the true identity was revealed by removing the what was defined as "filth," by the concerned citizens and reform-minded bureaucrats. As with other postcolonial states, in Syria "modern statecraft is largely a project of internal colonization often glossed, as it is in imperial rhetoric, as a "civilizing mission" (J. Scott 1998, 82). The promotion of order remains the "outward manifestation of authority," which is "necessary for the preservation of 'civilization'" (Herzfeld 2005a, 69).

Many Syrians today continue to worry about how visitors see their city and them, especially since they believe they are a "civilized" people, but the image one gets from the city is constantly one of "backwardness." Hence, the state and citizens fight against this image though they also clash over what causes "backwardness." It is this "cultural intimacy" (Herzfeld 2005a) where state and citizen converge in their national discourses to support gentrification and historic preservation. Not unlike in modern

Greece where Michael Herzfeld situated much of his discussion on "cultural intimacy" the preoccupation of Syrians with the pure past is also a reflection of "a deeply wounding sense of social, cultural, economic, and political dependency" (143). However, in Syria, political dependency is compounded by the lack of an effective political leadership that can withstand outside aggression. In addition, many Shuwam consider the current political leadership socially and culturally inferior and therefore unable to address the woes that afflict the nation. Several Damascenes did not think the state went far enough to remove "backwardness" but rather that it allowed it to flourish, thereby suffocating "civilization."

Despite this asymmetry where political power does not include social and cultural power, there were moments in the national history that brought the two sides together. George and Tariq, as two Syrians and Shuwam had no official capacity and visible links to the regime, yet they sided with the state when it removed the vendors from the center of Damascus. Many Damascenes did not show sympathy for dislocated residents when the state demolished certain neighborhoods in the city. Damascenes accepted these "improvements" regardless of the human costs since the displaced were considered not of the city and a source of pollution. Many Damascenes could be prevailed upon to accept state rhetoric owing to its power of persuasion (Ghannam 2002, 41) or its ability to induce citizens to "act as if" (Wedeen 1999, 6). Yet these explanations tend to view the subservient as homogeneous social actors, neglecting that they have competing interests as well as an ambiguous attitudes toward resistance (Ortner 1995, 175).

The rhetoric of pollution and cleanliness is embedded in the urban–rural divide and is used to construct social distinction. In the Old City this translates into the binary "civilization"–"backwardness." Furthermore, pollution and cleanliness underlines the relationship between Shuwam and the Ba'th regime because of its predominantly rural membership. However, the regime over the past forty years was also effective at infiltrating Syrian society and perhaps the resilience of the regime lies not only in its ability to coerce and enforce compliance but also in its ability to appropriate cultural behaviors from the Shuwam that furthers its political control. The situation in Syria provides an interesting case study where the political elite are not the social group with cultural capital. On the other hand, the Shuwam have the cultural capital but lost their political power when the Ba'th regime came to power. Although it is difficult to ascertain how this limitation shaped the outlook of the regime, it is indicative that the state initiated a series of "civilizing" projects approximating the Shami ideal city. The political elite in Syria, especially before economic liberalization, lived and socialized with other elites in Damascus, and their children studied in public schools and universities. The al-Asad sons and their cohort among the political elite were known in Damascus and socialized in hotels, restaurants, and even nightclubs where other Damascenes, including the Shuwam, went. Therefore, they were not immune from local discourses on "civilization" and "backwardness." As a regime that uses all means possible to ensure its survival, it is not above regurgitated local discourses in its public policy and social work.

The Old City became a designated heritage site because local activists called on the state to protect it from demolition. The state was able to comply with the demand of activists when the patrimony of the heritage site was appropriated for purposes of the regime. As I mentioned in chapter 2, Damascus eventually became "Dimashq al-Asad," as proclaimed on streets signs, much to the distaste of the Shuwam. As Talal Asad (1987, 606) explained, power does not seek to control the ways people "perceive reality," only the ways they act "autonomously." I would go further to add that power facilitates the process of domination if it appropriates people's "perception of reality" to induce actions that do not contradict with what people already do but that further the power of the state.

Therefore, it is no surprise many Syrians such as Tariq and George supported the gentrification of the Old City and the rest of Damascus because it brought back hadarah, not only in the historical sense, but also in the practices and behaviors considered "civilized" and appropriate for being in a city such as Damascus. Tariq considered the market to be too rustic and chaotic for many residents of Damascus. The barracks did not constitute nor reflect any particular civilization and the location in the center of the city was visible to visitors and travelers. Tariq thought it reflected poorly on Damascus and its inhabitants. The selling and buying that took place in the market in the center of Damascus was more appropriate in a village square or a temporary market on the outskirts of town. Its location harmed the sensibility of some Damascus residents such as Tariq; the appearance of the city reflected on him. The suq also covered the *wajh hadari* (civilized face) of the city and its inhabitants, and therefore, it had to be removed. Therefore, urban renewal revealed the "true face" of the city hidden under layers of rural pollution.

The Other in the City

It is significant that much of this local discourse on the "backward other" in Syria was in part the legacy of colonialism . National independence did not necessarily lead to the *"decolonization of representation"* or the dismantling of the "organized authoritative knowledge . . . that operated discursively to produce effects of Truth about the colonized" (D. Scott 1999, 12; emphasis in the original). Therefore, how local practices were categorized as "civilized" or "backward" reflected the established representations that emerged from the authoritative colonial knowledge in French urban planning. The French completed the process of isolating the Old City from the rest of Damascus, physically by ring roads but by also claiming it was unhygienic. On the other hand, its civilizational history should be preserved for their aesthetic and economic value. Therefore, under the French, the "backward" and "civilized" binary associated the lack of sanitation with the former and heritage with the latter.

Since Edward Said's seminal work *Orientalism* (1978) described how locating the other in the Orient allowed Europeans to formulate their geography of power, there were many variations on the power of representation. In his work on global consumerism in India, William Mazzarella (2003, 138) used "auto-orientalism" to describe the "use of globally recognized signifiers of Indian 'tradition' to facilitate the aspirational consumption, by Indians, of a culturally marked self." However, Herzfeld (2005a, 69; see also Herzfeld 1991, 16) used the term "practical orientalism" and its counterpart "practical occidentalism" to denote "the contested but authoritative valorization of Western cultural in people's daily life." In the Old City, both of these terms apply. "Auto-orientalism" is when members of the new class in Syria acquire a taste for an idealized Shami identity in the Old City. However, "practical orientalism" is a more immediate concern in the gentrification of the Old City because "civilizing" agents try to approximate Western ideals on sanitation and order in their urban planning. Orientalism "enters the encompassing realm of everyday sociality and sensual habit" (Herzfeld 2005a, 134) to reinforce the binary in the lived experiences of the "civilized" and the "backward."

Henri Lefebvre wrote how "the city, as consummate reality is falling apart" and the "historic city no longer has a coherent set of prescriptions, of use of time linked to symbols and to a style" (1996, 148). As a result, the historic city is an "object of cultural consumption for tourists, for a estheticism, avid for spectacles and the picturesque" and that it is "no longer lived" nor "understood practically" (148). Thus, the gentrification of the Old City imposed "estheticism" on a historic but viable city that privileged a culturally marked Shami identity, to reclaim "civilization" for a new emerging group of cultural consumers, marginalizing those who did not share or were unable to share the same consumption practices. Khost believed gentrification was challenging in an urban space that was not abandoned but teeming with daily life: "the problem with the Old City, it is too alive," and this created problems with the heritage preservation projects that aimed to stifle the thriving aspect of intramural neighborhoods that did not fit with the "civilized" image. Though historic preservation in the Old City of Damascus was about the return to "civilization" and rescuing the essence of being "civilized" from a polluted present, the process of gentrification and heritage preservation were being marred by concerns over ghazu thaqafi (cultural invasion). We see the external threat to the essence of "civilization" become prevalent among social actors who were concerned that some efforts at removing "backwardness" were actually doing the opposite.

Cultural Invasion

Lack of consistency in the interpretation of "civilization" alarmed some activists, who feared it was creating chaos in the Old City and diluting the local Shami identity. Muhannad was an architect who held several high-ranking positions in the Department of Antiquities. This is how he described preservation: "Protection and preservation for cities of a universal history is a kind of *takamul* [integration] that has to be compatible with the local region." By compatible, he meant socially, culturally, and technologically, with what came before. He was concerned that many restoration and renovation projects in the Old City lacked takamul because people were ignorant of the history of the local civilizations. He gave me an example:

> When Thahir [Baybars] built al-Thahiriyyah he did so using symbols that were in use and were known to the people. Today, there is *khalal* [gap or shortcoming] in the levels of thinking. Today, part of this *thaqafa* [culture or education] is missing. Of course, Thahir destroyed houses, but what he built was based on and from the city. The city was built from *muqawmat* [fundamentals] and whereas before there was a strategy, today there is *mizajya* [moodiness]; whatever I want to do, I do. This is where it is dangerous because there are ideas that are not from the region.[1]

Muhannad used the Mameluke leader as an example to demonstrate the authority of the past. His approach to the past is similar to Salim's, and Muhannad also believes in the past things were done in a correct manner when social actors were embedded in local social practices and did not deviate from the expected norms. The destruction of the city by Baybars, according to Muhannad, did not damage the essence of the local culture because what he built was a continuum with the built environment and spatial practices. Muhannad hermeneutically interpreted the past to give it the authority it needed in the present, though all civilizations were not sealed from one another and were known to exchange cultural knowledge. Yet he insists on a pure past to address concerns in the present where social actors bypass their history and borrow extensively from other cultures. Though the blame is on ignorance, it is more than that. Social actors who are ignorant can study their past; rather what concerns Muhannad

---

1. Thahir Baybrs was one of the Mameluke leaders, and al-Thahiriyyah was the library he built in Damascus and where he is also buried.

is the willful ignorance and the lack of respect for history that he attributes to the new mentality.

Muhannad was upset with the individualism he believed influences the course of the gentrification of the Old City. The moodiness he speaks of stems from rootless social actors who are concerned with their immediate comforts and needs. These individuals, much like Munir in chapter 4 who painted the outside of his courtyard house in bright colors, fragment the social fabric. The new economic conditions are encouraging a new idiosyncratic mentality that might be good for business but harms the communal and national well-being. However, it is also about further weakening an already fragmented society. To borrow new ideas and innovation when the nation is weak is dangerous because the new cannot be made to fit in with the local culture and remains either shadh or creates a gap between people and their culture. The gap can lead to alienation and the eventual destruction of local culture from within.

Although working with the government in a decision-making capacity, Muhannad implied he was powerless in preventing the idiosyncrasy of investors in their project. There was the strong implication the new alliance between the regime and private investors has left many bureaucrats vulnerable. Though the role of bureaucrats was to implement government policy, in this instance, the implementation of the preservation guidelines would harm business interests supported by the state. The regime was not interested in solving this impasse since it could be used to further its own dominance. Some of the staff at the Department of Antiquities and the Committee for the Protection of the Old City (CPOC) were concerned with the future of the Old City, yet felt helpless to do anything about it. However, the discourse over cultural invasion reflected local anxieties concerning the ability of the state to protect the nation-state from external threats. If it allows social fragmentation, how could it unite the nation against foreign aggression.

Ahmad, who also worked with the CPOC, expressed the same worry regarding cultural invasion when he advised me to "write history from the vocabulary of history," which he explained was the remains of the numerous empires in the cityscape. The vocabulary was the continuity in the theme from one civilization to the next. As Ibn Khaldun noted: "It is only with the passage of centuries of uninterrupted development that civilization takes roots in a city" (Mahdi 1964, 213). The similarities in views between the architect and historian reflect wider anxiety over the future of the city as a site of civilization. Although there have been several attempts at a temporal and spatial rupturing of the Old City, the current economic conditions might actually allow it to happen since preservation is privatized with the aim of producing and marketing a commodified local ethnic identity for global consumption.

Muhannad and Ahmad insist on an imagined continuous past to define what Ahmad called *wihdah hadarya* (oneness of civilization) that many argue gave Damascus its longevity, since it remained relevant to each successive layer. Because both men were not Syrian but Arab, they maintained the pan-Arab identity of Damascus, which included its Shami identity. Nonetheless, there is an element of essentialism in their discourse on "civilization," which harkens to the role of the past in the present and to the issue of authenticity in the gentrification of the Old City. Although we have seen earlier how Naji and others were disturbed by the innovations of some of the returnees in the restoration of the bayt 'arabi, here we have government officials expressing the same apprehension; however, their concern is for a more inclusive monumental past associated with pan-Arabism. They argue for the use of heritage to create national unity against "external interference or internal subversion, the effects of which can only be faced with a reassertion of the essence of the historical subjectivity" (Al-Azmeh 1993, 42).

Hani who worked with the CPOC was enraged by the lax standards of some of his colleagues when speaking about a house restored by a European. He worried many of the architects working in the government offices to protect the Old City lacked the experience and the knowledge of the local civilization, and unwittingly allowed for a cultural invasion to occur. He claimed an European returnee *shawah* (marred) Arab architecture: "There is a Quran verse in the bathroom; this is a direct violation of Arab traditions." He blamed the architects of the CPOC and the construction workers who he thought allowed this transgression. He believed the lack of standards in monitoring restoration projects derived from the ignorance of architects who were trained under the French. When I asked

Hani to explain he added, "They did not study architecture in theory or practice. This is all leading to the destruction of *the* built environment." He assumed the decolonization process is incomplete and believed the ignorance of the architect supervising the project as emblematic of the condition of the state. Any concession to heritage on part of the locals was part of the political concession by the state to foreign interests. Since the state is compromising on its territorial and geopolitical integrity, referring to the Israeli occupation of Golan, then one should not be surprised when employees of the state compromised on the purity of heritage. Moreover, by singling out a European returnee Hani implied people from the West are allowed certain liberties, even with the essence of the local "civilization," because they come from a powerful country and by association have power over locals. There is a refusal of the "valorization" of the West in local culture (Herzfeld 2005a, 68), but it is a rhetorical refusal because it cannot be supported with effective measures.

Hani believed a powerful and strong society that was able to protect its material culture could resist Western imperialism. Perhaps because he worked with the government he focused on external threats. Ghazu thaqafi underscored geopolitical concerns in a region not known for its stability where there have been periodic wars or civil unrest since the end of World War II. Although Syrian national struggles for independence occurred without bloodshed, the establishment of Israel in 1948 and the ensuing war began a series of conflicts that afflicted Syria, directly or indirectly. Fear of imperialism increased with globalization and neoliberalism, which created new economic opportunities for many but increased social and economic inequalities for most. What many believed was that a solid understanding of the history and an appreciation for the past is an effective weapon against external aggression and internal corruption.

Hence, cultural invasion underscores a fear of more loss in a nation that has not gained much. Hani, Muhannad, and Ahmad all bemoan loss—standards are lost, knowledge is lost, and eventually civilization is lost. As Muhannad summed his thoughts on the future of the Old City and Syria said: "Currently [Syrians] live under standards of lack, lack of technology and education. There is external control of these elements in which imperialism decides what kinds of standards it will give and to what end. They sometimes give inappropriate standards for a region. We have to be aware of this. In Damascus the archaeological remains are a reference." The belief in lack explains the appeal of nostalgia in the Syrian national practice. Perhaps, then it was no surprise that the weak national project should fall like a house of cards before the Arab uprising. There were already local concerns on the viability of national unity in the discourse of gentrification. Disagreements over the preservation of the courtyard house, the innovations in the restorations, and the liberties by investors in adding or removing essential elements in the house all belie the fragmentation of society.

What stops state bureaucrats, who should be in charge of overseeing the restoration of houses and the renovation of restaurants and hotels, from preventing this cultural invasion? State employees are aware of the dangers of innovations in the gentrification of Damascus, yet claim to be powerless. The role of the government and its representative in the preservation of the Old City was a contentious issue in the preservation of the Old City and showed the fissures between state and its employees, as the state became increasingly aligned with investors. Concerned government workers were also caught in interesting ways between the regime and the Shuwam on the one hand, and long-term residents on the other, as the gentrification of the Old City intensified. It is to this issue that we next turn.

Problems with the Government

The accusation of inefficiency and corruption by state bureaucrats can be seen as a lingering effect of the Ba'th regime employing rural migrants in government jobs on its assumption to power. Many long-term residents and investors did not think the CPOC was staffed by competent architects and experts in preservation and restoration. According to one architect, the CPOC "is run by people who are not qualified enough nor have enough power to enforce things." He went on to explain that there was neither direction nor a clear vision of how the Old City should be preserved. He also alluded to the lack of conservation experience and how most of the restoration work was done privately. He added, "It also did not make sense not to change the function of a room built 100 years ago. People these days like their bathrooms, next to, if not in their bedrooms and they should be able to have this."

Several investors I spoke to found obstruction to preservation work by the CPOC most frustrating. Officials took bribes to approve permits for restoration or renovations or to overlook violations. One long-term resident bragged how she paid over 1 million Syrian Pound to allow the violations in the rebuilding of a third story to her bayt 'arabi. However, some Syrians justified bribes as how employees compensate for their low public sector income. But corruption also allowed governments to be "constructed here in the imagination and the daily practices of ordinary people" (Gupta 1995, 390). It also channeled citizens' anger against the petty bureaucrats, instead of the regime. It is these public sector workers that become the obstacle to progress and development by their backward practice of accepting and demanding bribes. Bribe taking also showed their lack of concern for the common good, and by accepting kickbacks, they allowed foreign elements to mar the civilization of the Old City, which amounted to a crime of treason that largely went unpunished.

However, some Syrians claimed that the regime allowed corrupted bureaucrats because they were vested in maintaining a regime in place that overlooked their transgression. Furthermore, the regime could instigate campaigns to clean up corruption that gained public support, but were really about eliminating individuals that became a threat to the regime. This was happened before Bashar came to power and where he led a campaign to purge corruption from the regime, which many heralded as a break with the past but others saw it as eliminating any opposition to his succeeding his father. These disparate, and apparently contradictory aims, reinforced the power of the regime and the state by being inconsistent in their objectives and random in their exercise of power. They also revealed the complex layers in the workings of state power in Syria.

But as George reminded me on numerous occasions when I brought up the corruption of the CPOC, "even in Britain there is corruption and it's supposed to be a modern Western nation. [Mohamed] Fayed bribed a member of parliament to get citizenship, and this is Britain where it is a hundred times better than the US. So bribes happen everywhere." He wanted me to know that corruption was not endemic just to Syria.

Whereas corruption in Britain existed, the British still had faith in their government and its institutions. Moreover, they could speak against it, and there was a free press to criticize the British government in ways that was not possible to do in Syria.

In Rome, charges of corruption were also rampant against the state, but which Michael Herzfeld (2009, 119–20) understood as a form of social exchange: "Reading the laws as model texts and their infringement as instances of failure in practice, which prejudges the situation in terms of decontextualized concepts such as efficiency and democracy, I prefer to examine their content for evidence of what we can call 'structural collusion': the mutual engagement of legislators and citizens in pragmatic compromises that allow life to go on—not always satisfactorily to be sure, but at least comprehensively." In Damascus, corruption certainly becomes a form of social exchange that also allowed daily life to proceed.

Many restaurant owners also complained that the CPOC impeded rather than facilitated their work, especially when it came to the interpretation of the preservation law. The investors, long-term residents, and even architects of the CPOC acknowledged that the preservation law was *ta'baneh* (literally tired, outdated insufficient). The ineffectiveness of the guidelines is the result of their vagueness that allows for open interpretation. However, the inadequate guidelines have not hindered the gentrification of the Old City, and both investors and bureaucrats find ways to move forward. Moreover, the CPOC and the Department of Antiquities were trying to remedy the situation, but they always seem to lag behind global and local forces they could not control. An employee of the CPOC summed it up, "Residents have a problem with money and houses are now expensive after not being worth anything before, so we prefer not to show the master plan to people. Unfortunately, we are following the problem. We can't go ahead. We tried to pre-plan in the beginning in the mid-1980s and now you see what happened. I regret not being able to control everything but I can't. No one can when there is money." The government agencies supervising the heritage site lost their authority and ability to influence urban change.

Moreover, the rivalry among the various agencies that included tourism and the Department of Sanitation as well as the CPOC and the

Department of Antiquities revealed the lack of coordination within the government. A September 3, 2000, article in the newspaper *Al-Sharq al-'Wsat* described the bureaucracy facing many investors when several government ministries and agencies were involved in the preservation process. In addition to the CPOC and Department of Antiquities, to open a restaurant or hotel an investor required a license from the Ministry of Tourism. The Department of Health also had to weigh in on restoration efforts in ways that contradicted the CPOC and antiquities historic preservation guidelines. One owner of a restaurant complained about the many government agencies involved in the restoration process and how it led to confusion and stalemate. For instance, the Department of Antiquities did not want ceramic tiles in the kitchen and bathrooms, but the Department of Health insisted for hygienic reasons. Therefore, two representatives of the government agencies clashed until some decision was reached; meanwhile, work on the project came to a halt. However, inefficiency in bureaucratic procedure is not "only circumscribed from above" (Herzfeld 1991, 196) but is the result of different agendas by the different ministries. As mentioned earlier, the Ministry of Tourism emphasized investment (*taswih*) over the Ministry of Culture's concern for protecting the heritage site from overuse, which some quipped would dissipate (*tasyih*) the very heritage the tourist came to see. In addition, there was the Governorate of Damascus and its responsibility for the daily management of the Old City. These often contradicting aims of competing agencies caused confusion, despite the many committees formed to coordinate among the government ministries.

As a result, many investors and long-term residents blatantly disregarded preservation and renovation guidelines, a move that created different forms of heritage. Sometimes violators were never apprehended, their transgression ignored or overlooked; other times, bribery or the intercession of a high-ranking officials was required. But not all violators were lucky. A bayt 'arabi in Harat Hananya was being refurbished as a hotel, but I noticed that work had stopped for quite a while. I became curious since these projects were usually time sensitive. One day as I was walking by, I saw that the front door was open, and I slipped inside. I saw a guard talking to a worker who was hauling away stone tiles. The guard seemed friendly enough; he did not ask me to leave even though I was trespass-ing. I asked the guard, "Did the owner go bankrupt?" because I could not think of another reason for the lack of activity. "*Khalaf* (he violated)," he answered and pointed to the third floor that was illegally added using cement and steel beams visible from the street. I would not have thought a mustathmir would have been careless about this obvious violation and though I had seen the illegal third floor, I assumed he had found a willing government official to bribe. According to the guard, the owner was look-ing for a buyer who could deal with the CPOC and resolve the issue of the illegal floor. If the CPOC insisted on pressing charges on the violation, the third floor had to be removed.

Furthermore, government ministries owned some of buildings in the Old City, such as schools and mosques. With typical bureaucratic arro-gance, the Ministries of Religion and Education dismissed the preserva-tion laws when they were renovating or building schools and mosques. They also seemed to be immune to prosecution and beyond the juris-diction of the CPOC and Department of Antiquities. Several beautiful mosques from the nineteenth century were destroyed and rebuilt with stone, cement, and iron beams and much larger than their original size. Moreover, concessions were given to foreign governments that violated the preservation guidelines. The Iranian government was allowed to recon-struct a mosque in the Old City in a style inconsistent with the local built environment, and which required the destruction of dozens of nearby courtyard houses. Hence, the state worked in an "elusive, disorganized, and inchoate" manner that undermined its own efforts at planning (Bis-sell 2011, 113). Urban plans are not just about the built environment but "encoded within them are cultural visions and social statements that pro-vide blueprints for urban lives and space" (Bissell 2011, 315). Even the best intentions by state planners fail not only to achieve their stated objectives but also to make irreversible improvements in the daily lives of citizens (J. Scott 1998; Bissell 2011, 320). As the citizens in Syria were calling for the state to be more organized, efficient, and consistent in the preservation of the Old City, it became more random.

Mr. Turki, who we met in chapter 4, complained about another short-coming of the bureaucracy of the state when he described the ordeal of finalizing the sale of the house, which reflected the challenges of shifting from a command to a market economy. He described how he dealt with all the heirs when he bought the bayt 'arabi. These houses tended to be listed in the name of several owners, regardless of who actually lived in them. As he waited patiently for residents to figure out other living arrangements, he discovered that there were back taxes on the bayt for several years. He could not register the house in his name until the taxes were paid. State officials did not collect unpaid property taxes until the house was sold. Then they blocked the transaction until the back taxes were paid usually by the new owner. Although Mr. Turki considered this another example of government inefficiency and bureaucratic failure, it signals another important and significant aspect of Syrian bureaucracy. Bureaucrats conducted their work based on informal social relations and local social rhythm rather than imposing the bureaucratic rationality of order and organization. Therefore, they maintained relations in the neighborhoods. The employees in the tax revenue office waited for houses and businesses to be sold to collect overdue taxes. Bureaucracy in Syria had its own definition of efficiency and rationality that was in keeping with local practices and norms.

However, as Herzfeld (1991, 195; 2005a, 207–8) astutely noted, bureaucrats in general and those working in conservation are always beholden to their superiors where the capriciousness of authority is transmitted to their dealings with citizens. Government workers are caught in a delicate bind between their superiors and the people. They also tend to reside in the same community and neighborhoods as the people they serve. Hence, their exercise of power has to be well thought out because excessive use of power by the bureaucrat might lead to "social exclusion" (Herzfeld 1991, 196). Hence, the arbitrariness in which they execute the little power they have could be interpreted as the bureaucrat's attempt at performing "resistance" (Herzfeld 2005a, 208). In Damascus, the low-level bureaucrats who monitored the preservation of the Old City were not met with much respect. They were considered a nuisance to the investors and the fact that they were easily bribed contributed to this image. Many investors and long-term residents thought it was ironic that those in charge of protecting the Old City were also in charge of the many building violations. Yet because of the many contradictions in local bureaucracy, investors and long-term residents did not take the official guidelines and preservation laws seriously; they continued circumventing building codes and restrictions on building materials.

Several government employees I met seemed dedicated to their jobs and to protecting the Old City. As in Greece, they were trying to make the most of a situation where they were caught between the citizens who blamed them for their ineptitude and corruption and their superiors who could overturn any decision they made. The bureaucratic employees knew of the discrepancy in the guidelines for historic preservation in the Old City, but in many instances, they were helpless to bring about any real change. Karim worked with the Department of Antiquities and during an interview confirmed that the idea to preserve the Old City had been proposed for several years, even decades, but there had been no stipulations on how it should be done, even with the guidelines. He decried the serious lack of preservation experts working with the government and saw the lack of technical and planning expertise to be the real issue.

When I interviewed him in March 2004, he said, "We are still at the beginning. There are several obstacles to developing a plan for preservation because there are all these different concepts and plans, conservation versus preservation, prevention, etc. It is difficult to apply these concepts within a comprehensive plan." However, he also insisted that the project to preserve Damascus should be a local project using local expertise. The fast pace of gentrification made planning difficult, and getting local participation was not always productive. According to an employee of the CPOC, "even government agencies run into problems. We were working on a master plan of the city and about possible scenarios. We were doing it in a correct way by presenting it to people for their input. We had a meeting with people and talked about the plan. So what happened? People rushed to buy property on the proposed plan that was not yet approved and now we are being forced to implement it."

This adds another layer to the bureaucracy of conservation and preservation in the Old City of Damascus. Many investors want laws and rules applied but not to their own projects. Many investors and even long-term residents think they are above the law because they have a better understanding of preservation and of the Old City of Damascus than employees of CPOC or other agencies. Yet they want to see other investors and long-term residents fined when they violate the laws but keep violations in their restoration or preservation projects. The tension with the state bureaucracy is that for many investors and long-term residents it is unclear or what the role and authority of the state agencies should be. The regime deliberately remains obscure on the matter because its allows for flexibility in choosing allies and supporters.

Swirling Controversies

Rana Kabbani (2007) claimed Syrian government policies and global forces converged to eradicate historic neighborhoods within and beyond the wall. She addressed the controversial plan to open a motorway through King Faisal Street that runs parallel to the northern wall of the Old City, which would have destroyed large swaths of 'Amarah barraniyyah. Not only would a historic extramural neighborhood have been destroyed but many of the businesses lining the street, in the same family for generations, would have been devastated. The proposal was put forth by a private–public partnership that included funding from the Gulf and led to local outrage and worldwide protest. Eventually, the regime stopped the plan in response to the protest.

Nonetheless, Kabbani squarely blamed the regime and accused it of "trying to push through a 'modernization' and 're-development' scheme" that involved "the ripping out of the world's oldest city's heart, to replace it with banal and vulgar multi-story hotels, tower blocks, American-style shopping malls and motorways." She weighed in on the ongoing debate in Syria, and even around the Arab world, that equated modernization with westernization, which today under globalization is conflated with Americanization, and whether Syria should blindly follow Western models because they are assumed to be "modern."

Yet the changes in the intramural neighborhood are inextricably linked to wider urban changes in Damascus, as it is expanding at an alarming rate in all directions even creeping up Mount Qasyun and swallowing up more of the Ghutah. The growth of Damascus puts pressure on the already stressed municipal infrastructure with more power outages and water shortages. Some neighborhoods known as *'ashw'iyat* (informal urban areas) are not connected to municipal services, and many houses are not only illegally built but also violate health and safety codes, putting inhabitants at risk. Living in 'ashw'iyat also raised the risk of homelessness because homes could be destroyed by government bulldozers to open more ring roads to ease the pressure on city streets. During rush hour, which in 2008 seemed to last all day, some streets became massive parking lots. The current relationship between Damascus and the Old City is summed up by the architect Nasser Rabbat (2002, 299), who wrote, "The increase in population and creeping modernization have both conspired to bleed out resources for [Old City] and result in a tight tragicomedy race to shape, renew, protect, and preserve the city all at once."

The relevance of historic cities and districts is a global issue that has polarized communities around the world over whether to keep, demolish, or preserve. Urban planning for historic cities and districts remains "confrontational," as Dennis Rodwell (2007, 58) described in England, where "seeking to rebuild or at least very substantially remold them to a particular set of preconceived notions [is] time dated." In comparing approaches to planning in historic cities, he describes how top-down planning insists on implementing conceptual ideas with no relevance to real-life problems, whereas a bottom-up approach allows for the "chaos" of everyday life in a sustainable manner (196). In the Old City and since the late Ottoman period, a top-down approach has been adopted to manage modernization and preservation of the Old City that only continued to frustrate government officials and long-term residents. Whereas urban planners are thwarted in their efforts to impose order, discipline, and promote hygienic practices, long-term residents are exasperated by stringent laws that do not address their daily needs. Moreover, many of the approaches to managing the Old City have been adopted from Western examples or put forth by Western consultants. In 2008, I attended a meeting in Damascus between a European Union team of experts on municipal administration and modernization and a local cadre seeking to work on the outlines for their collaborative work on the management of the Old City. It was interesting to see how the tension over a proposed tourist walking route in the Old City arose between the European team leader and his Syrian counterpart. The European insisted that the route should remain within the wall and include stops at traditional artisan workshops. The Syrian argued that most of the traditional industries were outside the wall and the route should include stops in the extramural historic neighborhoods. The Syrian was aware of local politics where the artisans outside the wall will see this as an insidious attempt to deprive them of participating in the tourist industry. The European did not think the Old City extended beyond the wall.

Although many of these collaborations can be fruitful, much of the urban planning of the West comes after decades of experimentation, shifting ideas regarding heritage, past, urban space, and its management. Hence, the results are exchanged and implemented but not the process for how these results came about. The West did not wake up one morning and decide on the best course for municipal administration and management to export the rest of the world; rather, there was a process, and the experience of developing the process is lost in the exchange. Unfortunately for many Syrian urban planners, westernization is commensurate not only with modernity but is a panacea for current local socioeconomic and political challenges. Hence, the legacy of colonial dependency lingers.

Westernization had been complicated by the global flow of capital, especially after 9/11. The government began liberalizing the economy with a series of laws that encouraged the repatriation of the wealth and foreign direct investment. When 9/11 created an anti-Arab and anti-Muslim environment in the West, coupled with restrictions on states associated with terrorism, the pace of wealth repatriation accelerated. Much of the capital from oil-rich Gulf countries, usually invested in the West, was directed to the region, flooding oil-poor countries, including Syria, with investment capital. This explained the boom in real estate and construction as well as regional tourism in the first decade of the 2000s. Although the government encouraged this flow, it was difficult to control, especially when business partnerships were formed between foreign investors and individuals affiliated with the regime.

The official position of the government states that the Old City is a heritage site in its entirety and needs not only to be protected but preserved. Yet there was no consistent policy on how this should be done that considered the complicated issue of heritage preservations with numerous stakeholders and their competing agendas and needs. At the core of the issue is the regime, which has one purpose at all times, to survive regardless of the cost which allowed contradictory and often irresolvable discourses to take place on heritage and the future of the Old City. At times, the regime responded to popular sentiment and intervened to prevent the destruction of historic buildings and neighborhoods. But powerful business interest from the rich Gulf countries could not always be deterred. The regime has co-opted Damascus for its own purposes to confer cultural and political legitimacy to its rule and any regime will continue to do so in in the future. It has done so because "who has no old, has no new."

Concluding Remarks

This ethnography has focused on the gentrification of the Old City to illustrate the complexity of capital, culture, and place making in a volatile location where social divisions, history, and politics are implicated in the process of urban change. Social categories and hierarchies in many postcolonial countries are hinged on the legacy of colonialism that initiated forms of inclusion and exclusion based on class, sect, and ethnicity. In addition local forms of inclusion and exclusion complicate the social stratification in Damascus, especially in the urban-rural binary that had earlier manifestations in the precolonial period.

In my work, I have attempted not to reduce the intricate social and power hierarchy into Shami-Ba'th, Shami-Alawite, or Sunni-Alawite even though social actors themselves not only employ these divisions but sometimes insist on them. The Ba'th authoritarian regime is brutal and fixated on its own survival regardless of the cost, as the current civil war in Syria unfortunately demonstrates. However, to oversimplify the situation in Syria in terms of domination and resistance ignores the historic specificity for the current situation and the ways in which local social actors use binaries "to establish their own claims to power and distinction" and that the "binary tension" is constantly shifting (Herzfeld 2005a, 15, 20; see also Harms 2011). For many Shuwam, their "other" is found in rural migrants, and especially the Alawite political elite. Ironically, this binary then became the basis for the gentrification of the Old City but with cultural affinity for the urban heritage as the basis for affiliation. The urban–rural binary recast as "civilized"–"backward" allowed investors of a rural and even Alawite 'asl to engage in heritage preservation in the Old City.

Perhaps one of the fascinating outcomes of this study is how the political elite rely on the cultural elite for their moral authority and cultural capital. The government supported the preservation of the Old City and espoused its heritage and cultural significance, especially when it could mobilize the image of the historic center to further its own legitimacy, which only reinforces the superiority of the city to the village. The binary "civilized"–"backward" allows more fluidity in the membership of each group to meet new social alliance under new economic realities.

Moreover, architecture plays an important role in social processes, especially in social actors' use of the built environment to make declarations about themselves (Vellinga 2007, 756). Therefore, my study contributes to the understanding of architecture and cultural identification in the Middle East (Ghannam 2001; Bertram 2008). Furthermore, the contestation over the process of preservation illustrates the contestation among social actors in their definition of "civilized" and "backward." Unlike in other ethnographies on gentrification and preservation from the Mediterranean, mainly Rethemnos and Rome, both by Michael Herzfeld (1991, 2009), resistance is not always against government policies but against neighbors and their interpretation of those policies. Some social actors in the Old City want to see the government impose tougher sanctions against violations of the preservation codes and maintain consistency in applying the law.

Preserving the Old City of Damascus enhances our understanding of the urban process in the non-western world. The history of the Middle East is the history of cities that have always been the site of religious and economic power. Damascus, as one of the eminent centers of Islamic and Arab culture, has not been explored much in literature, and there are few historical works on Damascus (Rafeq 1966; Raymond 1984; Burns 2005; Degeorge 2005). Historic urban centers in the Middle East have been the target of much research in the past several decades focused on the role of the Islamic city, colonialism, and modernization of the built environment

(Abu Lughod 1971, 1980; Eickelman 1974; Celik 1986; Rabinow 1989; Wright 1991; Alsayyad 1992; Eldem, Goffman, and Masters 1999). In my approach to the study of social and cultural change in the Middle East, I departed from the usual dyad of modernity and tradition in Middle Eastern Studies that tends to "hegemonize" and "homogenize" discourses of modernity (Asad 1987, 603), seeking "other narratives of human connections" (Chakrabarty 2000, 46). It is the contradictions in modernity at once "indispensible and inadequate" for understanding social processes and change that compel us to seek other forms of explanation (6). Viewing social and cultural change in the Middle East through "civilization" and "backwardness" is my contribution to the scholarship on the urban setting in the region and an attempt at understanding local discourse on social categorization, power hierarchies, and social processes from the local vernacular vocabulary.

Furthermore, as nonindustrial historic urban cores, old cities in the Middle East are outside much of the literature of urban gentrification, which tends to focus on postindustrial cities (Harvey 1990; Sassen 1991; Smith 1996). The Old City remains a vibrant urban center that faces similar urban challenges as these cities without undergoing the same historical process. Moreover, much of the ethnographic research on contemporary cities in the Arab Middle East tends to be *in* rather than *of* the city. The few works available *of* the city tend to focus on emerging cities or neighborhoods that are the product of the twentieth century (Ghannam 2002; Elshestawy 2008; Sawalha 2010). Since Syrian cities are not only the political and economic centers but also where more than half the population resides, understanding everyday practices that take place in the city sheds light on local social actors' navigation of cultural and socioeconomic change. The focus of research on urban duality between new and old neighborhoods in cities of the Middle East not only creates a disconnect and artificial binary between the two neighborhoods that does not exist in reality but also ignores how historic city centers continue to evolve and deal with the same problems as newer neighborhoods even when they are protected by national heritage laws.

In *Preserving the Old City of Damascus*, I demonstrated how social actors navigate the relationship between the new and Old City to create their understanding of social change. Moreover, by approaching historic cities as viable urban settings, their transformation enhances our understanding of the processes and practices of place making in ways newer urban settings cannot. The Old City has survived for millennia because it continued to grow and evolve as an urban settlement, attracting new waves of people who adopted the city as the city adapted them to urban life. The past two decades have witnessed a continuation of the process of growth and change, although it may be in directions and in forms that leave many Shuwam upset and angered over the disappearance of "their" Damascus. But perhaps Damascus does not and cannot belong to a single group, which is the key to its longevity. It has always been able to adapt to a new power because it was always the center of civilization It is the prerogative of a city with so many histories to be able to "play" on its past. Yet urban planning under modernity attempts to control and direct change. Whereas there are plans for expansion and reordering city space, there is also insistence on preserving certain monuments or neighborhoods. This monumentalization of time (Herzfeld 1991) can only lead to more confusion and conflict between those who live in the city and those who want to order it. The designation as a World Heritage Site was both a blessing and a curse. It protected the intramural neighborhoods from complete annihilation, but it determined that the Old City remain fixed in the 1940s, when it was predominantly inhabited by the Shuwam. This in turn served to marginalize the current residents who maintain its residential aspects.

I concur with Herzfeld (2009, 310) and his observation on Rome when he wrote, "the irony of heritage; too often it entails the destruction of a local society in the name of preservation." Yet what remains striking, and unlike the Roman example, is that the gentrification of the Old City was about preserving its "Shaminess" despite the fact many of the long-term residents in the Old City were of rural descent. Moreover, the long-term residents were nonchalant about the preservation of the Old City though it meant the dislocation of many of them. There was an unspoken belief in the impermanence of change. Many of the long-term residents believe that this interest in the Old City will wane, as other plans to change and alter the intramural neighborhoods came to naught. A governor or minister might change and so will the policy toward the Old City. The current emphasis on investment and tourism will not always be the case, and the civil war has certainly put an end to it. The only permanence in the Old City is change, and this tends to be forgotten because of moniker "old" that gives the impression of a continuum from time immemorial.

Epilogue

Whither Syria?

Until early 2011, gentrification of the Old City continued at a rapid pace with more courtyard houses converted into restaurants, hotels, art galleries, cafés, and upscale boutiques. Neighborhood stores and workshops were also purchased by investors for the same purpose. Some neighborhoods such as Qimarriyyah and Harat Hananya have been transformed from predominantly residential to tourist areas. Groceries and workshops that served local residents transformed into souvenir stores filled with carpets, beads, shawls, and other tourist commodities, made mainly in India or China, all in anticipation of a boom in heritage tourism. However, tourism is a fickle business, and the Arab uprising has been the latest impediment to tourism in a region prone to political crises.

The current civil war in Syria is the latest political crisis to challenge economic development plans. It also questions the sustainability of the Ba'th authoritarian regime and highlights the frailty of the nation-state formed during the mandate period when sectarian and ethnic identities were institutionalized. Although these divisions remain strong in Syria, they are compounded by class alliances formed under new economic conditions that crisscross sectarian and ethnic differences. The demonstrations in support of the regime during the early days of the Syrian uprising should not be easily dismissed. The president does enjoy support among certain groups. The regime remains strongly embedded in the local social structures, and its interests dovetail with the interests of different segments of Syrian society. Many Syrians are vested in the survival of the regime and do not want to see political change, not because of a deep-seated loyalty but because they have benefited from its patronage. Moreover, among the warring parties in the current conflict, the regime for many is the least of bad options available. As I write these final words in late 2013, the regime seems stronger than ever in outlasting its opponents.

The civil war has spread throughout Syria, and there is no sign of its abatement. The government armed forces battle the Free Syrian Army as well as other groups, and violence has escalated in previously stable cities under state control. Most disturbing is that no side seems to be winning outright, which portends a drawn-out conflict with more casualties and destruction. In addition, the groups aligned against the regime are now fighting among themselves. Haythem al-Manna (2012), a leading Syrian figure in the opposition, does not seem to think the war will end with the fall of the regime but instead will initiate another long and protracted struggle among various factions. The Free Syrian Army is an umbrella for different armed groups who have a common goal in defeating government forces and bringing down the regime. Beyond that objective, the insurgent groups have no common agenda as to what will happen afterward. Rather, each faction promotes its individual agenda for the formation of a post–civil war state and that could take the form of anything from an Islamist to a secular government. However, in the past several months, there is less talk about the fall of the regime and more about the "new" Middle East and redrawing of the infamous Sykes-Picot map (Wright 2013). In Syria, this will result in the "Shamization" of Syria or the fragmentation of the country along major cities and provinces according to some combination of the Ottoman and French administrative units.

In late 2013, new developments prolonged the conflict. In addition to the infighting among the insurgent forces, the regime itself averted an attack from the United States and its allies when chemical weapons were discovered to have been used in the outskirts of Damascus. It is thought that by agreeing to dispose of its arsenal of chemical weapons and by cooperating with international inspectors, the regime has regained its strengthen. In late November, the Syrian army gained back territory lost to the insurgents. However, the struggle for Syria has also brought to the forefront new fault lines in the Middle East between secular and religious forces that could only complicate matters. What is most likely is that Syria, in for a long struggle among the different factions, will be eclipsed from the international headlines as new events gain the world's attention.

The situation in Syria today is light years from 2000 when Bashar al-Asad became president. I was amazed at how many people thought he would be different from his father and that he will truly be a reformer edging the country toward economic and political liberalization. Wishful thinking aside, he came to power in a plot cleverly orchestrated by his father to ensure continuity of the regime with an Asad at the top. In a discussion I had with a historian of Syria, he said of Bashar, "Look at him he is young and soft not hardened like his father. He will not kill people." I remember searching for a smirk, a wink, or some indication that he spoke with sarcasm or even irony but he was serious. The image of the young, nerdy optometrist who had spent six months in London and who loved computers was "seen" as different from his father because of his contact with Western civilization. Supposedly that contact should have made a larger impact than the thirty years he spent in his father's household and result in some kind of enlightenment. What I find fascinating is the belief that Western educated, Western attired, and possessing an affinity for Western technology Arab leaders will not kill civilians and suppress human rights. On the other hand, this belief also assumes that Western leaders are incapable of killing their own people. As Benjamin observed: "There is no document of civilization which is not at the same time a document of barbarism" (1968b, 256). Bashar al-Asad may not have the strategem of his father to overcome the impasse of the Syrian crisis but he is smart enough to know that to survive he must be the last man left standing.

What does this all mean for the Old City? Many of the new restaurants, hotels, and shops that opened in more optimistic times to serve the anticipated hordes of tourists now stand idle. There have been some bombings in the Christian quarter, the latest by a suicide bomber killing four preschool children and their bus driver. However, the fighting has for the most part spared Damascus proper. It is hoped the Old City will survive without major damage, though with all the carnage the country has seen this is little consolation. Nonetheless, its survival will be a testament to its resilience and perhaps due to divine intervention. Aleppo has not been lucky. Areas of the historic city center, including the suq, have been destroyed in the fighting between the government forces and the insurgents.

To return to the beginning, Damascus is a blessed city. It is a city of fada'l (virtues) as the populace would tell you. It was favored by the Prophet who said, "If the people of al-Sham become corrupt there is no good in any of you" (al-Makdisi 2003, 32). These are certainly trying times

15. A moment of tranquility in a bayt 'arabi, ca. 2004.

for Damascus and its people. And it will certainly be a different Damascus and people that survive the conflict. I am not sure how much good will remain. I still believe a resilient Old City will help mend what is left of a shattered country. I often think of the people of Damascus and hope they still have faith to write on the walls of the Old City, *Allah Hamyhah Ya Sham* (God is protecting you O Sham).

Glossary

References

Index

Glossary

'abraj: towers
'adabiyat al-mintaqah: local norms
'ajami: painted wood used in the decoration of the courtyard house
'akbiya: cellars
Allah Hamyhah Ya Sham: God is protecting you O Sham
ana raj'iyyeh: I am reactionary or returning
'ard al-diyar: courtyard
'arwa': more wonderful
'asala: authenticity
'ashw'iyat: informal neighborhoods
'asl: origin
'awda: return
badawi: Bedouin
baha: courtyard
baha al-samawiyya: courtyard
bahib al-balad: I love the country
al-balad al-qadimah: Old City
bayt 'arabi: Damascene traditional courtyard house abbreviated as *bayt*
bedu: Bedouin
'blaq: stone inlay used in the decoration of the courtyard house
al-day'ah: village
dhawq: taste, distinction
dihliz: corridor
Dimashq: Damascus
Dimashq al-mahrusah: Damascus the protected
Dimashq al-qadimah: Old Damascus
fada'l: virtues
frankat: from the word *Frank* meaning windows

fusha: opening as in courtyard
al-ghazu thaqafi: cultural invasion
hadarah: civilization
hadari: civilized
hadatha: modernization
hadr: urban dwellers
hammam: bathhouse
hammati: pigeon breeder
hanan 'umrani: kind buildings
haqarah: vulgar
harah: neighborhood
haram: forbidden or prohibited but in my usage "what a pity"
harb tabaqiyya: class warfare
haremlik: women's living space
hawiyya hadariyya: civilizational identity
hik inti kharabti al-dinya: with this you have ruined the world
hujrah: room
'ili ma lu qadim ma 'ilu jaded: who has no old has no new
'imara: building
intima' lil balad: belong to the country
'istthmar: investment
'iwan or *liwan:* a room with one side open
jinna: paradise
khalaf: he violated [the law]
khallal: fault
khanah 'idash: household eleven
kharab: ruin
khay: exclamation of thanks
khurafik: he pulled your leg
khususiyya: privacy
kulik dhawq: you are in good taste or good manners
la buda: must
madrassa: school
makbut: stifled
markiz: center
masturah: protected, guarded
min al-rif: from the countryside

min al-wadi: from the valley, a region in central Syria

Misr: Cairo or Egypt

mizajiyah: moodiness, idiosyncrasy

mukhabarat: secret intelligence

muqawamat: foundations

mustathmir: investor plural *mustathmirin*

mutakhalif: backward

muzarkash: overly decorated

namt haya: lifestyle

al-nasij al-'umrani: urban fabric

rahma: compassion

riad: courtyard house in Morocco

sabi' tabaqat: seven layers

sahn: courtyard

salimlik: men's living space

satr: protect, guard

shadh: deviant

Shaghur barrani

al-Sham: Damascus or greater Syria

al-Sham al-qadimah: old Sham

Shami: Damascene

shawah: marred

shu haram? kan hatha manzar hadari: What do you mean a pity? Was that a civilized sight?

Shuwam: Damascenes (plural of *Shami*)

siyaha: tourism

suba: heater

sukani: demographic

ta'baneh: tired or worn out

tabaqa: social class or layer

al-tabaqah al-jadida: new class

tabaqa tayarah: refers to the new class

tabaqat: social classes or layers plural of *tabaqa*

tabaqat hadariyyah: civilizational layers

tabiq: flat or apartment

tadamun: solidarity

tahdith: modernization

tajr: merchant
takaful: mutual responsibility
takamul: coherence
takhalluf: backwardness
tamwih: misleading
tashabu': satiation
tasih: melt
tasmim: design
taswih: make touristy
thaqafa: culture
traji' ila al-'asl: return to the origin
turath: heritage
'ulama: religious leaders
'umran: civilization or building
wajh hadari: civilized appearance
waskh: filth
wihdah hadariyyah: oneness of civilization
zakhrafa: ornament, decoration

References

Abboud, Samer. 2009. "The Transition Paradigm and the Case of Syria." In *Syria's Economy and the Transition Paradigm*, edited by Samer Abboud and Ferdinand Arslanian, 3–32. Fife, Scotland: University of St. Andrews Centre for Syrian Studies.

Abdulac, Samir. 1982. "Damas: Les Annees Ecochard (1932–1982)." *La cahiers de la recerche architecturale espaces et formes de l'Orient Arabe*, no. 10–11:32–42.

Abdul Nour, Antoine. 1982. *Introduction a l'histoire urbaine de la Syrie Ottoman (XVI–XVIII siecle)*. Beyrouth: Publications de l'Universite Libanaise Section des Etudes Historique.

Abu Lughod, Janet. 1971. *Cairo: 1001 Years of the City Victorious*. Princeton, NJ: Princeton University Press.

———. 1980. *Rabat: Urban Apartheid in Morocco*. Princeton, NJ: Princeton University Press.

———. 1987. "The Islamic City-Historic Myth, Islamic Essence and Contemporary Relevance." *International Journal of Middle East Studies* 19:155–76.

Abu Lughod, Lila. 1986. *Veiled Sentiments: Honor and Poetry in a Bedouin Society*. Berkeley: University of California Press.

———. 2005. *Dramas of Nationhood: The Politics of Television in Egypt*. Chicago: University of Chicago Press.

Agnew, John, John Mercer, and David E. Sopher. 1984. Introduction to *The City in Cultural Context*, edited by Johan Agnew, John Mercer, and David E. Sopher, 1–30. Boston: Allen & Unwin.

al-'Allaf, Ahmad. n.d. *Dimashq fi matla' al-qarn al-'Ishrin* [Damascus at the beginning of the twentieth century]. Damascus: Dar Dimashq.

Alsayyad, Nezar. 1992. "The Islamic City as a Colonial Enterprise." In *Forms of Dominance: On the Architecture and Urbanism of the Colonial Enterprise*, edited by Nezar Alsayyad, 27–43. Aldershot: Avebury.

———. 2001. "Global Norms and Urban Forms in the Age of Tourism: Manufacturing Heritage, Consuming Tradition." In *Consuming Tradition, Manufacturing Heritage: Global Norms and Urban Forms in the Age of Tourism*, edited by Neza Alsayyad, 1–33. London: Routledge.

al-'Ash, Abu Faraj. 1953. "Al-dour al-Athariyah al-Khasah fi Dimashq" [Private historical houses in Damascus]. *Al-Hawliyat Al-Al-Athariyah al-Suriyah* 3 (1–2): 47–58.

Altorki, Soraya, and Camillia Fawzi el-Solh, eds. 1988. *Arab Women in the Field: Studying Your Own Society*. Syracuse, NY: Syracuse University Press.

Asad, Talal. 1987. "Are There Histories of Peoples without Europe? A Review Article." *Comparative Studies in Society and History* 29 (3): 594–607.

Atkinson, Rowland, and Gary Bridge. 2005. Introduction to *Gentrification in a Global Context: The New Urban Colonialism*, edited by Rowland Atkinson and Cary Bridge, 1–17. London: Routledge.

al-Azmeh, Aziz. 1993. *Islams and Modernities*. New York: Verso.

Bachelard, Gaston. 1964. *Poetics of Space: The Classic Look at How We Experience Intimate Places*. Translated by Maria Jolas. Boston: Beacon Press.

al-Bahra, Nasr al-Din. 2001. *Dimashq al-Asrar* [Damascus of secrets]. Damascus: Dar Tlas.

Ball, Warwick. 1994. *Syria: A Historical and Architectural Guide*. Essex, England: Scorpion Publishing.

Bartu, Ayfer. 1999. "Who Owns the Old Quarters: Rewriting Histories in a Global Era." In *Istanbul: Between the Global and the Local*, edited by C. Keydar, 31–45. Lanham, MD: Rowman & Littlefield Publishers.

Basso, Keith. 1988. "Speaking with Names": Language and Landscape among the Western Apache. *Cultural Anthropology* 3 (2): 99–130.

Batatu, Hanna. 1981. "Some Observations on the Social Roots of Syria's Ruling Military Group and the Causes for Its Dominance." *Middle East Journal* 35 (3): 331–44.

———. 1999. *Syria's Peasantry, the Descendants of Its Lesser Rural Notables and Their Politics*. Princeton, NJ: Princeton University Press.

Benjamin, Walter. 1968a. "The Work of Art in the Age of Mechanical Reproduction." In *Illuminations: Essays and Reflections*, edited by Hannah Arendt, translated by Harry Zohn, 217–51. New York: Harcourt Brace Jovanovich.

———. 1968b. "Theses on the Philosophy of History." In *Illuminations: Essays and Reflections*, edited by Hannah Arendt, translated by Harry Zohn, 251–64. New York: Harcourt Brace Jovanovich.

———. 1978. "Naples." In *Reflections: Essays, Aphorisms, and Autobiographical Writings*, edited by Peter Demetz, translated by Edmund Jephcott, 163–73. New York: Harcourt Brace Jovanovich.

———. 1999. *The Arcades Project*. Translated by Howard Eiland and Kevin McLaughlin. Cambridge, MA: Harvard University Press.

Berger, John. 1972. *Ways of Seeing*. London: Penguin Books

Berman, Marshall. 1983. *All That Is Solid Melts into Air: The Experience of Modernity*. New York: Penguin.

Bertram, Carel. 2008. *Imagining the Turkish House: Collective Visions of Home*. Austin: University of Texas Press.

Bianco, Stefano. 1986. *Conservation of the Old City of Damascus*. Report to UNESCO.

Bill, James. A. 1972. "Class Analysis and the Dialectics of Modernization in the Middle East." *International Journal of Middle East Studies*, 3:417–34.

Bissell, William. 2011. *Urban Design, Chaos, and Colonial Power in Zanzibar*. Bloomington: Indiana University Press.

Bourdieu, Pierre. 1977. *Outline of a Theory of Practice*. Translated by Richard Nice. Cambridge: Cambridge University Press.

———. 1984. *Distinction: A Social Critique of the Judgment of Taste*. Translated by Richard Nice. Cambridge, MA: Harvard University Press.

———. 2003. "Kabayle House." In *The Anthropology of Space and Place,* edited by Setha Low and Denise Lawrence-Zúñiga, 131–41. Oxford: Blackwell.

Brubaker, Rogers. 2006. *Nationalist Politics and Everyday Ethnicity in a Transylvanian Town*. Princeton, NJ: Princeton University Press.

Brumann, Christoph. 2009. "Outside the Glass Case: The Social Life of Urban Heritage in Kyoto" *American Ethnologist* 36 (2): 276–99.

Buck-Morss, Susan. 1999. *The Dialectics of Seeing: Walter Benjamin and the Arcades Project*. Cambridge, MA: MIT Press.

Burns, Ross. 1999. *Monuments of Syria: A Historical Guide*. London: I. B. Tauris.

———. 2005. *Damascus: A History*. New York: Routledge.

Busquets, Joan. 2005. "Why Aleppo?" In *Aleppo: Rehabilitation of the Old City*, edited by Joan Busquets, 11–21. Cambridge, MA: Harvard University Graduate School of Design.

Celik, Zeynab. 1997. *Urban Forms and Colonial Confrontations: Algiers Under French Rule*. Berkeley: University of California Press.

Celik, Zeynab, Diane Favro, and Richard Ingersoll. 1994. Foreword to *Streets Critical Perspectives on Public Space*, edited by Zaynab Celik, Diane Favro, and Richard Ingersoll, 1–7. Berkeley: University of California Press.

Chakrabarty, Dipesh. 2000. *Provencializing Europe: Postcolonial Thought and Historical Difference*. Princeton, NJ: Princeton University Press.

Chatterjee, Partha. 1993. *The Nation and Its Fragments: Colonial and Postcolonial Histories*. Princeton, NJ: Princeton University Press.

Daher, Rami. 2007. "Reconceptualizing Tourism in the Middle East: Place, Heritage, Mobility and Competitiveness." In *Tourism in the Middle East: Continuity, Change and Transformation*, edited by Rami Daher, 1–69. Clevedon: Channel View Publications.

Daskalakis, Annie-Christine. 2004. "Damascus 18th and 19th Century Houses in the Ablaq-ʿAjami Style of Decoration: Local and International Significance." PhD diss., New York University.

Davila, Arlene. 2004. *Barrio Dreams: Puerto Ricans, Latinos, and the Neoliberal City*. Berkeley: University of California Press.

de Certeau, Michel. 1984. *The Practice of Everyday Life*. Translated by Steven Rendall. Berkeley: University of California Press.

Deeb, Lara. 2006. *An Enchanted Modern: Gender and Public Piety in Shi'i Lebanon*. Princeton, NJ: Princeton University Press.

Degeorge, Gerard. 1995. "The Damascus Massacre: Effects of Modernity on Old Buildings in Syria." *The Architectural Review*, 197 (1178): 68–72.

———. 2005. *Damascus*. Italy: Flammarion.

Devlin, John. 1976. *The Ba'th Party: A History from Its Origins to 1966*. Stanford, CA: Hoover Institution Press.

———. 1983. *Syria: Modern State in an Ancient Land*. Boulder, CO: Westview Press.

di Giovine, Michael. 2009. *The Heritage-scape: UNESCO, World Heritage, and Tourism*. Lanham, MD: Lexington Books.

Douglas, Mary. 1966. *Purity and Danger: An Analysis of Concepts of Pollution and Taboo*. Middlesex, England: Penguin Books.

Eickelman, Dale. 1974. "Is There an Islamic City?" *International Journal of Middle East Studies*, no. 5: 274–94.

———. 1981. *The Middle East: An Anthropological Approach*. Englewood Cliffs, NJ: Prentice Hall.

Eldem, Eldem, Daniel Goffman, and Bruce Masters. 1999. *The Ottoman City between East and West: Aleppo, Izmir, and Istanbul*. New York: Cambridge University Press.

Elias, Norbert. 1978. *The Civilizing Process: The History of Manners.* Translated by Edmund Jephcott. New York: Urizen Books.

Elsheshtawy, Yasser, 2008. "Cities of Sand and Fog: Abu Dhabi's Global Ambitions." In *The Evolving Arab City: Tradition, Modernity and Urban Development,* edited by Yasser Elshestaway, 258–304. London: Routledge.

Erman, Tahire. 1998. "Becoming 'Urban.' or Remaining 'Rural': The Views of Turkish Rural-to-Urban Migrants on the 'Integration' Question." *International Journal of Middle Eastern Studies,* no. 30: 541–561.

Fabian, Johannes. 1983. *Time and the Other: How Anthropology Makes Its Object.* New York: Columbia University Press.

Faneslow, Frank S. 1990. "The Bazaar Economy or How Bizarre Is the Bazaar Really?" *Man,* no. 25: 250–65.

Feld, Steven, and Keith H. Basso, eds. 1996. *Senses of Place.* Santa Fe, NM: School of American Research Press.

Ferguson, James. 1992. "The Country and the City on the Copperbelt." *Cultural Anthropology* 7 (1): 80–92.

Fernandez, James. 1988. Andalusia on Our Minds: Two Contrasting Places in Spain as Seen in a Vernacular Poetic Duel of the Late 19th Century. *Cultural Anthropology* 3 (1): 21–35.

Fitch, Martin. 1990. *Historic Preservation: Curatorial Management of the Built World.* Charlottesville: University Press of Virginia.

Flood, Finbarr Barry. 2001. *The Great Mosque of Damascus: Studies on the Makings of an Umayyad Visual Culture.* Leiden: Brill.

Flores, Richard. 2002. *Remembering the Alamo: Memory, Modernity, and the Master Symbol.* Austin: University of Texas Press.

Freud, Sigmund. 1946. *Civilization and Its Discontents.* Translated by Joan Riviere. London: Hogarth Press.

Fries, Franck. 1993. "Le Reglement Ottoman de construction après incendi aux prises avec les Francais a Damas sous le Mandat Francais (1925–1926)." *La Ville en feu: actes de la journée du 4 Juin 1993,* edited by S. Yerasimos and F. Fries, 53–66. Champs-sur-Marne: Laboratoire Théorie des mutations urbaines, Institut français d'urbanisme.

———. 1994. "Les plans d'Alep et de Damas, un banc d'essai por l'urbanime des freres Danger (1931–1937)." *Revue de Monde Musulmad et de la Mediterranee* 73–74 (3–4): 311–25.

Fromkin, David. 1989. *A Peace to End All Peace: Creating the Modern Middle East 1914–1922.* New York: Holt.

Fuller, Mia. 1992. "Building Power: Italian Architecture and Urbanism in Libya and Ethiopia." In *Forms of Dominance: On Architecture and Urbanism of the Colonial Experience*, edited by Nezar Alsayyad, 211–39. Aldershot: Avebury.

———. 2007. *Moderns Abroad: Architecture, Cities, and Italian Imperialism.* New York: Routledge.

Gable, Eric, and Richard Handler. 1996. "After Authenticity at an American Heritage Site." *American Anthropologist* 98 (3): 568–78.

Gandolfo, Daniella. 2009. *The City at Its Limits: Taboo, Transgression, and Urban Renewal in Lima.* Chicago: University of Chicago Press.

Gaonkar, Dilip. 1999. "On Alternative Modernities." *Public Culture* 11 (1): 1–18.

Gaudin, Jean-Pierre. 1992. "L'Urbanisme au Levant et le Mandat Francais." In *Architectures Francaises Outre-Mer*, edited by Pierre Mardaga, 177–205. Institut Francais D'Architeture.

Geertz, Clifford. 1973. "Thick Description: Toward an Interpretive Theory of Culture. In *The Interpretations of Cultures*, 3–30. n.p.: Basic Books, 3–30.

———. 1979. "Suq: The Bazaar Economy in Sefrou." In *Meaning and Order in Moroccan Society*, edited by Clifford Geertz, Hildred Geertz, and Lawrence Rosen, 123–313. Cambridge: Cambridge University Press

———. 1989. "Toutes Directions: Reading the Signs in an Urban Sprawl." In *International Journal of Middle East Studies* 21 (3): 291–306.

Ghannam, Farha. 2002. *Remaking the Modern: Space, Relocation, and the Politics of Identity in a Global Cairo.* Berkeley: University of California Press.

Gilloch, Graeme. 2002. "Benjamin's Moscow, Baudrillard's America." In *Hieroglyphics of Space: Reading and Experiencing the Modern Metropolis*, edited by Neil Leach, 164–84. New York: Routledge.

Gluck, John. 1963. "Images of an Arab City." *Journal of the American Planning Association* 29 (3): 179–98.

Gupta, Akhil. 1995. "Blurred Boundaries: The Discourse of Corruption, the Culture of Politics, and the Imagined State." *American Ethnologist* 22 (2): 375–402.

Gupta, Akhil, and James Ferguson, eds. 1997a. *Culture, Power, Place: Explorations in Critical Anthropology*, Durham, NC: Duke University Press.

———. 1997b. "Beyond 'Culture': Space, Identity, and the Politics of Difference." In *Culture, Power, Place: Explorations in Critical Anthropology*, edited by A. Gupta and J. Ferguson, 33–51. Durham, NC: Duke University Press.

Hakki, Haitham. 2003. *Dhikryat Al-Zamn Al-Qadm* [Memories for the time to come]. Thirty-episode serial. Damascus: Al Rahba Production.

Halbwachs, Maurice. 1992. *On Collective Memory*. Translated by Lewis A. Coser. Chicago: University of Chicago Press.

Hamadeh, Shirine. 1992. "Creating the Traditional City: A French Project." In *Forms of Dominance: On the Architecture and Urbanism of the Colonial Enterprise*, edited by N. Alsayyad, 241–59. London: Avebury.

Handler, Richard. 1986. "Authenticity." *Anthropology Today* 2 (1): 2–4.

———. 1988. *Nationalism and the Politics of Culture in Quebec*. Madison: University of Wisconsin Press.

Handler, Richard, and Eric Gable. 1997. *The New History in an Old Museum: Creating the Past at Colonial Williamsburg*. Durham, NC: Duke University Press.

Hanna, Abdullah. 1985. *Harakt al-Amah al-Dimashqiyeh fi al-qarnyen al- thamin ashr wa al-tasieh ashr* [Social Damascene movements in the eighteenth and nineteenth centuries]. Beirut: Dar Ibn Khaldun.

Hannerz, Ulf. 1996. *Transnational Connections*. London: Routledge.

Harms, Erik. 2011. *Saigon's Edge: On the Margins of Ho Chi Minh City*. Minneapolis: University of Minnesota Press.

Hartigan, John, Jr. 1999. *Racial Situations: Class Predicaments of Whiteness in Detroit*. Princeton, NJ: Princeton University Press.

Harvey, David. 1985. "Paris, 1850–1870." In *Consciousness and the Urban Experience*, 63–220. Baltimore: John Hopkins University Press.

———. 1989. "From Managerialism to Entrepreneurism: The Transformation in Urban Governance in Late Capitalism." *Geografiska Annaler, Series B, Human Geography* 71 (1): 3–17.

———. 1990. *The Condition of Postmodernity*. Oxford: Blackwell.

———. 2005. *A Brief History of Neoliberalism*. Oxford: Oxford University Press.

Hassan, Kamal. 1985. "Nadwat Dimashq al-Qadimah: Ifkar wa Nat'j" [Conference on Old Damascus: ideas and conclusions]. *Al-Hawaliyat Al-'thariyah*, no. 35:443–47.

Hazbun, Waleed. 2008. *Beaches, Ruins, Resorts: The Politics of Tourism in the Arab World*. Minneapolis: University of Minnesota Press.

Herzfeld, Michael. 1991. *A Place in History: Social and Monumental Time in a Cretan Town*. Princeton, NJ: Princeton University Press.

———. 2005a. *Cultural Intimacy: Social Poetics in the Nation-State*. New York: Routledge.

———. 2005b. "Political Optics and the Occlusion of Intimate Knowledge." *American Anthropologist* 107 (3): 369–76.

———. 2009. *Evicted from Eternity: The Restructuring of Modern Rome*. Chicago: University of Chicago Press.

Hill, Matthew. 2004. "Globalizing Havana: World Heritage and Urban Redevelopment in Late Socialist Cuba." Ph.D. Diss., University of Chicago.

———. 2007. "Reimagining Old Havana: World Heritage and the Production of Scale in Late Socialist Cuba." In *Deciphering the Global: Its Scales, Spaces, and Subjects*, edited by Saskia Sassen, 59–77. New York: Routledge.

Hinnebusch, Raymond. 2001. *Syria: Revolution from Above*. London: Routledge.

———. 2009. "Syria under the Ba'th: The Political Economy of Populist Authoritarianism." In *The State and the Political Economy of Reform in Syria*, edited by Raymond Hinnebusch and Soren Schmidt, 5–24. Fife, Scotland: University of St. Andrews Center for Syrian Studies.

Hitti, Philip. 1959. *Syria a Short History: Being a Condensation of the Author's "History of Syria including Lebanon and Palestine."* New York: Macmillan.

Hobsbawm, Eric, and Terrance Ranger, eds. 1983. *The Invention of Tradition*. Cambridge: Cambridge University Press.

Holleran, Michael. 1998. *Boston's "Changeful Times": Origins of Preservation and Planning in America*. Baltimore: John Hopkins University Press.

Holston, James. 1989. *The Modernist City: An Anthropological Critique of Brasilia*. Chicago: University of Chicago Press.

Hourani, Albert. 1968. "Ottoman Reform and the Politics of the Notables." In *Beginnings of Modernization in the Middle East*, edited by William R. Polk and Richard L. Chambers, 41–68. Chicago: University of Chicago Press.

Hudson, Leila. 2008. *Transforming Damascus: Space and Modernity in an Islamic City*. London: Tauris Academic Studies.

Humphrey, Caroline. 1988. "No Place Like Home in Anthropology: The Neglect of Architecture." *Anthropology Today* 4 (1): 16–18.

Huyssen, Andreas. 2003. *Present Pasts: Urban Palimpsests and the Politics of Memory*. Stanford, CA: Stanford University Press.

Idlibi, Ulfat. 1980. *Dimashq: Ya basmat al-huzn* [Damascus: The smile of tears]. Damascus: Ministry of Culture Publications.

Islam, Tolga. 2005. "Outside the Core: Gentrification in Istanbul." In *Gentrification in a Global Context*, edited by Rowland Atkinson and Gary Bridge, 121–36. London: Routledge.

Ivy, Marilyn. 1995. *Discourses of the Vanishing: Modernity, Phantasm, Japan*. Chicago: University of Chicago Press.

al-Jabari, Muhammad Abed. 1991. *Al-turath wa al-hadathah: Dirasat wa Munaqashat.* Beirut: Markiz al-Dirasat Al-wuhdah al-'arabiyyah.

Jackson, John L., Jr. 2002. *Harlemworld: Doing Race and Class in Contemporary Black America.* Chicago: University of Chicago Press.

Jager, Michael. 1986. "Class Definition and the Esthetics of Gentrification: Victorian in Melbourne." In *Gentrification of the City,* edited by Neil Smith and Peter Williams, 78–91. Boston: Allen & Unwin.

Jones, G. A., and A. Varley. 1999. "The Reconquest of the Historic Centre: Urban Conservation and Gentrification in Puebla, Mexico. *Environment and Planning A,* no. 31:1547–66.

Ibn Jubayr. 1980. *Rihlat Ibn Jubayr* [Travels by Ibn Jubayr]. Beirut: Dar Sadir.

al-Jundi, Sami. 1969. *Al-Ba'th* [The Ba'th]. Beirut: Dar al-Nahar.

Kabbani, Rana. 2008. "Old Damascus: A Plan to Destroy Paradise." http://www.IslamiCity.com/forum/forum_posts.asp?TID=12870

Kapchan, Deborah. 1996. *Gender on the Market.* Philadelphia: University of Pennsylvania Press.

Kayali, Hasan. 1998. "Wartime Regional and Imperial Integration of Greater Syria During World War I." In *The Syrian Land: Processes of Integration and Fragmentation,* edited by T. Philipp and B. Schaebler, 295–306. Stuttgart: Franz Steiner

Keenan, Bridget. 2000. *Damascus: Hidden Treasures of the Old City.* London: Thomas & Hudson.

———. 2007. "Damascene Conversions." *Telegraph Magazine,* November, 98–104.

Keydar, Caglar. 1999. "Synopsis". In *Istanbul: Between the Global and the Local,* edited by Caglar Keydar, 187–97. Lanham, ND: Rowman & Littlefield Publishers.

Ibn Khaldun. n.d. *Al-Muqaddamah* [The promulgation]. Beirut: Dar al-'Rqam

Khechen, Mona. 2005. "Spatial Restructuring and Participatory Public Action." In *Aleppo: Rehabilitation of the Old City,* edited by Joan Busquets, 55–67. Cambridge, MA: Harvard University Graduate School of Design.

Khost, Nadia. 1989. *Al-Hijra min al-jinna* [Exodus from paradise]. Damascus: Al-Ahali Press.

———. 1993. *Dimashq: Dhakirat al-Insan was al-Hajr* [Damascus: memory of humans and stone]. Damascus: Dar Daniya.

Khoury, Philip S. 1983. *Urban Notables and Arab Nationalism.* New York: Cambridge University Press.

————. 1987. *Syrian Urban Politics in Transition: The Quarters of Damascus during the French Mandate*. London: Tauris and Co.

King, Anthony. 1990. *Urbanism, Colonialism and the World Economy: Culture and Spatial Foundations of the Urban World System*. New York: Routledge.

————. 2007. "Boundaries, Networks, and Cities: Playing and Replaying Disaporas and Histories." In *Urban Imaginaries: Locating the Modern City*, edited by Thomas Bender and Alev Cinar, 1–14. Minneapolis: University of Minnesota Press.

Kirshenblatt-Gimblett, Barbara. 1998. *Destination Culture: Tourism, Museums, and Heritage*. Berkeley: University of California Press.

Knauft, Bruce. 2002. "Critically Modern: An Introduction." In *Critically Modern: Alternatives, Alterities Anthropologies*, edited by Bruce Knauft, 1–56. Bloomington: Indiana University Press.

al-Kodmany, Kheir. 1999. "Residential Visual Privacy: Traditional and Modern Architecture and Urban Design." *Journal of Urban Design* 4 (3): 283–311.

Koning, Anouk de. 2009. "Gender, Public Space and Social Segregation in Cairo: Of Taxi Drivers, Prostitutes and Professional Women." *Antipode* 41 (3): 533–56.

Kurd 'Ali, Muhammad. 1983. *Khitat al-Sham* [Design of al-Sham]. Damascus: Maktabat al-Nouri.

————. n.d. *Dimashq: Madinat al-sihr wa al-shi'r*. Damascus: Dar al-Fikr.

Kurzac-Souali, Anne-Claire. 2007. "Rumeurs et cohabitation en medina de Marrakech: L'etranger ou on ne L'attendait pas." *Herodote* 4 (127): 64–88.

Lapidus, Ira, ed. 1969. *Middle Eastern Cities: A Symposium on Ancient, Islamic, and Contemporary Middle Eastern Urbanism*. Berkeley: University of California Press.

Lawrence, Denise, and Setha Low. 1990. "The Built Environment and Spatial Form." *Annual Review of Anthropology*, no. 19:453–505.

Lawrence-Zúñiga, Denise. 2010. "Cosmologies of Bungalow Preservation: Identity, Lifestyle, and Civic Virtue." *City and Society* 22 (2): 211–36.

Lees, Loretta. 2000. "A Reappraisal of Gentrification: Towards a 'Geography of Gentrification.'" *Progress in Human Geography* 24 (3): 389–408.

Lefebvre, Henri. 1991. *The Production of Space*. Cambridge, MA: Blackwell.

————. 1996. "Rhythmanalysis of Mediterranean Cities." In *Writings on Cities*, 228–40. Oxford: Blackwell.

Low, Setha. 1996. "Spatializing Culture: The Social Production and Social Construction of Public Space in Costa Rica." *American Ethnologist*, 23 (4): 861–79.

———. 2000. *On the Plaza: The Politics of Public Space and Culture.* Austin: University of Texas Press.

Low, Setha, and Denise L. Lawrence-Zúñiga. 2003. "Locating Culture." In *The Anthropology of Space and Place: Locating Culture*, edited by Setha Low and D. Lawrence-Zúñiga, 1–48. Oxford: Blackwell.

Lowenthal, David. 1985. *The Past Is a Foreign Country.* Cambridge: Cambridge University Press.

———. 1996. *Possessed by the Past: The Heritage Crusade and the Spoils of History.* New York: Free Press.

Lynch, Kevin. 1960. *The Image of the City.* Cambridge, MA: MIT Press.

Mahdi, Muhsin. 1964. *Ibn Khaldun's Philosophy of History.* Chicago: University of Chicago Press (Phoenix Books).

al-Makdisi. 2003. *Fad'il al-Sham* [Virtues of al-Sham]. Edited by Hassan al-Tahan. Dimashq: Dar L'ay.

Makdisi, Ussama. 2002. "Rethinking Ottoman Imperialism: Modernity, Violence and the Cultural Logic of Ottoman Reform." In *The Empire in the City: Arab Provincial Capitals in the Late Ottoman Empire*, edited by J. Hanssen, T. Philipp, and S. Weber, 29–48. Beirut: Ergon Verlag Wurzburg.

al-Malouf, Fawzi. 2004. "Proposition for Investment in Bayt Nizam, Quwatli and Siba'I." *Al-Thawara Newspaper*, November 21.

al-Manna, Haytham. 2012. "Syria: After Assad Falls, What Then?" *The Guardian*, December 17. http://www.guardian.co.uk/commentisfree/2012/dec/18/after-assad-falls-what-then?INTCMP=SRCH.

Marcus, Abraham. 1986. "Privacy in Eighteenth-Century Aleppo: The Limits of Cultural Ideals." *International Journal of Middle East Studies*, no. 18:165–83.

Marino, Brigitte. 2000. *Hay Al-Midan fi al-'asr Al-'uthmani* [Midan during the Ottoman period]. Translated by M. Al-Sahrif. Damascus: Al-Mada.

Martin, Kevin. 2010. "Presenting the 'True Face of Syria' to the World: Urban Disorder and Civilizational Anxieties at the First Damascus International Exposition." *International Journal of Middle East Studies*, no. 42:391–411.

Massad, Joseph. 2007. *Desiring Arabs.* Chicago: Chicago University Press.

Massey, Doreen. 1994. *Space, Place, and Gender.* Minneapolis: University of Minnesota Press.

Mathews, Annie-Christine Daskalakis. 1997. "A Room of 'Splendor and Generosity' from Ottoman Damascus." *Metropolitan Museum Journal*, no. 32:111–39.

Mazzarella, William. 2003. *Shoveling Smoke: Advertising and Globalization in Contemporary India.* Durham, NC: Duke University Press.

McConnell, Phil. 1982. "Restoration of Damascus." *Saudi Aramco World*, March/April. http://www.saudiaramcoworld.com/issue/198202/restoration.of.damascus.htm).

Mennell, Stephen, and Johan Goudsblom. 1998. Introduction to *On Civilization, Power, and Knowledge: Selected Writings*, by Norbert Elias, 1–45, edited by Stephen Mennell and Johan Goudsblom. Chicago: University of Chicago Press.

Miller, Judith. 1982. "Tempers Rise as Shops Fall in Damascus Restoration." *New York Times*, April 15, Sec.1.

Mitchell, Timothy. 2000. "The Stages of Modernity." In *Questions of Modernity*, edited by Timothy Mitchell, 1–34. Minneapolis: Minnesota University Press.

Mufti, Aamir. 2000. "The Aura of Authenticity." *Social Text* 18 (3): 87–103.

al-Nahawi, Ali. 2000. "Das Damaszener Haus." In *Damaskus Aleppo: 5000 Jahre Stadtentwicklung in Syrien*, 348–52. Mainz: Philipp von Zabern.

Newcomb, Rachel. 2009. *Women in Fes: Ambiguities of Urban Life in Morocco.* Philadelphia: University of Pennsylvania Press.

Nora, Pierre. 1989. "Between Memory and History: Les lieux de memoire." *Representations*, no. 26:7–24.

Orbasli, Aylin. 2000. *Tourists in Historic Towns: Urban Conservation and Heritage Management.* London: E&FN SPON.

Ortner, Sherry. 1995. "Resistance and the Problem of Ethnographic Refusal." *Society for Comparative Studies in Society and History* 37 (1): 173–93.

Ossman, Susan. 1994. *Picturing Casablanca: Portrait of Power in a Modern City.* Berkeley: University of California Press.

Ouroussoff, Nicolai. 2010. "Preserving Heritage, and the Fabric of Life, in Syria." *New York Times*, December 26. http://www.nytimes.com/2010/12/27/arts/design/27preserv.html?_r=1&emc+eta1&page . . .

Ozyurek, Esra. *Nostalgia for the Modern: State Secularism and Everyday Politics in Turkey.* Durham, NC: Duke University Press.

Page, Max, and Randall Mason. 2004. "Rethinking the Roots of the Historic Preservation Movement." In *Giving Preservation a History: Histories of Historic Preservation in the United States*, edited by Max Page and Randall Mason, 3–16. New York: Routledge.

Paul, Robert A. 1998. "The Genealogy of Civilization." *American Anthropologist* 100 (2): 387–96.

Perthes, Volker. 1991. "A Look at Syria's Upper Class: The Bourgeoisie and the Ba'th." *Middle East Report* 21 (3): 31–37.

————. 2004. "Syria: Difficult Inheritance." In *Arab Elites: Negotiating the Politics of Change*, edited by Volker Perthes, 87–114. Boulder, CO: Lynne Rienner.

Petran, Tabitha. 1972. *Syria*. New York: Praeger.

Pini, Daniele, Didier Repellin, and Franca Miglioli. 2008. *Ancient City of Damascus Mission Report*. UNESCO and ICOMOS, Damascus, April 23–29. whc.unesco.org/en/documents/100687/.

Potuoglu-Cook, Oyku. 2006. "Beyond the Glitter: Belly Dance and Neoliberal Gentrification in Istanbul." *Cultural Anthropology* 21 (4): 633–60.

Qabbani, Nizar. 1995. *Dimashq Nizar Qabbani* [Nizar Qabbani's Damascus]. Damascus: Al-Ahali lil Nashr.

Qasatili, Nuʻman. 1879. *Kitab al-Rawdah al-Ghanaʾfi Dimashq al- Fayhaʾ* [The book on the happy garden in redolent Damascus]. Damascus, Syria: Tlas Publishing House, 2004.

Rabbat, Nasser. 1997. "Al-ʾiwan: maʻnahu al-faraghi wa madlulahu al- tidhkari" [The ʾiwan its meaning and historical significance]. *Bulletin d'Etudes Orientales* 49:249–67.

————. 2002. *Thaqafit al-binaʾ wa binaʾ al-thaqafah* [The culture of buildings and the building of culture]. Beirut: Riad El-Rayys Books.

Rabinow, Paul. 1989. *French Modern: Norms and Forms of Missionary and Didactic Pathos*. Cambridge, MA: MIT Press.

Rafeq, Abdul Karim. 1966. *The Province of Damascus*. Beirut: Khayts.

————. 1989. "City and Countryside in Ottoman Syria." In *Urbanism in Islam: Proceedings of the International Conference on Urbanism in Islam (ICUIT), October 22–23, 1989*. Vol. 3, 97–144, Tokyo: Middle Eastern Cultural Center.

Rapoport, Amos. 1969. *House Form and Culture*. Englewood Cliffs, NJ: Prentice Hall.

————. 1990. *Meaning of the Built Environment*. Tucson: University of Arizona Press.

————. 2007. "The Nature of the Courtyard House: A Conceptual Analysis." *Traditional Dwelling and Settlement Review* 18 (2): 57–72.

Raymond, Andre. 1984. *The Great Arab Cities in the 16th–18th Centuries: An Introduction*. New York: New York University Press.

Redfern, P. A. 2003. "What Makes Gentrification 'Gentrification'?" *Urban Studies* 40 (12): 2351–66.

Reichl, Alexander. 1999. *Reconstructing Times Square: Politics and Culture in Urban Development*. Lawrence: University Press of Kansas.

Reilly, James. 1991. "The Modern Birth of Traditional Damascus." Unpublished manuscript.

Richardson, Miles. [1982] 2003. "Being-in-the-Market versus Being-in-the-Plaza: Material Culture and the Construction of Social Reality in Spanish America." In *The Anthropology of Space and Place: Locating Culture*, edited by Setha Low and Dennis Lawrence- Zúñiga, 74–91. Oxford: Blackwell.

al-Rihawi, Abdul Qadir. 1969. *Madinat Dimashq: Turathuha wa Malamiha al-Tarikhiyyah* [City of Damascus: its heritage and historical monuments]. Damascus.

Robinson, Mike. 2001. "Tourism Encounters: Inter- and Intra-cultural Conflicts and the World's Largest Industry." In *Consuming Tradition, Manufacturing Heritage: Global Norms and Urban Forms in the Age of Tourism*, edited by Nezar Alsayyad, 34–67. London: Routledge.

Rodman, Margaret C. 1992. "Empowering Space: Multilocality and Multivocality." *American Anthropologist* 94 (3): 640–56.

Rodwell, Dennis. 2007. *Conservation and Sustainability in Historic Cities*. Oxford: Blackwell.

Rofel, Lisa. 1999. *Other Modernities: Gendered Yearnings in China after Socialism*. Berkeley: University of California Press.

Rosen, Lawrence. 1979. "Social Identity and points of Attachment: Approaches to Social Organization." In *Meaning and Order in Moroccan Society: Three Essays in Cultural Analysis*, edited by Clifford Geertz, Hildred Geertz, and Lawrence Rosen, 19–122. Cambridge: University of Cambridge Press.

Roy, Ananya. 2004. "Nostalgias of the Modern." In *The End of Tradition?*, edited by Nezar Alsayyad, 63–86. New York: Routledge.

Sack, Dorothee. 1998. "The Historic Fabric Of Damascus and Its Changes in the 19th-Century Damascus." In *The Syrian Land: Processes of Integration and Fragmentation*, edited by T. Philipp and B. Schaebler, 185–202. Stuttgart: Franz Steiner Verlag.

———. 2005. *Dimashq: Tatwr wa Binayan Madiant Mushreqyeh 'Islamiyeh*. Translated by Qasem Tuwyr. Dimashq: IFPO.

Said, Edward. 1978. *Orientalism*. New York: Penguin Books.

Salamandra, Christa. 1998. "Moustache Hairs Lost: Ramadan Television Serials and the Construction of Identity in Damascus, Syria." *Visual Anthropology* 10 (2–4): 227–45.

———. 2000. "Consuming Damascus: Public Culture and the Construction of Social Identity. In *Mass Mediations: New Approaches to Popular Culture in the Middle East and Beyond*, edited by Walter Armbrust, 182–202. Berkeley: University of California Press.

———. 2004. *A New Old Damascus: Authenticity and Distinction in Urban Syria.* Bloomington: Indiana University Press.

———. 2006. "Chastity Capital: Hierarchy and Distinction in Damascus." In *Sexuality in the Arab World*, edited by Samir Khalaf and John Gagnon. Beirut: Saqi Press.

———. 2008. "Through the Back Door: Syrian Television Makers between Secularism and Islamization." In *Arab Media: Power and Weakness*, edited by Kai Hafez, 252–62. New York: Continuum.

———. 2011. "Arab Television Drama Production in the Satellite Era." In *Soap Operas and Telenovelas in the Digital Age: Global Industries, Hybrid Content, and New Audiences*, edited by Diana I. Rios and Mari Castaneda, 275–90. New York: Peter Lang.

Sassen, Saskia. 1991. *Global City: New York, London, Tokyo.* Princeton, NJ: Princeton University Press.

Sauvaget, Jean. 1934. "Esquisse d'une histoire de la ville de Damas." *Reveue des Etudes Islamique* 8:421–80.

Sawalha, Aseel. 2010. *Reconstructing Beirut: Memory and Space in a Postwar Arab City.* Austin: University of Texas Press.

Schilcher, Linda Schatkowski. 1985. *Families in Politics: Shuwam Factions and Estates of the 18th and 19th Centuries.* Stuttgart: Franz Steiner.

Schorske, Carl. 1979. *Fin-de-Siècle Vienna Politics and Culture.* New York: Knopf.

Scott, David. 1999. *Refashioning Futures: Criticism after Postcoloniality.* Princeton: NJ: Princeton University Press.

Scott, James. 1998. *Seeing Like a State: How Certain Schemes to Improve the Human Condition Have Failed.* New Haven, CT: Yale University Press.

Selvik, Kjetil. 2009. "It's the Mentality, Stupid: Syria's Turn to the Private Sector." In *Changing Regime Discourse and Reform in Syria*, edited Aurora Sottimano and Kjetil Selvik, 41–70. Fife, Scotland: University of St. Andrews Centre for Syrian Studies.

Semerdjian, Elyse. 2008. *"Off the Straight Path": Illicit Sex, Law, and Community in Ottoman Aleppo.* Syracuse, NY: Syracuse University Press.

Sennett, Richard. 1990. *The Conscious of the Eye: The Design and Social Life of Cities.* New York: Knopf.

Shackley, Myra. 1998. "Visitors to the World's Oldest Cities: Aleppo and Damascus Syria." In *Managing Tourism in Cities: Policy, Process and Practice*, edited by D. Tyler, Y. Guerrier, and M. Robertson, 109–23. Chichester, West Sussex: Wiley.

Shannon, Jonathan H. 2005. "Metonyms of Modernity in Contemporary Syrian Music and Painting." *Ethnos* 70 (3): 361–86.

———. 2006. *Among the Jasmine Trees: Music and Modernity in Contemporary Syria*. Middletown, CT: Wesleyan University Press.

Shatta, Hikmat. 1999. "Ma Zalat mustamirah hijrat dimashq al-qadimah ila shiqaq al-binayat" [The exodus from old Damascus continues]. *al-Hayat*, March 12.

———. 2005. "Wijhat Nathr 'iqtisadiyyah" [Economic point of view]. *al-Hayat*, August 24. http://internationaldaralhayat.com/print/92430/archive.

Smith, Neil. 1996. *The New Urban Frontier: Gentrification and the Revanchist City*. London: Routledge.

———. 2002. "New Globalism, New Urbanism Gentrification as Global Urban Strategy." *Antipode* 34 (3): 427–50.

———. 2006. "Gentrification Generalized: From Local Anomaly to Urban 'Regeneration' as Global Urban Strategy." In *Frontiers of Capital: Ethnographic Reflections on the New Economy*, edited by Melissa Fisher and Greg Downey, 191–208. Durham, NC: Duke University Press.

Smith, Neil, and Peter Williams. 1986. "Alternatives to Orthodoxy: Invitation to a Debate." In *Gentrification of the City*, edited by Neil Smith and Peter Williams, 1–12. Boston: Allen & Unwin.

Soja, Edward. 1989. *Postmodern Geographies: The Reassertion of Space in Critical Social Theory*. New York: Verso.

Sorkin, Michael. 1992. "Introduction: Variations on a Theme Park." In *Variations on a Theme Park: The New American City and the End of Pubic Space*, xi–xv. New York: Hill and Wang.

Sovich, Nina. 2005. "Syria Moves to Attract Investors." *Wall Street Journal*. October 10, A11.

Stewart, Kathleen. 1988. "Nostalgia: A Polemic." *Cultural Anthropology* 3 (3): 227–41.

———. 1996. *A Space on the Side of the Road: Cultural Poetics in an "Other" America*. Princeton, NJ: Princeton University Press.

Stewart, Susan. 1999. *On Longing: Narratives of the Miniature, the Gigantic, the Souvenir, the Collection*. Durham, NC: Duke University Press.

Sudermann, Yannick. 2012. "Contested Heritage? Gentrification and Authoritarian Resilience in Damascus." In *Syria's Contrasting Neighborhoods: Gentrification and Informal Settlements*, edited by Balsam Ahmad and Yannick Sudermann, 29–60. Fife, Scotland: University of St. Andrews Center for Syrian Studies.

Taraki, Lisa. 2008. "Urban Modernity on the Periphery: A New Middle Class Reinvents the Palestinian City." *Social Text* 26 (2): 61–81.

Tarazi, Leila Fawaz. 1994. *An Occasion for War: Civil Conflict in Lebanon and Damascus in 1860*. Berkeley: University of California Press.

Tergeman, Siham. 1969, *Ya Mal al-Sham* [Oh bounty that is Damascus]. Damascus: Press of Directorate for Moral Instruction in the Ministry of War.

———. 1994. *Daughter of Damascus*. Translated by Andrea Rugh. Austin: Center for Middle eastern Studies University of Texas at Austin.

Thompson, Elizabeth. 2000. *Colonial Citizens: Republican Rights, Paternal Privilege, and Gender in French Syria and Lebanon*. New York: Columbia Press.

Till, Karen. 2005. *The New Berlin: Memory, Politics, Place*. Minneapolis: University of Minnesota Press.

Tsing, Anna. 2000. The Global Situation. *Cultural Anthropology* 15 (3): 327–60.

Tuan, Yi-Fu. 1977. *Space and Place*. Minneapolis: University of Minnesota Press.

Twain, Mark. 2003. *The Innocents Abroad, or The New Pilgrims' Progress*. New York: Modern Library.

UNESCO. 1953. "Dimashq." *Al-huwliyat al-'athariyyah al-suriyyah* 3 (1–2): 29–45.

Vellinga, Marcel. 2007. Anthropology and the Materiality of Architecture. *American Ethnologist* 34 (4): 756–66.

Verdeil, Eric. 2012. "Michel Ecochard in Lebanon and Syria (1956–1968): The Spread of Modernism, the Building of the Independent States and the Rise of Local Professionals of Planning." *Planning Perspectives* 27 (2): 249–66.

Watenpaugh, Heghnar. 2004. *The Images of an Ottoman City: Imperial Architecture and Urban Experience in Aleppo in the 16th and 17th Centuries*. Leiden: Brill.

Watzinger, Carl, and Karl Wulzinger. 1921–1924. *Damaskus*. Berlin: W. de Gruyter.

Weber, Stefan. 1997–1998. "The Creation of Ottoman Damascus: Architecture and Urban Development of Damascus in the 16th and 17th Centuries." *ARAM*, nos. 9–10:431–70.

———. 2002. "Images of Imagined Worlds." In *The Empire in the City: Arab Provincial Capitals in the Late Ottoman Empire*, edited by J. Hanssen, T. Philipp, and S. Weber, 145–71. Beirut: Ergon Verlag Wurzburg.

———. 2004. "Reshaping Damascus: Social Change and Patterns of Architecture in Late Ottoman Times." In *From the Syrian Land to the States of Syria and Lebanon*, edited by Thomas Philipp and Christoph Schumann, 41–58. Beirut: Erogon Verlag Wurzburg in Kommission.

Wedeen, Lisa. 1999. *Ambiguities of Domination: Politics, Rhetoric, and Symbols in Contemporary Syria*. Chicago: University of Chicago Press.

Weulersse, Jacques. 1946. *Paysans de Syrie et du Proche-Orient*. n.p.: Gallimard.

Williams, Brett. 1988. *Upscaling Downtown: Stalled Gentrification in Washington, D.C.* Ithaca, NY: Cornell University Press.

Williams, Raymond. 1973. *Country and the City*. New York: Oxford University Press.

———. 1977. *Marxism and literature*. Oxford: Oxford University Press.

Wirth, Louis. 1938. "Urbanism as a Way of Life." *American Journal of Sociology* 44 (1): 1–24.

Wise, Michael. 2012. "The Ritz-Carlton of Failed States." *Foreign Policy*, March/April. http://www.foreignpolicy.com/articles/2012/02/27/the_ritz_carlton_of _failed_states.

Wright, Gwendolyn. 1991. *The Politics of Design in French Colonial Urbanism*. Chicago: University of Chicago Press.

Wright, Robin. 2103. "Imagining a Remapped Middle East." *New York Times*. September 29. http://www.nytimes.com/2013/09/29/opinion/sunday/imagining -a-remapped-middle-east.html?_r=0

Zeifa, Hayma. 2004. "Les Elites Techniques Locales Durant le Mandat Francais en Syrie (1920–1945)." In *The British and French Mandate in Comparative Perspectives*, edited by Nadine Meouchy and Peter Sluglett, 497–536. London: Brill.

Zenlund, Darrow. 1994. "Post-Colonial Aleppo, Syria: Struggles in Representation and Identity." PhD diss., University of Texas at Austin.

Zukin, Sharon. 1987. "Gentrification: Culture and Capital in the Urban Core." *Annual Review of Sociology*, no. 13:129–47.

———. 1995. *The Culture of Cities*. Cambridge: Blackwell.

———. 2010. *Naked City: The Death and Life of Authentic Urban Places*. New York: Oxford University Press.

Index

Disney urban model, 203–4
dispossession, 14–15
domestic space, 135
door, 139
dual city, 215

Ecochard, Michel, 53, 66, 68–72; master
    plan of, 68–69; Verdeil on, 69–70
Elias, Norbert, 24
emergency laws, 193
enclosure, 200
epithets written on walls, xvi, *xvii*, 248
Erman, Tahire, 77
"estheticism," 224
Euromed Heritage Project, 5n5

façade, 174, *174*; corruption of, 175; of
    courtyard house, 172; Geertz on,
    172–73
Fairuz, 204–6
Faisal, Amir, xv
falsification, 200
felicitous space, 163, 201, 202
fleeting class, 173
Flores, Richard, 63
foreign direct investment, 218, 238
free press, 231
Free Syrian Army, 245
French Mandate, xxi–xxii, 40, 81–83;
    leader class and, 82; ruralization
    during, 82
French modernization, xxii, 49, 50,
    65–68

Gandolfo, Daniella, 19
garden, 110–14
Geertz, Clifford, 172–73

gender: communication and, 139; court-
    yard house and, 119–22, 134–39;
    Massey on, 136; restaurants and,
    212–13; shopping and, 121; walking
    and, 45–46. *See also haremlik; salem-
    lik;* women
gentrification, xi–xii; aesthetic differ-
    ences and, 5; in Aleppo, xii, 6–7;
    anxiety and, 15–16; authenticity and,
    21, 154; as authoritarian upgrading,
    20, 22; in Beirut, 16–17; civilization
    brought about through, 222–23; class
    and, 15, 151; as colonialism, 14–15;
    conscientious, 167–68; contamina-
    tion from, 19; Davila on, 21; dispos-
    session from, 14–15; of East Harlem,
    21; "estheticism" imposed by, 224;
    Gandolfo on, 19; generalizations
    of, 13–17; globalization of, 14–19;
    of Havana, Cuba, 18; individualism
    influencing, 226; in Istanbul, Turkey,
    16, 79; Jager on, 15, 151; Khost on,
    224; Law No. 10 of 1991 and, 5; of
    Lima, Peru, 19; of Marrakesh, 18;
    neoliberalism and, 14–15; power
    relations and, 23; for promotion,
    xix; in Pueblo, Mexico, 16; of Rome,
    18–19; ruralization facilitating, 79;
    Salamandra on, 20–21; as saving,
    5; sectarian differences and, xxvi;
    Smith on, 14; social status and, 5–9;
    Sudermann on, 20, 22, 186; tourism
    encouraged through, 5–6; UNESCO
    World Heritage designation as,
    17–19; variance in, 14; violence and,
    14–15
German Organization for Technical
    Cooperation (GTZ), 6, 7
Ghannam, Farha, 113; on door, 139; on
    modernity, 54; on privacy, 122–23